The Financial Markets of Roman Egypt

Risk and Return

Liverpool Studies in Ancient History 2

LIVERPOOL STUDIES IN ANCIENT HISTORY

The Financial Markets of Roman Egypt

Risk and Return

PAUL V. KELLY

LIVERPOOL UNIVERSITY PRESS

First published 2023 by
Liverpool University Press
4 Cambridge Street
Liverpool
L69 7ZU

British Library Cataloguing-in-Publication data
A British Library CIP record is available

ISBN 978-1-80207-833-6 cased

Typeset by Carnegie Book Production, Lancaster
Printed and bound by CPI Group (UK) Ltd, Croydon CR0 4YY

Contents

Acknowledgements

This book had its origins in the doctoral thesis I undertook under the guidance of Professor Rathbone at King's College London and I would particularly like to thank him for his patience. He helped me adapt my corporate, financial perspective to the different and occasionally frustrating norms of academia. I would also like to acknowledge the financial and other support provided by the London Arts and Humanities Partnership during the completion of my thesis.

Daniel Jew and Myles Lavan showed me how my professional expertise in stochastic modelling could be relevant to the study of ancient history, and the staff at Birkbeck College of the University of London fuelled my enthusiasm and interest in Roman history when I completed my BA and MA there as a mature student. I am very grateful for the help and input from the team at Liverpool University Press, Carnegie Book Production and the anonymous readers. Thanks are also due to the staff at the wonderful Institute of Classical Studies joint library, where much of this book was written, and to the friends who helped me test ideas over convivial lunches. You know who you are.

My daughter Rona provided useful comments, helping me hopefully avoid any inadvertent sexism in the chapter on women, but the main thanks are due to my wife Linda, for all her kindness and practical support in reading and re-reading each and every word of this book multiple times. Any errors are, of course, my own responsibility.

Papyri Checklist

When papyri are referenced I use the conventional abbreviations. The full checklist of papyri can be found at https://papyri.info/docs/checklist#.

Chapter 1

Introduction

This is a book about the financial markets of Roman Egypt, specifically the credit and real estate markets in all their aspects. Egypt is the one place in the ancient world where we have sufficient data to examine, on a microeconomic level, the way in which the markets operated. But it is more than a book about the markets as institutions. It concentrates on the behaviours that drove individuals to make some of the most important decisions of their lives: to lend money to a neighbour, to buy an apartment or to rent a plot for farming. This book lays more emphasis on behaviours rather than institutions, on the individual rather than the larger order, on decisions made by ordinary people rather than by the elite and the anonymous state. It particularly addresses questions of the 'universality' of human nature – did the people of Roman Egypt think and act in similar ways to our modern selves?

This book has its roots in my doctoral work, but whilst the original thesis concentrated on those who held capital (the landlords and lenders), this book adds balance by considering the impact on, and the perspective of, those who were dependent on such capital (the tenants and borrowers).[1] I have also moved away from the simple yes/no question of the thesis: 'Were the markets driven by financial rationality?' to consider a wider range of potential motivations and market drivers. Were the markets driven by reciprocity or redistribution, by family or societal considerations, or by the profit motive? Through this examination of the behaviours of individuals in the past we can empathise with what connects us to them and understand what separates us from them, which for me at least is what history is all about.

Apart from the central question of the behaviours that drove the markets, the book will also provide conclusions on the wider Roman economy and the impact of that economic system on society. It challenges the accepted views on price inflation and economic indicators of growth and decline. It considers how economic structures such as interest rate levels hindered social mobility, discriminated on gender grounds, led to newborn abandonment and concentrated wealth in those who already possessed it.

[1] Kelly 2020.

But it also shows how mutually advantageous credit and lease structures linked lender and borrower, landlord and tenant in symbiotic relations that reduced financial risk for the poorest and helped social stability.

Theories of the market

Since this book is about the 'markets', perhaps I should deal first with the question of whether 'markets' really existed. The term 'market' brings, in an economic context, some unfortunate baggage. It calls to mind a market economy as opposed to a planned economy, with all the consequent political connotations. Nevertheless, provided we define the term market in a wide context without any presumption as to its specific nature, it is a useful, indeed unavoidable, concept when we discuss the exchange of goods, services and assets between people. If we define a market as the means by which this exchange occurred it is an undeniable fact that financial markets existed in Roman Egypt since we know that people frequently bought and sold real estate, leased that real estate and loaned and borrowed money and commodities. However, just because these markets existed does not mean that they formed part of a market economy or were driven by the behaviours we associate with that concept, that is those 'free market' behaviours which are based on exchange value judgements and reflect the participants' pursuit of profit or utility. When these behaviours drive a market, forces of supply and demand then determine market pricing.

To expand on the concept of the free market a little, in neoclassical economic theory there are three key pre-requisites for an effective exchange value-based market to exist:

- frictional costs of transactions should be minimised
- sufficient information should be available to all participants, and
- participants should act in a 'rational' manner.[2]

In neoclassical theory, *homo economicus*, who seeks to maximise profit or utility in a rational manner, is the central actor in the market. This approach may be considered to be 'formalist'.[3]

[2] See Hollis & Nell 1975: 209–15 for a discussion of the assumptions underlying neoclassical economics.

[3] This orthodoxy was challenged by Weber who rejected the emphasis on *homo economicus* and stressed instead the wider environment in which humans interact. Specifically, in the ancient world, he sought to emphasise that *homo politicus* was driven by considerations of 'status' and he saw a clear distinction between that world and the pre-modern or modern societies where *homo economicus* operated. He defined status to mean 'an effective claim to social esteem in terms of positive or negative privileges'.

However, historical examples of markets that did not exhibit these features are numerous and often include power imbalances or status stratification between the parties concerned that inhibited the ability of both to arrive at 'fair' prices. Consider the grain markets of nineteenth-century England, where prices were fixed by the Corn Laws at levels designed to benefit the elite. Or the modern narcotics markets, where even if the vendor is driven by profit-maximisation the buyer will purchase at any price to feed their habit. Or colonial markets, where, by the exertion of physical power, western nations exploited indigenous peoples and extorted human capital as slaves. Even religious markets, where, by the use of threats and promises, the established churches in western Europe obtained tithes and assets in exchange for spiritual advantages and absolutions.

Weber's view of the markets, which covered millennia within a single simple sweeping statement, was that 'where stratification by status permeates a community as strongly was the case in all political communities of Antiquity and the Middle Ages, one can never speak of a genuinely free market competition as we understand it today'.[4] The markets of Roman Egypt were by no means exempt from such influences, but I will challenge his generalisation by demonstrating that some markets exhibited many features consistent with, and indicative of, markets driven by the pursuit of profit.

But power imbalances are not the only reasons why a market may not exhibit exchange value characteristics. Markets may simply not be efficient enough to allow rational judgements to be made due to information deficits between the parties often associated with illiquidity in the marketplace, where the infrequency of the transaction, or a difficulty in commoditising the item to be traded, limits the ability of the parties to make a reasoned judgement. Frictional costs can also be so high as to preclude either party from making a profit.

Finally, and perhaps most importantly, markets can be driven by 'embedded' human behaviours that have nothing to do with the pursuit of profit.[5] Polanyi saw a distinction between the market and the institutions that were contained within it. His view was that 'although market institutions, therefore, are exchange institutions, market and exchange are not coterminous'.[6] Within pre-modern markets, he saw socially driven

Weber 1978: 305. He did not associate this form of status directly with wealth or class but thought that it was founded on style of life, formal education or hereditary or occupational prestige. Weber 1978: 305–6.

[4] Weber 1978: 937.

[5] Polanyi developed the concept of 'substantivism' which emphasised that any economy is 'embedded' within the society which surrounds it. Polanyi et al. 1957: 242. This contrasts with the 'formalism' inherent within neoclassical economic theory.

[6] Polanyi 1957: 267.

redistribution and reciprocity as being stronger drivers of economic behaviour than the exchange value drivers of the neoclassical approach.[7] I would certainly agree that markets, when defined as the means of making an exchange, are not coterminous with exchange value, but whether redistribution and reciprocity were *stronger* than exchange value is the principal subject of this book.

The terms redistribution and reciprocity are worthy of more discussion. By redistribution, Polanyi particularly saw a system where transfers of goods, assets and wealth operated through a central authority figure such as a tribal chief or feudal lord. Within the context of Roman Egypt, this concept may perhaps best be understood as relating to the Roman state.

By reciprocity, Polanyi refers to the exchange or gift of goods or services that provide the donor no immediate tangible benefit but where they may expect to gain by actions of a reciprocal nature. In his exploration of the concept, he places this firmly within a family context and also, although he does not use the term, includes the acquisition of 'social capital' within the potential benefits likely to be provided to the donor.[8] In this book we will see many examples of intra-family transactions that I believe go beyond Polanyi's examples, and that do not fit comfortably into his reciprocity framework. There is no evident reciprocity in the actions of Herais who bought a house for her daughter Taaphochis in the Pammenes' Garden quarter of Oxyrhynchus around AD 167.[9] A simpler explanation for Herais's actions is that her affection for her daughter led her to want to secure her future and this was an altruistic gift without any expectation of reciprocity rather than being the result of inter-generational solidarity.[10] As for the acquisition of social capital, this was a central feature of Roman morality exemplified by the concept of euergetism, where wealthier parties donated capital to acquire by reciprocity social status from the wider community.[11]

7 Polanyi 1944: 47. He also proposes a third aspect of the pre-modern economy 'householding', which he describes as 'production for one's own use'. Polanyi 1944: 55.

8 For more on the intangible forms of relationship-driven social capital and prestige-driven cultural capital, see Bourdieu 1986.

9 *P.Oxy.* XIV 1648 l.13–25 (late second century).

10 The concept of inter-generational solidarity is one which has considerably more power in the francophone world than the Anglo-Saxon. The clearest example of the relative power of *solidarité entre les générations* is the preference in France for 'pay-as-you-go' pension systems where the pensions of the older generation are paid from the taxation of the active working generation, as opposed to the preference in the UK and US for pensions which are pre-funded in pension funds from contributions previously made by the pensioner generation during their working lifetime. See Huebner 2013: 66–72 for a discussion of parental love in Roman Egypt.

11 See van Minnen 1997 for a discussion of euergetism in Roman Egypt.

Institutions and drivers

Turning to institutional constraints, the debate on the nature of any economy has been modified by the concepts developed within New Institutional Economics (NIE). As Temin noted, 'this body of thought grows out of a belated recognition by economists that institutions affect economic activity – and are in turn affected by economic pressures. Douglass North won a Nobel Prize for making this point over and over again'.[12] Most scholars of the ancient economy feel the need to reference NIE, but it is far from a 'new' conceptual framework, having been first mooted some 30 years ago, and some of its precepts are simple common sense and others anticipated by Marx's work on the institutions of the superstructure. Institutions within the context of Roman Egypt may include not only the physical institutions and apparatus of the state such as the army and records offices, but, more importantly, intangible institutions such as the legal system. In North's words, 'institutions are the rules of the game in a society, or, more formally, are the humanly devised constraints that shape human interaction'.[13]

Under NIE it is recognised that not all market participants will operate in a manner that seeks to maximise profit, but may adopt 'bounded rationality' strategies that may be described in a somewhat clumsy expression as 'satisficing': providing a financial outcome that satisfies a party within a transaction since their needs have been met, although profit may not have been maximised.[14] It is a general principle of NIE that in any situation the ability for an individual to act perfectly rationally is constrained by the time that they have to make the decision, the information at their disposal and cognitive limitations. NIE also recognises that an individual's actions may be 'path dependent' in that an action may be pre-conditioned by the choices and the outcomes that the individual or those known to him within his social group may have made in the past. However, I would agree with Lewis, who noted, in a recent summary of the state of the debate on the ancient economy, it is appropriate to look beyond NIE and include consideration of the theoretical advances in behavioural and financial economics in our assessment of the Roman economy.[15]

We can certainly see that markets are not solely driven by institutions or by bounded rationality, and that on occasions human behaviours, irrational even when they are driven by the profit motive, can hugely impact the market concerned. Think of the Dutch tulip bulb mania of the

[12] Temin 2012: 49.

[13] North 1990: 3.

[14] This concept was originally set out in Simon 1947 and was described within the context of the ancient economy in Frier & Kehoe 2007: 121.

[15] Lewis 2018: 39. This recognition of the importance of socioeconomic behaviours has echoes in the francophone school of Andreau and Maucourant. See Maucourant 2004.

1630s, the South Sea bubble of 1720 or the dotcom tech bubble at the end of the last century, where human nature led individuals to make entirely irrational judgements on the suitability of investments.[16] Thus, in looking at the markets I have tried to be sensitive to some of the other risk biases and heuristics that have been identified within behavioural finance. These include overconfidence as a cognitive bias, gender-differentiated attitudes to risk and the use of heuristic short cuts or rules of thumb to reach a decision.[17] I have also sought to give due weight to altruism, including that within a family setting. It has proved more difficult, however, since my data generally relate to the outcomes rather than the process of decision-making itself, to show the impact of emotions and fairness at work within the markets, which is another aspect of behavioural finance.

However, whilst accepting the importance of the institutional constraints, this work gives greater prominence to the behaviours of individuals. It also recognises that decisions are shaped by social networks, particularly gendered networks, since I believe, along with Fourcade, that 'it is the quality of ties between actors, the general shape of the social networks they are part of, and their own position within these networks, that determine many individual and collective market outcomes'.[18]

Bringing together these themes, and allowing for the limitations of the data, I will look for five different drivers of behaviours within the financial transactions we have available for Roman Egypt:

- pursuit of profit, or the maximisation of utility, by the exercise of financial rationality in an exchange value market
- reciprocity where the individual is motivated by the expectation that in the future they will receive a tangible or intangible gain
- altruistic familial actions
- actions designed to gain social capital, and
- redistributive actions that are necessary due to institutional constraints from the Roman state.

I have also sought to identify where the market is distorted by attitudes to gender and the associated discrimination.

I adopt tools borrowed from financial economics (that have only recently started to be used to study the ancient economy) to reach conclusions, not

16 Interestingly, these 'bubbles' of irrationality were all enabled by the ability of individuals to borrow money to make investments, or 'gearing', which we will see was not a strong feature of the economy of Roman Egypt.

17 See Kahneman & Tversky 1979 for the seminal work on behavioural economics.

18 Fourcade 2007: 1017.

only on these drivers, but also on the nature of the economy and wider society.[19] These tools include Modern Portfolio Theory (MPT), itself as much a misnomer as New Institutional Economics since Markowitz introduced it in 1952, although it took him until 1990 to be recognised by a Nobel prize.[20] I am influenced by MPT when thinking and analysing how an individual builds a 'portfolio' of investments to increase return and decrease risk. However, the Egyptian in Roman times could not build a 'portfolio' in the modern way of stocks, shares and bonds, but could construct a portfolio of loans, land, houses and tenancies (acting both as tenant and landlord) that could satisfy their financial or social aims, and this concept is considered in Chapter 7. I also use stochastic techniques, which are currently common in financial modelling to project financial outcomes for modern institutions (such as pension funds or insurance companies), to simulate the financial outcomes of ordinary families and what that meant for wider societal structures.[21]

Histories of the ancient economy

I have described above the wider context of theories about the markets and the tools that can be used to analyse their nature. However, there are particular positions and scholarship that dominate the mindsets and debate on the Roman economy and that need to be addressed. But when examining the historiography of the ancient economy, we are faced with the question of when to start? From the ancient writers themselves, such as Columella describing the investment preferences of the Roman elite, or Tacitus commenting on a Roman monetary crisis?[22] From the founders of classical economics such as Adam Smith, who drew on ancient texts to help them formulate their own ideas?[23] From the neoclassicists like Alfred Marshall, who built on earlier work to produce models of the market?[24] From Max Weber and Karl Polanyi, whose influence on the economists and historians of the ancient world was so profound?

I will return to the attitudes displayed by the ancient writers whilst the later scholars discussed above, although they were interested in the ancient world, they studied a wide range of societies and timeframes. But their ideas influenced two specialist scholars of the ancient world: Moses I. Finley and Michael Rostovtzeff, whose opposing attitudes provide the key dialectic

[19] See Lavan et al. (forthcoming).

[20] Markowitz 1952.

[21] For ease of reference, a glossary is provided at the end of this book of technical terms, whether they are mathematical, financial or specific to Roman Egypt.

[22] Columella, *De Re Rustica* 3.3.9–10; Tacitus, *Annals* 6.16–17.

[23] See, for instance, Smith 1976 [1776]: 111 on usury in the Roman Empire.

[24] Marshall 1890: 883–90.

within which this book is based. The 'modernist' approach to the Roman economy drew on the neoclassical economists and saw the motivations and actions of individuals as being similar to those of people within a 'modern' market economy. This viewpoint was adopted by Rostovtzeff.[25] It assumes that people in the ancient world were exemplified by the *homo economicus*. The 'primitive' approach, developed by Finley, and drawing on both Weber and Polanyi, stressed that there were other, more important, drivers for an individual's behaviour within the ancient economy, such as the 'very large non-economic element in the preference' for investment in land.[26] Whilst Rostovtzeff and Finley were strongly influenced by formalist and substantivist concepts in the development of their modernist and primitivist positioning, there is a danger of conflating terms. For instance, 'substantivism' is not identical to 'primitivism'. A substantivist economy may certainly be embedded within wider society, and its markets not subject to formulaic neoclassical drivers, without it being 'primitive'.[27] Consider, for instance, the planned economies of the communist states of the twentieth century. Similarly, 'formalism' and 'modernism' should not be conflated. As Lewis pointed out, 'modern economic actors are also embedded in social norms', a position that Williamson viewed as being 'taken as a given for most institutional economists'.[28]

Semantically the primitive vs modern debate is fundamentally flawed since it opposes two concepts that are not opposites. The opposite of modern is ancient, not primitive, and no one would deny that the Roman economy was ancient. Add the pejorative connotations of the word primitive, and its use cheapens and confuses the debate. I would thus reject entirely any attempt to categorise a market as being intrinsically 'modern' or 'primitive'. The word primitive will not be used in the remainder of this book, unless of course I am quoting the exact words of previous scholars.

I do, however, throughout the book use both modern and historical comparators for specific elements of the markets.[29] I do so for a number of reasons, not least of which is to add colour and interest to the text. However, there are three other reasons. First, modern-day terms such as pied-à-terre or buy-to-let can express succinctly the same actions and motivations as were

[25] See, for example, Rostovtzeff 1957: xiv for an example of his positive view of the 'city-capitalism' of the early empire.

[26] Finley 1999: 116.

[27] See Granovetter 1985: 482–3 for a rejection of a clear distinction between ancient embedded and modern disembedded markets.

[28] Lewis 2018: 24, Williamson 2000: 596.

[29] I recognise that using modern comparators places the book within a specific early twenty-first-century context, which might lessen its impact as conditions change, but all academic books have a limited shelf life.

seen in the ancient world and thus aid our understanding.[30] Second, when a market exhibits features that are very different to our own experience, a comparison with modern-day norms can help remind us to change our mindset and perspective as to the financial markets. An example of this can be seen when I consider the relative affordability of housing. Finally, when, on the contrary, features of the market have a commonality with the modern world and this may indicate similar motivations and behaviours, then a modern comparison is entirely appropriate and may be an indicator of 'universality', particularly if supported by evidence from other locales and times. I also draw a distinction here between the modern 'developed' and 'developing' worlds where markets can be very different. This is particularly the case when I consider the rationality of a framework for risk and return or the relative impact of microfinance institutions.

Moving beyond Finley vs Rostovtzeff, within the debate on the nature of the market in the Roman world there is an evident division of opinion between francophone and anglophone scholars as to the drivers of the market. Andreau and Lerouxel would question the degree to which evidence for a competitive market can be seen, whilst Rathbone, Scheidel, Temin and others would be more positive as to the prevalence of market forces.[31] As a bilingual scholar who has lived and worked in the francophone world for a number of years, I will confess to having a foot in both camps.

Modelling

As I hope will have been evident from the preceding paragraphs, I will mix the techniques of both narrative and social scientific history telling in this book using comparative metaphors and modelling in equal measure.[32] In the use of these modelling techniques I have been inspired by the approach adopted by Hopkins, even if his models were more conceptual than mathematical, and it is worth quoting his own justification for the use of models in full:

> Some of the greatest fun I have had in Roman history has been in constructing models. A model is, roughly speaking, a simplification of a complex reality, designed to show up the logical relationships between its constituent parts. The utility of models in Roman history, as I see it, is twofold. First, models allow us to perceive the structures or repeated

[30] I further recognise that the implied primary audience for this book is therefore that of the modern developed world, with a bias towards the West, but that again is a practical fact.

[31] Andreau 2010; Lerouxel 2016; Rathbone 1991; Scheidel 2012: 10; Temin 2013.

[32] See McCloskey for a lively discussion of 'the old battle of the sciences against art, the humanities, refought in history as analysis model against story, number against word'. McCloskey 1990: 289.

> patterns which lie behind the superficial flow of individual actors and events, which fill the pages of traditional Roman narrative histories. Second, models allow us to construct whole pictures, into which the surviving fragments of ancient source material can be plausibly fitted. The model is a sort of master picture as on the front of a jigsaw puzzle box; the fragments of surviving ancient sources provide only a few of the jigsaw pieces.[33]

Hopkins, I believe, overstated the utility of models somewhat. If a model does present a 'master picture' it is one that must inevitably be somewhat fuzzy and out of focus, and it is here that stochastic techniques, rather than the deterministic, best-estimate approaches adopted by Hopkins, come into their own. Stochastic models have inputs and outputs that 'are probability distributions rather than discrete values. The underlying principle is that one first represents the uncertainty about the underlying processes or input variables mathematically and then calculates the implied uncertainty about the outcome measure—a method called the forward propagation of uncertainty'.[34] It is this ability to deal with uncertainty that makes these models so valuable, and at the time of writing they have perhaps been most visible in the current global Covid-19 emergency to project the likely outcomes of the course of the pandemic. They are also used in the financial world to project financial outcomes for investments or institutions. I, however, use models based on stochastic techniques to 'project' what might have been the likely financial outcomes for landlords and farming families based on the remarkable data we have available for Roman Egypt.

Overall, I hope that, following Lewis's approach of methodological pluralism, and using a toolbox that includes economic sociology, previous ancient history scholarship, NIE, behavioural finance, MPT and stochastic modelling for my analysis, our understanding of the ancient economy may be improved. I am primarily interested in how people in the ancient world thought about key financial decisions that would have a great impact on their lives and those of their family. Adherence to a single academic viewpoint would hinder this investigation and a pluralist conceptual framework is the best approach. I will thus draw from a number of different disciplines, although my emphasis will be more on behaviours than institutions as I examine these key financial decisions.

33 Hopkins 1995–96: 41.
34 Lavan 2016: 21–2.

Who were the people concerned?

This a book about the 9,743 individuals who participated in the transactions I collected. But who were the people who did these deals? They come predominantly from the rural nomes of Middle Egypt, reflecting the pattern of survival of the papyrological texts. Papyrus survives best in undisturbed dry conditions and the accidents of survival mean that they have been found in a variety of contexts: in ancient rubbish dumps, in abandoned villages lost to the desert towards the end of the Roman period, even used as the stuffing to preserve sacred crocodiles. Most of the data we have available come from the areas south of, but relatively near to, modern Cairo. We have very little from the largest city in Roman Egypt, Alexandria, simply because much of the ancient city is now under the Mediterranean sea. The most common source locations are the Arsinoite nome (the Fayuum), literally a backwater region, away from the Nile valley, and the Oxyrhynchite nome, which lay on the Nile valley itself. In both of these nomes we have data from both cities and villages. The papyri are generally written in Greek, reflecting the history of Alexander's conquest of Egypt and the subsequent establishment of the Ptolemaic dynasty as the rulers of Egypt and the colonisation of certain regions, including the Fayuum, by Greek-speaking plantations. Greek was also the lingua franca of all the Eastern half of the Roman world. However, just because a document was written in Greek does not mean that the parties were descendants of Greek settlers and many of the people concerned would have been indigenous Egyptians. We get clues from names but no certainty of their background or ethnicity.[35]

But despite these geographical and ethnic constraints, the great advantage of the papyrological information is that, like the Vindolanda tablets, they can be regarded as documentary evidence about ordinary people, rather than the art, inscriptions and histories dealing with the elite that dominate the classical interpretation of the Roman world.[36] Papyrological studies have been considered to focus 'on the urban and rural middle classes ... individuals who owned some property but were not rich, small and moderate landowners, veterans, craftsmen, merchants'.[37] I

[35] This book does not deal in any detail with religious or ethnic issues, which is not to underestimate the significant contribution of different groups to the economy, which will, for instance, have been impacted by the aftermath of the Jewish revolt and the gradual introduction of Christianity. It is simply difficult to quantify these impacts.

[36] In passing, even the most respected historians can sometimes be in error. The famous Vindolanda tablets are mostly ink on wood, not, as Mary Beard states, scratched on wax: Beard 2015: 490.

[37] Huebner 2013: 5.

did have some concerns therefore, that the costs to the scribe of drawing up documents, and language preferences, may overly bias the data to a Greek-speaking sub-elite rather than the ordinary Egyptian farming families who made up the vast bulk of the population. I was reassured, however, by an accidental discovery made when extracting the data from financial records.

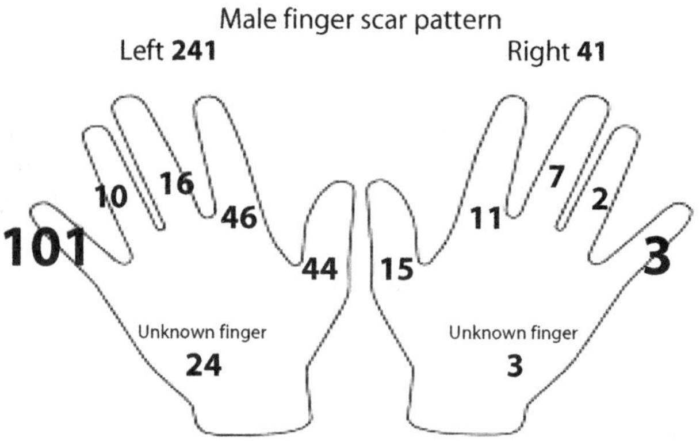

Figure 1 Scar distribution

The process of data mining can be mind-numbingly dull but satisfying. It was through the process of gathering information on the ages and sexes contained within the data that I began to notice a pattern in the descriptions of the people concerned. The descriptions that were used to identify someone often included scars, much as passports used to have a section on distinguishing features. Not only did a surprisingly high number of people have scars, but more men had scars on their left hand than their right, and a high proportion of these were on their little finger. I gathered the data and produced Figure 1.[38] I puzzled over this pattern for some time. Did it relate to a ritual practice or violence of some kind? Eventually, in discussion over lunch with a friend we arrived at a convincing explanation of both the prevalence of scarring on the left rather than the right hand and the high number of injuries to the little finger of the left hand. The prevalence of left- rather than right-hand injuries could certainly be explained by tool use; but why the high number of injuries to the little finger?[39] If the injuries resulted

[38] In total, I extracted data from some 2,568 descriptions. Unfortunately, there are insufficient data to produce figures for women.

[39] The greater frequency of scars to the little finger of the left hand rather than the right hand is statistically significant at a probability level of in excess of 99.9 per cent

from holding an item in the left hand whilst using a tool, like a hammer, surely the most frequent injuries would occur in the thumb and forefinger?

One of the most frequently employed tools in Egyptian farming was the sickle, which was generally used for harvesting corn rather than a scythe. The process of harvesting is illustrated in a number of pieces of tomb art and there was a gendered division of labour, with the man reaping and the woman gathering the ears of corn.[40] I believe that the most likely reason for the very significant prevalence of scars on the little finger of the left hand for men is that this was the most vulnerable point on the body for a harvesting worker using a sickle in his right hand making horizontal cuts to the standing corn being held by the left hand. As Shaw put it:

> as the weariness of long hours of cutting and sheaving dragged on and exhaustion set in … it was possible to miss the mark and hit one's hand or fingers. It happened to a reaper in late sixth-century Gaul. He cut through one of his own fingers, but he was lucky enough to have a holy man nearby who was able to heal the digit dangling from his hand by a thin strip of skin.[41]

The little finger of the left hand would be the part of the hand closest to the blade as it cut and thus that part most likely to be injured. That this risk was real is illustrated by the use, within living memory, of hand guards for the left hand when harvesting with a sickle in Southern Europe, such as a *zoqueta* from the Basque country.

So, for our purposes, the association of this particular scar type with the physical activity of reaping provides an important 'marker' of such activity. I believe, given the rareness of little finger injuries to the right hand, which suggests that the little finger was not a part of the body at significant risk of injury in everyday life, that someone with a scar to the little finger of the left hand was someone who in all likelihood had at some point undertaken physical harvesting work and in particular reaped crops. The same may also be assumed but with less absolute certainty for those who had injuries on their left hand more generally and some 16 per cent of men had scars on their left hand. Of course, not all people who had reaped would have been clumsy enough to have injured their hand, so the high prevalence indicates that, particularly in the villages, many men involved in the financial

– a level of scientific confirmation that archaeologists and ancient historians can usually only dream of.

40 For a particular clear example, see the Tomb of Sennedjem, 1280 BC, Deir el-Medeina, Thebes, at The Metropolitan Museum of Art, New York. For a Roman period example of harvesting and division of labour by gender and age, see the Tomb of Petosiris, as shown in Venit 2016: 38 (Fig. 1.32).

41 Shaw 2013: 40–1.

transactions that this book is concerned with, would have physically farmed the land themselves.[42] This is backed up by the fact that 91 per cent of males had some, presumably substantial, scarring used for identification purposes, which I would suggest is most likely to have resulted from their occupation, given the proportion of their time spent at work.[43] We are therefore dealing with very ordinary agrarian people, many of them tenants, who had a direct physical connection to the land, as well as Huebner's 'middle classes'.

'Big data' for the Roman world

A reasonable question would be why concentrate on Egypt? And the simple answer is the unique quality and quantity of data available. It is, in the expression I first heard Roger Bagnall apply in this context, the ancient historian's version of 'big data'. I do, however, need to define the scope of what I have interpreted as being 'Roman Egypt'. I have chosen to define the time period for study as being between AD 1 and 350. The start date allows time for Roman institutions and attitudes to have embedded themselves within Egyptian society in the 30 years following Augustus' conquest in 30 BC. The end date of AD 350 was chosen to allow for study of the higher inflation period of the fourth century, whilst the geographical scope is defined by the province or provinces of Roman Egypt.

The data come mostly from papyri, which is similar to our modern-day paper, and is the source of the word, but it was thicker and made from the pith of the papyrus plant that flourished in the Nile wetlands. These documents would generally be written for the principals by a scribe for a fee. We also find generally shorter, more informal documents, written or inscribed on *ostraca*, or small pieces of pottery or stone. These may be as simple as the IOU written by Epithymetos, a soldier at the Mons Claudianus quarries in the Eastern Desert, on 3 September AD 140, recognising that he owes 5 drachma to Flavius Isidoros, a soldier with the Alexandrian fleet.[44]

The data available reflect the patterns of survival, publication preference and other variables outside my control.[45] At the time of compilation of the

[42] Of the 1,378 men from Arsinoite villages with descriptions, 94 per cent had scars of some sort and 5 per cent had the little left finger scar. The figures for the city of Arsinoe are lower, 83 per cent and 2 per cent respectively (n = 254), but still high enough to indicate significant numbers of farmers. However, with a smaller sample (n = 100), the numbers for the city of Oxyrhynchus are lower at 80 per cent and 0 per cent respectively. This may indicate a difference in the nature of the populations of the two cities concerned. Arsinoe appears to be directly connected to the rural community, whereas Oxyrhynchus may have a more truly urban character.

[43] Females were by no means exempt from injury, as 71 per cent of women had identifying scars.

[44] *O.Claud.* III 540 (AD 140).

[45] See Lerouxel 2016: 3–8 for a discussion of the issues involved in constructing a

data there were 18,962 published documentary papyri where the date of the source could fall within the period from AD 1 to 350. First, I needed to categorise all these papyri to form a 'normative' database.[46] Then I needed to extract a subset of these data to establish smaller databases of documents of particular interest. This data subset was then 'mined' to identify relevant features and trends. For this quantitative approach to be effective, it was essential that a strictly objective methodology was used and this methodology is described in my thesis.[47] However, this quantitative approach needed to be allied with a qualitative, and inevitably subjective, analysis of particular texts.

The database from which the data were collected is the Duke Databank of Documentary Papyri (DDbDP), as set out within 'Papyri.info' (http://papyri.info/), including most published papyri collections. Whilst, as noted by van Minnen, no database can be regarded as covering all the relevant papyri in existence and there may be published documentary papyri that have been omitted, the vast bulk of published papyri are included within the DDbDP.[48] As regards the provenance of the documents concerned, it should be noted that we have few papyri from Alexandria and that the bulk of the papyri from the Oxyrhynchite nome come from the nome capital – Oxyrhynchus.[49] It should also be noted that the number of papyri, by type and location, vary over the period, but by adopting a normative approach and examining trends over time I have sought to take account of these diachronic changes within the sample.

Transactions of particular interest

The details of the transactions that were particularly relevant (land sales, house sales, loans and deposits, land leases and house leases) were placed within excel databases. Entries in the databases were not limited solely to the contracts themselves, and documents that referred to a specific transaction were also included. Examples of these references are petitions or letters referring to a transaction, offers to complete a transaction, contract

database of documentary papyri documents.

[46] For a description of the process of normalisation of data within a Roman papyrological context, see Bagnall 2011: 65 and for the procedures that should be adopted in the interpretation of the data, see Bagnall 2011: 74.

[47] See Kelly 2020. A listing and partial description of the data may be found in the appendices to my doctorate, which are available at www.academia.edu/80342215. At more than 200 pages long, these appendices were too large to include in this book.

[48] van Minnen 2009: 652. See Duke Databank of Documentary Papyri. https://papyri.info/docs/ddbdp.

[49] I use the term 'city' to refer not only to Alexandria and the other three *poleis* but also the nome capitals (for instance, Oxyrhynchus). See Tacoma 2008: 87 for a discussion of this categorisation. All other settlements are categorised as villages.

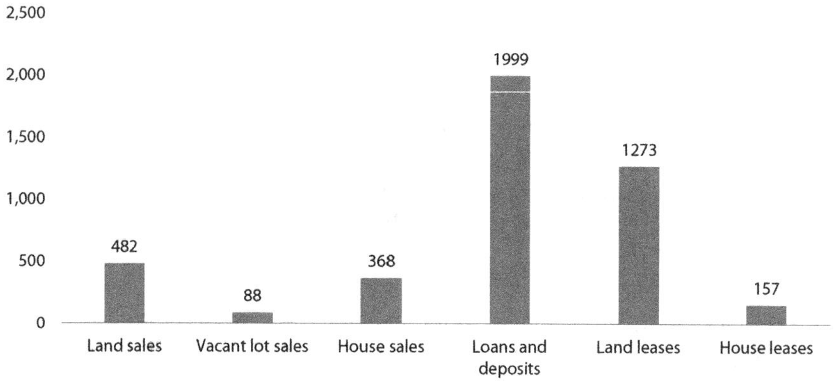

Figure 2 Number of transactions of particular interest

registers or receipts for payments. Five interconnected databases were thus established, derived from 2,941 documents. In total, a remarkable 4,367 transactions were included in these databases and their distribution is shown in Figure 2. Nowhere else in the ancient world does such a large body of diverse financial data survive.

Having established the five transactional databases, they needed to be analysed. The database format had been chosen as a set of inter-connected excel spreadsheets so as to make this analysis process as easy as possible. Using a spreadsheet allowed medians, averages and other attributes of the data such as distributions to be relatively easily calculated and displayed. It also allowed a number of the conclusions to be tested for statistical significance. It might be thought that the databases constructed would be suitable for the application of social network analysis (SNA) given that the documents contain much information on the individuals concerned and their geographical location. However, in practice it has not proven useful to use the normal techniques to identify standard clustering or density measures, or to display nodal information in network diagrams, partly due to the fact that the inclusion of information on individuals, particularly their location, is highly selective, and varies according to circumstances.[50] For instance, when two principals in a transaction were resident in the same village there may not have been any need to record their locations in the contract. Lerouxel adopted an approach where he used the document's

[50] This may reflect my own visual perception bias, but I frequently find SNA charts more confusing than elucidating. In any event, most of my data are of an isolated, distinct nature and cannot be tied directly to the rest of the data, with the exception of family archives. I have, however, examined social networks by looking at the geographical and gender distributions.

provenance to determine the location of the principals in some circumstances, but I have only assigned an individual's location when it is stated or it is implied by the description of the individual concerned.[51]

I make no claims that the databases thus established are exhaustive, since human error inevitably means that some documents may be missed or misclassified. I hope, however, that the systematic process undertaken will have eliminated any unconscious bias in the identification of the documents of particular interest and ensured that the vast bulk of relevant transactions will have been included.

[51] Lerouxel assumed that where no location is specified for any of the principals, then their locations were the same as the location where the transaction took place. Lerouxel 2016: 128. This is not an unreasonable assumption, but I have preferred to be more conservative and not make assumptions which depend on scribal habits. I have, however, assumed locations for the participants from their personal description, even if it is not explicit. For instance, in *P.Tebt.* II 395 (AD 150), a document from the village of Tebtunis, which mentions a bank in the city of Arsinoe, one of the principals, Pappion, is described as a gymnasiarch-designate, which is a function that was city-based, and I have thus assigned a location of Arsinoe to that individual.

Chapter 2

The Drachma in Your Pocket

> 'It does not mean, of course, that the pound here in Britain, in your pocket or purse, or in your bank, has been devalued.'
>
> Harold Wilson, British Prime Minister, 19 November 1967

Leaving aside for the moment whether people in Roman Egypt had pockets, I believe the title of this chapter has relevance and resonance.[1] In 1967, Harold Wilson tried to explain to the British public what the devaluation of the pound by 14 per cent against foreign currencies meant for ordinary people, and he failed. That is why his quote about 'the pound in your pocket' is remembered, and it is relevant to Roman Egypt, where in the late third century there was a crisis in public confidence in the coinage, which led to substantial price inflation.

Price inflation and its importance

Before I move on the main themes of the book I need to establish the economic background to the long time period I am analysing and in particular it is important to understand how prices evolved. This is the subject of this short chapter and is important for two reasons. First, an individual's perception and financial aims as to risk and return may be influenced by the general economic and inflationary situation. If inflation is high and trust in money is low, individuals may shy away from commercial or investment opportunities that provide a monetary return and prefer to keep their wealth in 'real' assets such as land ownership. Since this book is primarily about behaviours, I need to understand what external forces might have influenced decision-making. I also need a mathematical framework that allows me to compare the return on different financial items and terms over a long period. For instance, a plot of land under fodder realised a rent of 36 drachmas per aroura (a measure of land size)

[1] They certainly had purses, but apart from the *sinus*, a fold in the toga that could be used for carrying things, I have been unable to find any evidence for pockets as such.

in AD 121.[2] How does this compare in real terms to another plot in the same area that realised 50 drachmas per aroura in AD 269?[3] If I do not have a measure for inflation I cannot reasonably compare the return to the landlord in these two situations.

However, I recognise that inflation numbers may not be the most scintillating of subjects, and the uninterested reader may safely skip this chapter, although I would draw their attention to Figure 20 and the conclusion to this chapter, which summarise my view of inflation.[4]

The accepted view

First, the accepted view is that there was a jump in prices in the 270s when there was a 'brusque leap in price levels around 274 by a factor of ten or more'.[5] In addition, based on Rathbone's work, it is thought that the 'distribution of prices of particularly well-documented goods – wheat, wine, and donkeys – points to the existence of two distinct periods of price stability, from the late first century CE to the 160s CE or a bit later and from the 190s to the early 270s CE'.[6] This is repeated as 'there is also Rathbone's study of Egyptian prices, the only useable series from anywhere in the Empire, which sees the doubling between A.D. 160 and 190 as the only significant change between A.D. 45 and A.D. 274/5'.[7] This view of static prices up to AD 274 was restated recently 'as is well known, inflation starts in 274'.[8]

2 *P.Oxy.* III 499.

3 *P.Oxy.* XIV 1646.

4 For those readers with more interest in the subject I would draw their attention to Kelly 2021a, a paper where prices for the period prior to AD 274 are analysed in detail. For an analysis of the whole period, see Kelly 2020: 30–74.

5 Rathbone 1997: 215.

6 Rathbone 1997; Rathbone & von Reden 2014; Scheidel 2010: 428.

7 Howgego et al. 2010: 1. See Lerouxel 2016: 42 for a similar statement and also Temin 2013: 87–88 for a mathematical proof of price stability after AD 190 but note that he based his corroboration only on wheat prices, and it is thus, I would suggest, flawed. However, he also, based purely on the existence of army pay increases, suggested continued inflation over the third century. Temin 2013: 74. Harper 2016: 816 modelled two periods of level prices for wheat but sees a 'sharp increase in price variability across a range of goods and services in the entire period AD 250–275'. But see the Appendix to Kelly 2021a for comments on Harper's methodology, and thus conclusions, for land prices and rents.

8 Cuvigny & Lach-Urgacz 2020: 321n.35.

Did AD 274 really see a step-change in prices?

The first question is whether AD 274 is an appropriate step-change date, but the data for the 270s are sparse and in order to determine if there was a jump in prices all data related to monetary amounts need to be taken into account. The criteria I have adopted for selecting the data are very strict so as to avoid the implications of circular logic. For instance, *P.Kellis* I 62, which has amounts of rent payments, is stated to date to AD 275 under papyri.info, based in part on Rathbone's proposal that AD 274 was the year of a great jump in prices. To consider such a document as securely dated is inappropriate when the proposition that there was such a jump in prices is the very proposition that is being tested. Therefore, only sources where the dating of the year concerned may be considered secure and not based on comparative prices have been included.

Price data containing indicators of prices that can be securely dated to the decade of the 270s are set out in Table 1, together with a commentary as to whether there is clear evidence for an abrupt jump to a very much higher set of prices. It it is clear that there was a step-change in prices that occurred sometime in this decade. A possible *terminus ante quem* for such a jump is provided at AD 275 by *P.Cair.Isid.* 85 but this is not definitive. A more secure date for such a jump is AD 276, when there are two sources that clearly show a change in wheat and donkey prices. It is more problematic to determine a *terminus post quem* since there may be transactions that were proposed at prices in line with the 260s and these may be 'hang-overs' from previous practice between market participants where the parties had not realised that the 'rules of the monetary game' had changed.[9]

Of interest is *P.Oxy.* XII 1414, which is a record of the proceedings of the Senate of Oxyrhynchus. This text was originally dated to the period between AD 270 and 275 by the editors but can be refined to AD 270–271 in BL VII 138 if the 'tentative' argumentation proposed by Bowman is accepted.[10] The dating of this document is critical since it contains one of the rare references to physical action as a result of price and wage inflation, since the Senate agrees to make a payment in excess of 200 drachmas in response to a petition from the city cloth-workers that 'more drachmae should be given to them on account of the rise in the value of the materials and in the wages of their workmen'.[11] If the dating proposed for this source were to be accepted then it would reaffirm that prior to Aurelian's currency reform of AD 274 there were already systemic

9 Haklai 2011: 18.
10 Bowman 1971: 152–3.
11 *P.Oxy.* XIV 1414.

Table 1 Price indicators in the 270s

Date	Description	Clear evidence for price jump?	Reference
270	Offer to lease house, including five workshops, for a monthly rent of 180 dr.	No. This is the highest house rent known prior to AD 271 and substantially higher than the typical house rents of the period to that date. However, it is not an order of magnitude difference in rent from *BGU* I 253 dating from AD 244 to 248 of the lease of part of a house, court, dining room and bedroom for 100 dr. per month. Furthermore, this is a substantial metropolite house with a number of opportunities for sub-leasing or other use of workshops which might have been expected to command a high rent and thus it does not constitute clear evidence for a price jump in or before AD 270.	*P.Turner* 37
271	House sale at 3,000 dr.	No, see prices in chapter on housing.	*SPP* XX 72
271	Apprentice contract with terminal payment of 60 dr. to the apprentice.	No, amount of terminal payment is small by comparison with cost of living after jump in prices.	*SB* XVIII 13305
271–272	Receipt for the purchase of dates – price is 16 dr., though amount is unknown.	No.	*O.Kellis* 66
271–272, see BL VII p 138	Report of proceedings of senate.	No, though inflationary pressures are clear. See below.	*P.Oxy.* XII 1414
272	Lease of a house at a yearly rent of 400 dr.	No, this level of rent is of a similar magnitude to earlier house rents such as SPP XX 53, where two-thirds of a house was rented for a yearly rent of 160 dr. in AD 246.	*P.Oxy.* VII 1036
After March 272 – following BL VII, S. 215 and APF 44, 1998 p 274	Sale of two donkeys for 4 talents.	Yes, given previous prices, but cannot provide a firm date as to jump in prices, simply that it occurred after March 272.	*SB* VIII 9829

Date	Description	Clear evidence for price jump?	Reference
274	Sale of land – half of 25 and 11/16th arouras for 30,000 dr.	No, at *c*.2,336 dr. per aroura this is higher than attested land sale prices in the 260's – *P.Ryl.* II 165 at 400 dr. per aroura and *P.Oxy.* XII 1475 at 821 dr. per aroura – but not an order of magnitude higher.	*P.Oxy.* XLIX 3498
275	Sale of mare for 5,000 dr.	Questionable. Although the price is considerably higher than the typical range of horse prices in the period up to AD 270, which vary from 72 to 400 dr., there is one example of a horse sale at 2,800 dr. in AD 77, *PSI* VI 729, which presumably reflects the quality of the animal concerned.[a] Thus, although 5,000 dr. is a high price indicating inflationary pressures it is not an order of magnitude difference from the AD 77 example and may partly reflect the quality of the animal rather than an abrupt jump in prices.	*P.Cair.Isid.* 85
275	Bid to purchase private land in possession of state (800 dr. plus extra charges for 11 arouras).	No, though a bid to purchase state land was typically at rates lower than that for private land.	*P.Oxy.* XIV 1633
276	*adaeratio* (the conversion of in-kind taxes to cash) at a price of 200 dr. per artaba.	Yes, given previous prices.	*O.Mich.* I 157 with TAPhA 76 (1945) 144–6
276	Sale of adult donkey at a price of 3,800 dr.	Probably, given previous prices.	*P.Stras.* III 139
c.279	Sale of pitch at 3,400 dr. per talent.	Yes, given prices per talent in *P.Lond.* III 1177 and *P.Oxy.* XXXI 2580 in the tens of drachmas per talent of pitch, or BGU I 14, which has a rate of 240 dr. per talent for dry pitch in AD 255.	*P.Oxy.* XII 1497
279	Cash deposit of 148 talents and 1,280 dr.	Yes, this is an enormous and unprecedented amount by earlier standards and equal to almost 890,000 dr.	*P.Oxy.* XIV 1713

[a] Other available prices for horses in the period prior to AD 270 are: *SB* XVIII 13303 (first century), 200 dr.; *PSI* XIV 1405, AD 133, 80 dr.; *PSI* IX 1031, AD 134, 72 dr.; *P.Ross.Georg.* II 18, AD 140, 400 dr.; *PSI* I 39, AD 148, 188 dr.; *P.Fay* 301, AD 167, 220 dr.; *BGU* XI 2049 (second century), 120 dr.; and *P.Laur* I 11, AD 248–258, 220 dr. 1 ob.

inflationary pressures that manifested themselves in price increases for both free-market goods and wages. However, the small amount of the payment of a few hundred drachmas when in the same document there is discussion of multiples of talents would not seem to point to a change in prices of an order of magnitude and therefore this would imply that the 'jump' in prices came after 270-1. Note that *P.Oxy* VII 1036, a transaction from AD 272, is concluded at rates consistent with those that pre-date AD 270, which would support the proposal that the jump in prices post-dated AD 272.

It appears logical therefore to conclude that the jump in prices occurred between AD 273 and 275. A tenfold jump in prices is a one-off event compared to the endemic and systemic low inflation of earlier years and can only have been caused by an exogenous driver. As to which external event triggered such a change, I address that later in this chapter.

Prices pre-AD 274

Having determined that AD 274 was a potential step-change date, we need to consider prices prior to that date. To determine the pattern of price increases, I examined both prices of goods that could be included in a consumption basket for measuring inflation (barley, donkeys, wheat, wine) and economic indicators, which may reasonably be expected to have a relationship with price inflation. Those indicators where sufficient data exist to allow analysis are donkey rents, earnings, house prices/rents, land prices/rents, loan sizes and slave prices. Note that donkeys, slaves and houses are not homogeneous goods like wheat, where a price can be defined by reference to a price per unit of volume. Some slaves and donkeys will have been in better health than others and houses will have varied in size and quality.[12] These complex goods will also have been subject to different economic supply and demand pressures than staple goods. Therefore, price data from complex goods and the development of other indicators may not be expected to have a 'one-to-one' relationship with commodity prices but may be expected to follow similar patterns over the medium to long term. Thus, they are more useful for indicating the shape and medium-term timing of price increases than the absolute amount of such inflation.

When dealing with multiple time series with relatively few datapoints it is exceptionally difficult to associate specific probabilities with a proposition that a common trend does or does not exist. It is even more difficult – indeed I believe impossible – to combine findings for different commodities

[12] See Kelly 2021b for more discussion on the methodology used to reflect these constraints and for a discussion on the best way to present the data.

and price indicators to arrive at a statistically valid single probability that generally prices did or did not increase. I have therefore taken the approach to work from the patterns and shapes of best-fit lines through the whole period under consideration in order to test whether the accepted view of inflation is correct.[13] When we look for patterns within the curves and statistics shown below we must be aware that, given the small number of observations and the non-chronological price variations that will have existed in our data as a result of regional or other differences, the curves cannot represent fluctuations in prices over the short term. There will have been short-term price differences caused by good and poor harvests, or political and monetary events, and a curve simply represents a smoothed indication of price levels over the longer term. Given these provisos, the development over time of prices and their associated indicators are shown in Figures 3–14.[14]

A visual comparison of the best-fit lines shows that there are different patterns for the first century AD, although the prices of goods are generally flat. All the charts show increases from the middle of the second century and thus far the accepted view is validated. However, all the commodities and economic indicators, other than wheat, show increases that do not stop after AD 190, but continue into the third century, which is contrary to the accepted view. The best-fit line for wheat, however, is largely consistent with Rathbone's conclusion that there were two periods of price stability for wheat: up to AD 160 and from AD 190 to 274, with a doubling of prices in the interim. This conclusion is confirmed by examination of the trends from AD 190 for each of the goods concerned on a logarithmic transformed basis, where wheat shows no upward trend, but all other goods do so, although the number of data points are relatively few. The wheat data shown in Figure 3 are for private sales and a comparison with sales where the state was involved is shown in Figure 15.

The variability of state prices is low and it looks as though prices were conventionally set, typically at 8 drachmas, rather than established by negotiation and the operation of market forces. The drivers for these trades are likely to fall within 'redistribution', as Polanyi defines it, reflecting the power of the state. For instance, the state as buyer requisitioned wheat at a price of its choosing. Other forms of state intervention other than simple

[13] The best-fit line in the figures is a second-order polynomial, which is the simplest curve that can be used to test the accepted view.

[14] The R^2 coefficient shown in each chart is an indicator of the degree of fit of the data to the line drawn, although it is not a direct indicator of statistical significance. Note that the charts are not drawn to the same vertical scale but to fit the available space. Differences in the effective rates of increase are listed in Figure 17.

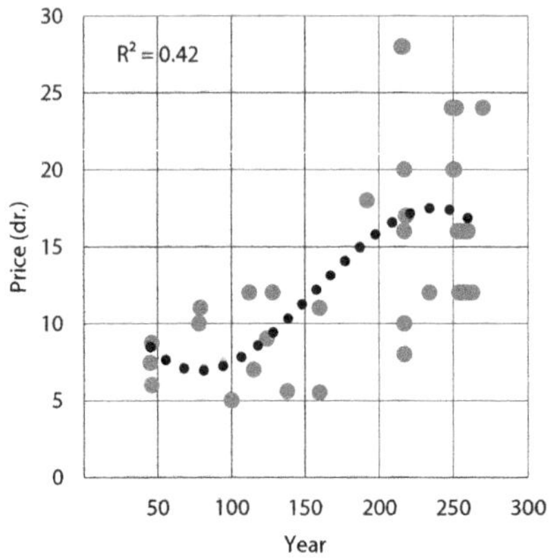

Figure 3 Private wheat prices n = 40

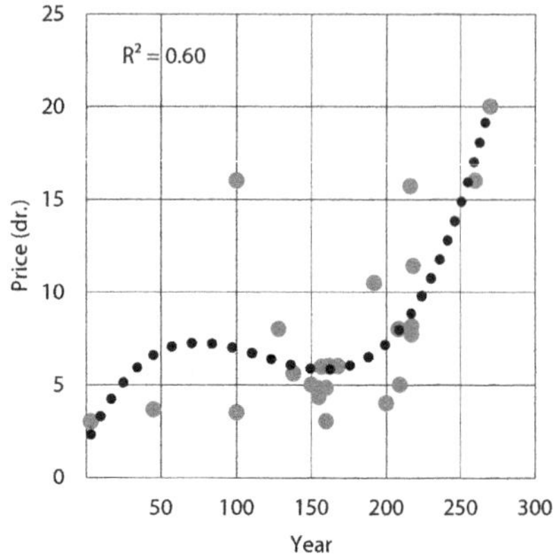

Figure 4 Barley prices n = 25

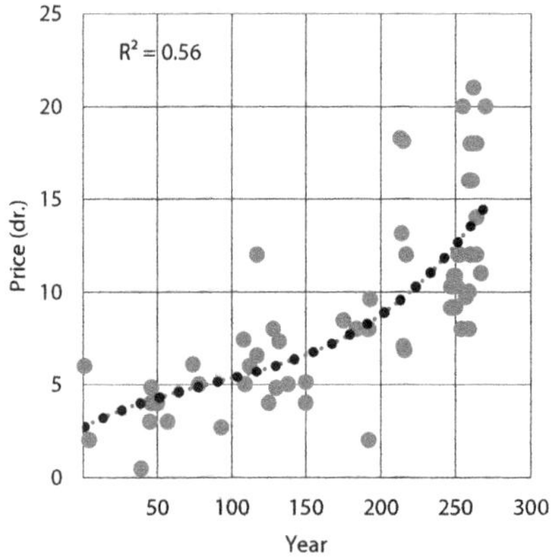

Figure 5 Wine prices n = 65

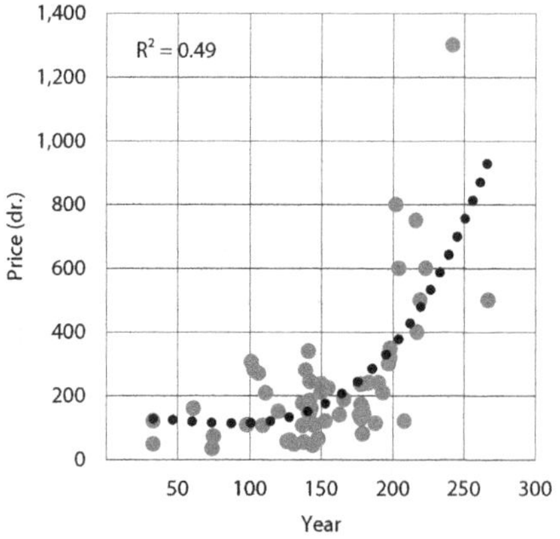

Figure 6 Donkey prices n = 57

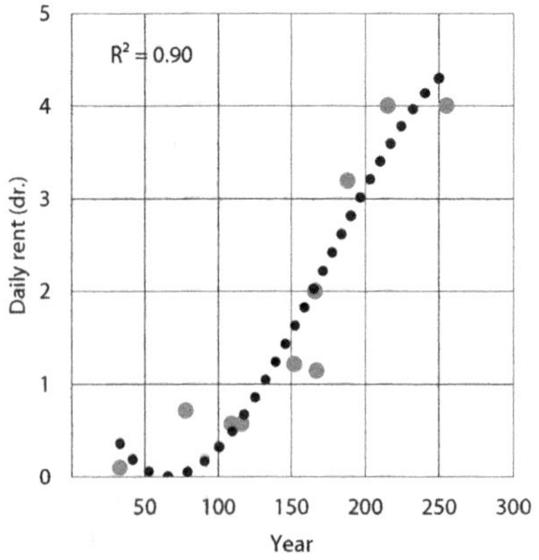

Figure 7 Donkey rents n = 10

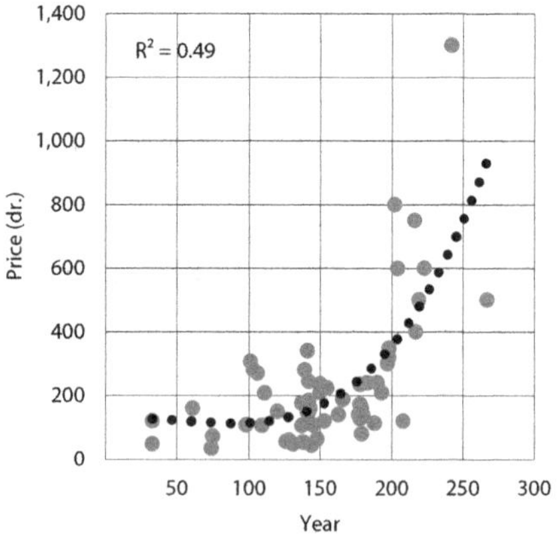

Figure 8 Slave prices n = 25

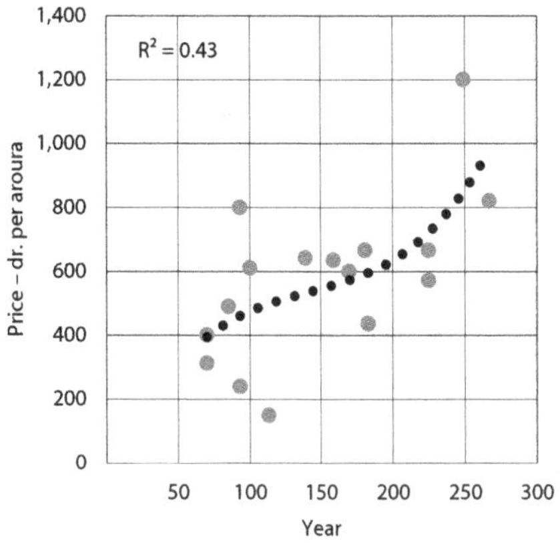

Figure 9 Land prices n = 17

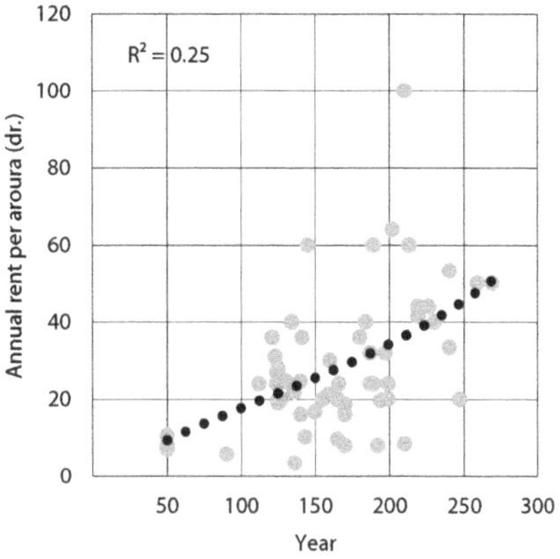

Figure 10 Fodder cash rents n = 54

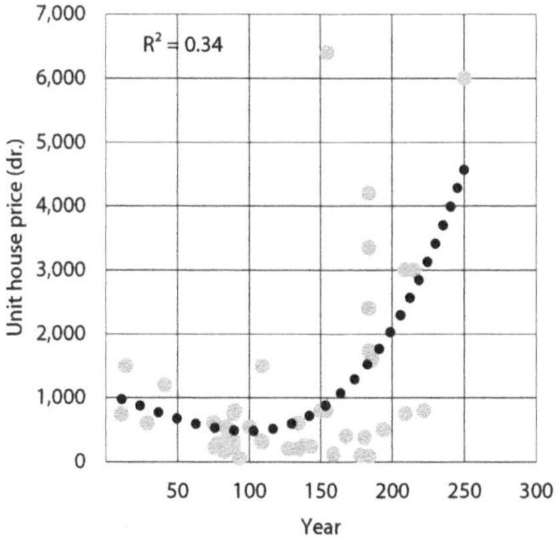

Figure 11 House prices n = 46

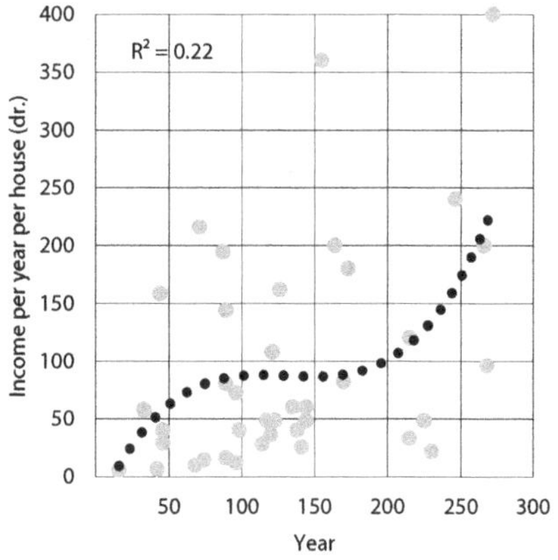

Figure 12 House rents n = 36

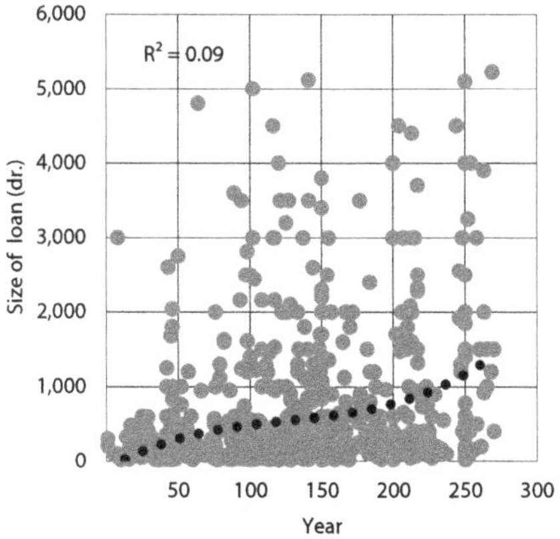

Figure 13 Loans n = 1,008

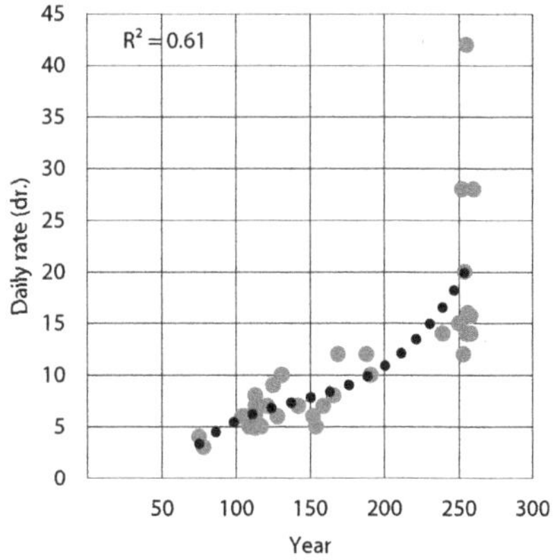

Figure 14 Earnings n = 33

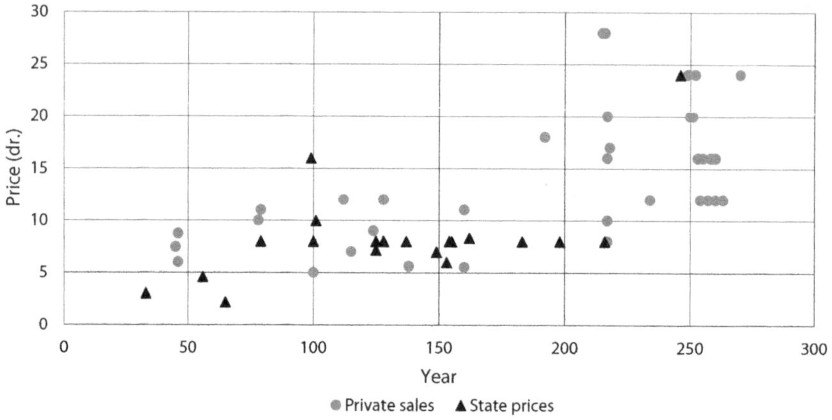

Figure 15 Private and state wheat prices

requisitions or sales from public granaries existed, as in the case shown in *P.Oxy.* XLII 3048, where in AD 246 the Prefect ordered that all private stocks of wheat in the Oxyrhynchite nome be declared and potentially acquired on behalf of the state at a rate of 24 drachmas. As a major actor in the economy, the state's pricing position might dampen average prices if it was slower to react to increasing prices than private individuals or generally made purchases at the lower end of the private market price range.[15] Evidence for such behaviour can be seen in Figure 15 around the beginning of the third century when state prices were maintained at the conventional price of 8 drachma whilst private prices generally increased to around 10 to 20 drachmas per artaba.

However, there is another way, other than in their development over time, that prices of wheat seem to differ from other commodities and that is in their numerical format. In any economic sector where prices are determined by supply and demand and there is significant competition in the marketplace, we would expect to see prices whose numerical format reflects the competition between, and among, buyers and sellers. The format of a market price needs to allow for relatively small changes in the marginal pricing of commodities to facilitate offer and bid processes. Therefore in Roman Egyptian terms, for commodities such as barley, wheat or wine, where the per unit price was typically under 20 drachmas, it would be an indication of free market activity if prices were expressed in fractions of drachmas, or obols. Such 'fractional' pricing is clearly present in wine transactions where many of the prices include obols. Fractional pricing in obols is also present in a number of the barley sources such as *P.Louvre* I 51 (AD 217–218?). Given the higher per unit pricing of donkeys and slaves,

15 Rathbone 1997: 198.

fractional pricing at the obol level was not necessary to allow market prices to be struck but the prices show sufficient 'marginal' variability to allow market processes to function. However, for wheat, the pattern is different. Fractional pricing in obols is relatively rare even within private sales, where there are no examples after AD 160 and where prices tend to be expressed in tetradrachm steps such as 8, 12 or 16 drachmas. State wheat pricing exhibits few signs of fractional or market pricing and the vast majority of prices seem conventionally set at 8 drachmas. Note that there is little or no evidence for conventional pricing of barley, wine, donkeys or slaves, other than in the 'stepping' of prices in multiples appropriate to the coinage system.[16]

Why do wheat prices show a different pattern?

We have seen that there are significant differences between the patterns of wheat prices and those for other goods, and that it appears to be linked to state action, but what could have caused such variation? What was different about wheat? First, it will be noted that bread made from wheat was the staple element of the diet of the ordinary people of Roman Egypt and thus it had a particular social importance. It was also, critically, a commodity where the state intervened to a greater extent than in relation to other commodities. This state intervention took a number of forms. Taxes or rents from state lands were usually assessed and mostly paid in wheat.[17] State tenants were frequently supplied with seed loans for wheat but I am not aware of any state loan for other commodities. The greater interest of the state in wheat compared to other goods can be demonstrated by the simple evidence of the number of price points we have for private and state sources for wheat and barley. For wheat we have a total of 40 private price points within our sample and 31 for state, so state prices represent 44 per cent of our overall total. For barley we have a total of 21 private price points and 4 for state, so state prices form a much smaller proportion of the admittedly small sample: 16 per cent. These figures support a conclusion that the level of state intervention in wheat transactions was greater than for barley. The absence of state prices for wine or donkeys in our sample would also support the conclusion of greater state interest in wheat than other commodities. To support this interest in wheat there was an 'organization involving the whole province from local farmers and village granary keepers up to the Procurator Neaspoleos at Alexandria, all tightly under the surveillance of the Prefect of Egypt'.[18] Given this extensive state apparatus embedded

16 Rathbone 1997: 195.

17 Erdkamp 2005: 222.

18 Rickman 1980: 82. The authorities monitored wheat prices right up until the end of the Empire (Bransbourg 2012: #p92). This is not to say that there was no state

within key actors in society, I would agree with Rathbone 'that the wheat market was not entirely free is not surprising'.[19]

Given the lack of evidence for substantial state intervention for barley, wine and donkeys and the patterns within the prices – where there is marginal pricing, a clear increasing trend over time and no sign of pricing by convention – these commodities may be regarded as goods where 'exchange value' was the dominant feature in their market.[20] What this analysis shows then is a co-existence of two economic sectors, with the prices of wheat being influenced by economic interventions by the state, whilst other commodities were largely left to float to find their own market price. It should be stressed for wheat that this was in no sense an attempt to fix prices as in Diocletian's Edict. We have no evidence in the period concerned for any central state directives coming from Rome requiring that wheat prices be set at a certain level and there is little evidence for central government grain agents operating at a provincial level.[21] This pattern of prices seems rather the result of local state interventions, which appear to have had the effect of encouraging wheat production at the expense of other crops. State intervention also seems to have dampened both the level and variability of the average price of wheat, given the policy of state prices being generally lower than private ones at the beginning of the third century and being conventionally set at 8 drachmas for the bulk of the period.

Numerical estimates of inflation

The discussion above has concentrated on the patterns and shapes of the development of typical prices and indicators, but how would this translate into numerical estimates of inflation as measured by the increase in the price of goods?[22] The typical increase rates for individual commodities and indicators can be estimated by examining the best-fit lines for each item. But what general measure of price inflation would be appropriate as a rule of thumb? I have constructed a general 'blended' inflation measure that combines the best-fit lines for wheat, barley, wine and donkeys, and where the weightings given to each line are determined by the number

involvement in the market for commodities other than wheat. The state did require, and on occasion, requisition donkeys, barley and wine for military and civilian purposes. For example, *PSI* X 1123 (AD 152) shows the state requisitioning wine for Alexandria from the Oxyrhynchite nome, but the extent of this intervention was less than that for wheat.

19 Rathbone & von Reden 2014: 189.

20 Rathbone 1997: 183.

21 Rickman 1980: 224.

22 Inflation can, of course, also be construed to include the costs of services and housing.

Table 2a–b Average inflation rates (per cent per annum)

Period (AD)	Commodities				Index
	Wheat	Barley	Wine	Donkeys	Blended
50–160	0.4	−0.1	0.4	0.4	0.3
160–190	0.7	0.4	0.6	1.5	0.8
190–270	0.1	1.4	0.7	1.5	1.1

Period (AD)	Indicators									
	Wheat	Barley	Donkey rent	Slaves	Land price	Land rent	House price	House rent	Loans	Earnings
50–160	0.4	−0.1	NA[a]	NA	NA	1.0	0.4	0.3	0.7	NA
160–190	0.7	0.4	1.4	0.4	0.3	0.6	1.9	0.3	0.5	0.6
190–270	0.1	1.4	0.6	0.7	0.6	0.6	1.6	1.1	0.8	1.1

[a] There are too few data points for any conclusion to be drawn on donkey rents, slave prices, land prices or earnings in the period from AD 50 to 160.

of points in each set.[23] Note that this blended line is not a price index in the common meaning of a measure that is based on a basket composed of commodities and that reflects the cost of living for a certain type of individual. Constructing such an index is fraught with difficulties and requires knowledge of the consumption patterns of individuals to determine the weighting of individual components within a basket. Whilst by no means perfect, and open to criticism for the weighting it gives to donkey prices, using the number of observations means that greater weight is given to the components where there is a more robust statistical expectation that the data reflects the experience, and thus, I believe, the line is more likely to reflect 'reality'.[24] The geometric average inflation rate for different commodities and indicators and a blended index, based on the best-fit lines, are shown in Table 2, where it will be noted that the blended index provides a middle-ground estimate of inflation when compared to the individual prices and indicators.

[23] The information from the first half of the first century is too sparse to construct an analysis.

[24] An alternative approach could be to give equal weighting to each commodity as a component of the index, but this would ignore the quality of the information provided. Imagine if you had two commodities x and y, where for x you had two data points separated by 200 years and for y had 100 evenly spread over the period. If you weight both of these equally you are giving equal credence to both sets of data whereas the quality of information is much better for y than for x.

If wheat increases are compared to other items, the clear outlier is the period from AD 190 to 270 when, as we have noted, wheat prices are steady but all the other commodities and indicators continue to show price increases. Although the per annum figures appear small, the cumulative effect is significant. Another feature of note is that earnings appear broadly to keep pace with price inflation as measured by the blended index. If a general levelling off of prices truly did occur in the first 70 years of the third century, then the increase in earnings seen would imply a substantial improvement in living standards for ordinary people over that time, which is questionable given the lack of any other evidence for real economic growth during that period.

Conclusions for the period prior to AD 274

Ideally I would have liked to provide the reader with solid probability likelihoods to test a specific set of propositions as to price trends, including whether prices continued to rise after AD 190, but the limitations of the data and the difficulty of linking trends in prices of goods to other indicators makes this impossible to do in a strict mathematical way. However, 11 out of 12 prices or indicators show increases in the period after AD 190 and I believe it is reasonable therefore to conclude that prices in the period were more likely to have risen than remain steady. The average levels of general price inflation are low in absolute terms, never being much above 1 per cent per annum, and in relative terms are considerably lower than those that have often occurred in modern economies. The differential patterns of wheat prices against other commodities mean that this was an economy where the state influenced the price of the politically and fiscally vital commodity of wheat, but largely left other commodities to find their own level, and these two market sectors co-existed.

Conditions and prices after the inflation shock of AD 274

Interest in the changes in coinage and monetary policy during the whole period under consideration has generated an extensive bibliography from numismatists, papyrologists and ancient historians.[25] It is beyond the scope of this chapter to consider relationships between money and inflation in any detail, whether it relates to issues of coinage debasement, reform or re-tariffication. However, we need to understand monetary conditions if we are to develop inflation measures for the period after the inflation shock. The changes in coinage in the later part of the period were extensive and before considering their nature it is helpful to set out certain monetary concepts.

[25] See Haklai 2011: 33–9 for a recent comprehensive list.

'Money' can broadly have four functions: a medium of exchange, a store of value when its purchasing power remains stable, a standard of deferred payment in the form of credit and as a money of account 'or standard of value used in reckoning prices, costs and values'.[26] It is this final category to which most of the sources in this period relate. For the purposes of this chapter it will also be noted that there were two important changes in coinage with Aurelian's (AD 274) and Diocletian's reforms (AD 295–296).[27] These changes in coinage mean that a peculiarity of this period is that the units used as a medium of exchange, e.g. Diocletianic *nummi*, could be different from the units used as a money of account where the documents typically retained the drachmas and talents that were largely used for both purposes in the period prior to AD 274. The most significant state intervention in prices was, of course, Diocletian's attempt at price fixing, in his Price Edict of AD 301. That this attempt failed will be evident in the discussion that follows.[28]

The data for this period are few, and wheat, barley, wine and donkeys are the only commodities with a sufficient number and spread of prices. Displaying the data in Figures 16–19 shows that price increases were generally exponential in nature since they show a relatively good fit to a straight line when transformed into a logarithmic scale.[29] We can track the average inflation rate over the period from AD 275 to 350, which is reflected in the best-fit lines in Figures 16–19 and these are fairly tightly defined for wheat, barley and wine at between 13 per cent and 15 per cent per annum.[30] The increase rate for donkeys is lower at 8 per cent per annum. I suspect that the lower increase rate may reflect the lack of data in the later years, since the vast bulk of the data are clustered around AD 310. The R^2 coefficient is significantly weaker than for barley, wheat and wine and this could reflect the greater heterogeneity of the commodity since donkey prices vary not only over time but according to sex, age and condition of the donkey itself. The implications of this weaker R^2 coefficient are explored further below.

Given the rapidly changing prices over time it is not possible to come to any conclusions as to whether state or private wheat prices were lower but it is clear that the state could not maintain the conventional prices set in low multiples of 8 drachmas and had to follow the market as is evidenced by

26 Munro 2012: 1.

27 Harl 2012: 37–8.

28 For a discussion of the background and details of the Edict, see Ermatinger 1996: 67–108.

29 See Kelly 2020: Appendix 2.2 for underlying data. A logarithmic scale is necessary to display data when inflation is high.

30 The average rates are 13.3 per cent for wheat, 13.5 per cent for barley and 14.9 per cent for wine.

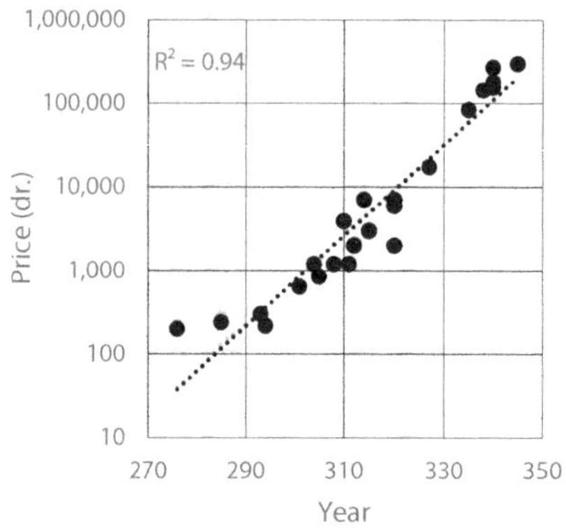

Figure 16 Wheat prices, AD 274–350

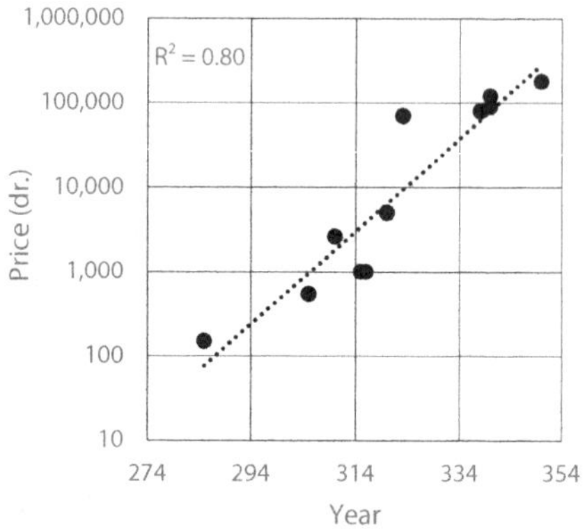

Figure 17 Barley prices, AD 274–350

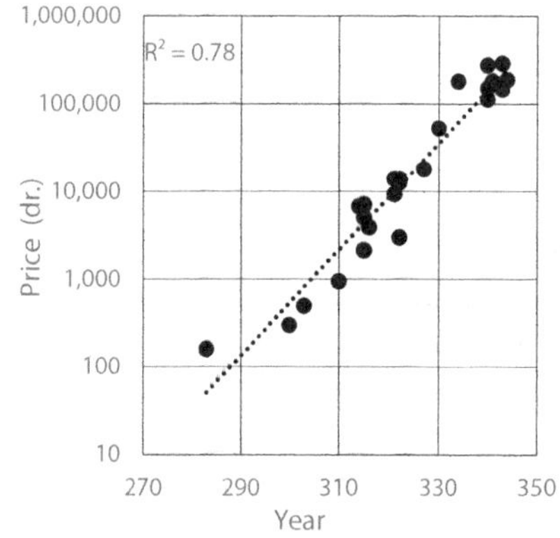

Figure 18 Wine prices, AD 274–350

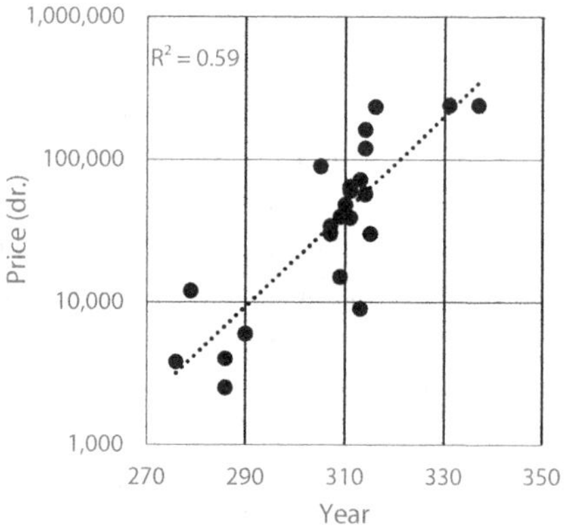

Figure 19 Donkey prices, AD 274–350

O.Mich. I 157, where the adaeratio price (the price for commuting taxes in kind into cash) had grown to 200 drachmas.

The rates of inflation are very much higher than those of the earlier period but do not, at least when averaged, indicate hyperinflationary conditions.[31] Rathbone postulated that after the jump in prices in AD 274 there would have been a pause in price increase until Diocletian's replacement of the Alexandrian tetradrachm with his new imperial coinage in around AD 296.[32] When the graphs above are examined visually there does seem to be a relatively level period in prices up to around AD 300 when the price points follow the trend line upwards thereafter. If there

[31] Cagan 1956: 25.
[32] Rathbone & von Reden 2014: 178.

was a period of relative price stability between the two coinage reforms, this would potentially mean that there were higher rates of inflation in the period after AD 296 than the 13 per cent to 15 per cent noted above. Bagnall and Bransbourg would take a contrary view in relation to the first half of the fourth century and stated:

> That half century saw what has often been described as inflation, but was in fact ... instead a series of steps in which the metallic value of the everyday coinage was reduced, partly by a reduction in the amount of the amount of silver in the coins and partly by a decline in the overall weight of the coins. Each such step led to a noticeable rise in prices.[33]

I would agree that monetary debasement is a very good candidate as to an underlying reason for the increase in prices but believe that it is perhaps inadvisable to assign a single cause to explain all price increases – particularly when, as we will see below for donkeys, there is not an absolute correlation between prices and debasement changes.

Why are donkey prices different? Roman Egypt's used car salesmen?

Unlike the earlier period, the commodity that displays a different pattern to the others is donkeys not wheat. Donkeys show not only a much lower R^2 coefficient but they also have a very different average inflation. The lower R^2 coefficient implies a greater variability of prices for donkeys than for other commodities and I would suggest that in turn this variability has two causes: the natural heterogeneity caused by age, sex and condition referred to above but also inefficiency in the price formation mechanism. The evidence for this inefficiency is best illustrated by considering the variability of the prices for donkeys in the earlier period and for the third century as shown by the 'relative standard deviation' or RSD, a statistical measure where the higher the RSD, the higher the variability of the data.[34] In the earlier period, the RSD for donkey prices is 0.58 for all data points during the 'stable' price period up to AD 150. For the period in the fourth century where we have the bulk of the data, the 12 years from AD 305 to 316, the RSD is 0.90, a much higher variability for a much shorter period of time that cannot be explained solely by the greater variability caused by higher inflation. To give a practical example of this variability, the price for

[33] Bagnall & Bransbourg 2020: 368, citing Bagnall 1985b: 27–48.

[34] Note that this definition of variability is far preferable to the use of the difference between the highest and lowest data point, which overemphasises outlier data and which was adopted by Bang 2008: 161.

a donkey in AD 305 was 15 talents in *P.Oxy.* XLIII 3145 and in AD 309 when other evidence would suggest a higher price by around 50 per cent, the price for another donkey was only two talents and 3,000 drachmas in *SB* VI 9179. Both prices cannot be 'right' and someone took advantage of an information deficit to strike a very advantageous deal.[35]

I would attribute this greater volatility to the inefficiency of the price mechanisms in the marketplace to deal with 'complex', yet mobile, goods such as donkeys.[36] In times of high inflation even a simple marketplace can provide pricing information to market participants on commonly traded, locally produced commodities like wheat, barley or wine, with clear per unit pricing in artabas or jars. The bid and offer process for such commodities is relatively simple, with little room for debate between market participants as to quality, and the likelihood is that there was relative equality in information between buyers and sellers. Both parties would be likely to have known the prices of recent transactions and there may have been multiple counterparties for the buyer or seller to test the market as to the price bid or offered. Donkeys are a more complex good whose variability by age, sex and condition makes pricing a more nuanced decision. The information exchange for donkeys within the market appears to have been far from perfect and both buyers and sellers seem to have struggled to strike prices that were consistent in real terms from year to year in a period of high inflation and I believe that the high variability of the prices struck compared to earlier periods reflects this market inefficiency.

Inflation summary

As regards the pattern of price increases prior to AD 274, my view of the price trends for 'free market' items in Roman Egypt in the private sector is perhaps a simpler one than that suggested by Rathbone and accepted by Scheidel and Howgego et al.[37] There was indeed a period of price stability from around AD 50 to 150 at which point prices started to rise moderately all through the period to AD 270, when thereafter there was a sharp jump in prices. This conclusion is contrary to the commonly held view that the years from AD 190 to 270 were a period of price stability since the cost of living would have roughly doubled over this period. On a macroeconomic

35 Note that the difference cannot be explained by the currency changes outlined by Bagnall 1985b: 31–32 and illustrates that price changes did not simply directly reflect changes in the metallic content of coinage.

36 The mobility of donkeys would suggest that the market would have been more geographically integrated than bulk goods such as wheat, which may have been more expensive or difficult to transport but is not apparent within the pricing evidence.

37 Scheidel 2008: 3 and Howgego et al. 2010: 1.

level it provides a framework for considering whether army pay increases in the period were simply inflationary or whether the army took an increasing share of the available resources at others' expense.[38] Perhaps most importantly, it also contributes to the debate on the effects of coinage debasement on the economy.[39]

I have identified differential patterns of wheat prices against other commodities, which means that this was an economy where the state influenced the price of the politically and fiscally vital commodity of wheat but left other commodities to find their own level and these market sectors co-existed. We will see this theme of there being different sectors that were driven by different drivers in the other purely financial markets.

The analysis laid out above has shown that Rathbone's proposition that there was a jump in prices in AD 274 is supported by the available evidence, although I am unable to pin down the exact timing of such a jump to a more exact date range than AD 273–275. For the period between AD 274 and 296, after Diocletian's coinage changes took effect, we lack sufficient evidence to come to a definite conclusion, but the available information would seem to indicate a period of price stability or lower inflation compared to that which followed. For instance, for wheat, we have an official price of 200 drachmas in AD 276 and by AD 294 there had not been a substantial price increase for official purposes with prices ranging from around 208 to 232 drachmas per artaba.[40] By contrast, for the first half of the fourth century there is clear and remarkably consistent evidence within staple goods' prices of sustained inflation at levels in the order of 15 per cent per annum. This is a high level of price increase but is not indicative of hyperinflationary conditions. The suggested shape of the price developments for 'free market' goods over the period covered can thus be presented in the schematic in Figure 20.

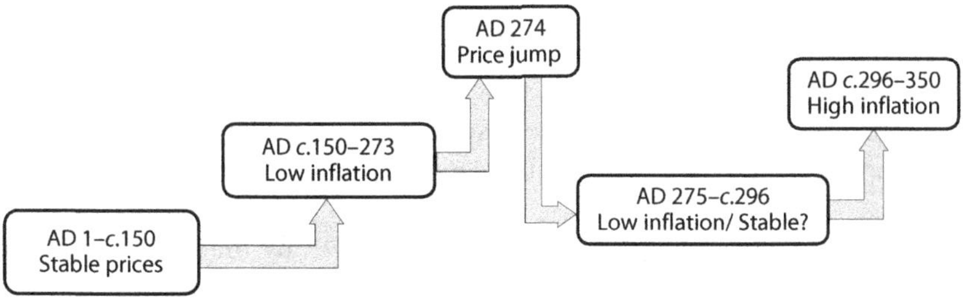

Figure 20 Price schematic

38 For a summary of the debate on the levels of pay and increases, see Speidel 2014.

39 Bransbourg 2012: #p157; Elliott 2020: 126–41; Haklai 2011; Temin 2013: 70–1.

40 *O.Mich.* I 157 (AD 276), *P.Harr.* I 93 (AD 294).

As Bagnall noted, a number of earlier works have suggested that there were periods of deflation in the first half of the fourth century.[41] I can, however, within the data I have analysed, see no statistically significant evidence for such conclusions.

Correlation is not causation

Turning to what caused these price changes, we should remember that price inflation is a function of individual and group behaviours. Individuals tried to buy and sell at certain prices and their attitudes and behaviours, driven by supply and demand circumstances as to money and goods, caused the price increases. But on a macroeconomic level there are many potential causes for inflation. Higher wages can drive an inflationary spiral as can increases in the tax burden, the money supply or in the cost of imported goods. Inflation can also be caused by a loss of confidence in the coinage, particularly when it is perceived to be devalued, as people seek to obtain more units of a devalued currency for the same good. But even if we can identify a correlation between, say, price increases and debasement of coinage, this does not in itself imply causality, since it is simply one of a number of potential causes.

As to why the period after the middle of the second century started to exhibit inflationary increases, in other historical contexts a plague has led to an inflationary spurt – for instance in medieval England after the Black Death – and as Rathbone noted, it could well be that the Antonine Plague was the trigger for this change.[42] However, whilst this external event may have been the trigger to start prices increasing, the continued trend over a period of more than 100 years would point to underlying endogenous systemic economic drivers, linked to fundamental supply and demand issues, which sustained inflation over such a long period. It is tempting to correlate my new findings as to continued inflation after AD 190 against the decline in silver content of the coinage and suggest that the devaluation was the cause. However, as noted above, loss of confidence in the currency is only one of a number of possible drivers for inflation and we simply lack the data to eliminate other plausible causes for the continued inflationary trends.

But what caused the jump in prices *c.*AD 274? By that date the silver content within Roman 'silver' coinage had declined so much that it was increasingly 'fiduciary' in nature (that is money whose value depends on

[41] Bagnall 1985b: 2, citing Mickwitz 1932: 98–114; West and Johnson 1944: 124; Rémondon 1957: 130–46.

[42] Munro 2004: 11; Rathbone 1996: 334.

it being trusted as an accepted medium of exchange).[43] But I believe that the sudden price jump *c.*AD 274 would have needed an extraneous event, probably monetary in nature, as a cause. Roman Egypt in the first half of the 270s was a period of significant political and social disruption. These five years included the period of the Palmyrene coup, then Roman re-conquest and Aurelian's currency reform. The currency reform is the event that Rathbone views as the likeliest reason for the jump in prices and the diachronic analysis above would support this conclusion since the Palmyrene coup and re-conquest date to AD 270–272.[44]

It is tempting similarly to identify coinage reforms as being the cause for the higher inflation of the fourth century. However, the sustained nature of the inflationary conditions for at least 50 years would also argue that inflation was systemic in nature, with price increases being caused by supply and demand imbalances within the economy, although monetary changes could have acted as triggers for price shocks.

Inflation and the markets

Turning to the effects of the price increases on ordinary people; in the period up to AD 274 there would have been strong fluctuations in prices of goods on a year on year basis due largely to the quality of the harvest, which was heavily dependent on the success or failure of the Nile flood (which in turn was largely determined by climate). However, the longer-term trends would have generally been imperceptible and would be unlikely to have influenced market behaviours. People would have been aware of and keen to avoid or exploit short-term price fluctuations. The woman who writes to her husband in around AD 117 about the price of wine and vineyards was certainly aware of the opportunities and risks of price movements and also understood the supply and demand features that caused such changes.[45] The price jump of AD 274 would have shaken consumer confidence in coinage and in the high inflation period of the first half of the fourth century it is likely that they would have been very aware of rising prices. It must, however, be remembered that the 'inflation' that is being dealt with in this section is that of prices in money as 'units of account' not the coinage that circulated at the time. Unfortunately, little can be gathered from the available data as to the equivalence or otherwise of these two forms of money. In passing, van Minnen's statement that inhabitants of the cities

[43] However, as Haklai pointed out, it was never purely fiduciary in that 'it enfolded a promise that it could be converted into a valuable good, i.e. into metal, whether precious or base', no matter the degree of debasement. Haklai 2011: 3–4.

[44] Rathbone 1996: 335.

[45] *P.Giss* I 79 (*c.*AD 117).

in Roman Egypt would have 'died in large numbers, because wheat prices soared' after AD 275 is not logical since an increase in prices does not, of itself, imply famine.[46]

Inflation would also have impacted on the efficiency of the market. If the internal consistency of a market in the way in which it prices goods can be regarded as a measure of its efficiency, in that similar goods were priced at similar prices at similar times, then it appears that the market managed, even in times of high inflation, to operate effectively for simple goods such as barley, wheat and wine. However, the wider variety of pricing of a more complex good, donkeys, would indicate that people struggled to price such goods at this time probably due to inefficiencies in the pricing mechanism of the market.

However, from the evidence described above, there is little, other than the inefficiency of the market to deal with complex goods, to support Bagnall's claim that the 'cause and effects of the price rises … can be seen as characteristic of the relatively primitive ancient economy'.[47] Prices seem to have been driven by exogenous changes in monetary policy or systemic imbalances in the economy and there is nothing inherently 'primitive' about either feature. Periods of sustained high inflation have been noted in modern economies, sometimes fuelled by inappropriate monetary changes or by exogenous events such as the current Ukrainian war. For instance, following on from Harold Wilson's 'pound in your pocket' speech, in a ten-year period from September 1972, price inflation in the UK as measured by the retail price index never fell below 7 per cent per annum, and peaked at 26.9 per cent in August 1975, higher than the average rates seen in the fourth century.[48] The UK economy in the 1970s was certainly inefficient, perhaps broken, but surely not primitive?

[46] van Minnen 2008: 228. Unprecedented increases in prices tend to hurt those with cash reserves more than those who are already living hand to mouth, if wages and agricultural produce prices also rise. See, for instance, the hyper-inflationary conditions of 1920s Germany, which diminished the financial well-being of the middle classes to a great degree.

[47] Bagnall 1985b: 55.

[48] 'UK inflation since 1948'. www.theguardian.com/news/datablog/2009/mar/09/inflation-economics#data (accessed 3 January 2017).

Chapter 3

Housing

Markets within Markets

This chapter deals with the housing markets, whether in cities and villages, for sale or rental, or bought by investors or owner-occupiers.[1]

Types of housing

Properties varied in the size of their footprint, but most houses were of mud-brick construction with timber used for framing and roof beams.[2] Many incorporated yards that Huebner described as 'the center of activity and socialization' and the houses themselves were typically of two to three storeys.[3] They were simple, impermanent buildings and Husson noted that there are only three cases where houses are stated to have been built in stone in the papyri from the Roman era.[4] All of these were in Oxyrhynchus and are likely to have been considerably more expensive to build than the typical house, and this is reflected in the higher price of a stone-built house from AD 222, which at 21,600 drachmas is more than ten times the typical price of houses at that date.[5] In general, the available sale documents provide only limited details as to the nature of the housing being sold, including the location, a brief description and the proportion of the total property included in the transaction. It should be stressed, even if the cities and villages had 'blocks' of housing, these are very different from the high multi-storied apartment blocks of Rome and possibly Alexandria, although none of the data we have comes from that city. There was also, in common with much of the rest of the Roman world, a blurred distinction between

[1] The chapter title comes from a quote by Australian financial analyst Paul Clitheroe: 'Before you start trying to work out [in] which direction the property market is headed, you should be aware that there are markets within markets'.

[2] Bagnall 1993b: 49; Alston 2002: 59.

[3] Huebner 2013: 41.

[4] Husson 1983: 310, citing *P.Oxy.* III 489 l.7 and l.15 (AD 116–117) and *P.Oxy.* XIV 1634 (AD 222).

[5] *P.Oxy.* XIV 1634.

commercial and residential spaces and property and a number of sales and rentals include commercial premises.[6] Housing was not, however, generally tied to land tenancy, which does occur in other societies. This has a number of important implications for the real estate markets. First, it means that we can treat the housing and land markets separately, second, it should in theory have increased liquidity in the housing market and finally it reduced the dependence of the agricultural tenant on his landlord since they were not reliant on the landlord for accommodation as well as the land.

Who lived in the houses?

Houses were occupied by relatively large numbers of people and often by more than one family grouping.[7] And we need to be careful here in our understanding of households, family groups and economic units of production. As Huebner stated, 'households were not necessarily a unit of production that shared its means of production such as livestock, farming equipment, and land and did not inevitably hold all its property jointly'.[8] Add the propensity for houses to contain lodgers with no familial connection, and the fragmentation of houses into differently owned or rented spaces and the complexities increase.[9] In general in this book I will concentrate on, and model, the economic unit that shared its resources and debts, rather than be tied to a wider family or household definition. These economic units would have evolved over time as family circumstances changed but the pattern that appears from family archives and individual transactions is that there was typically a male, patriarchal, head of the economic unit, although through widowhood and divorce economic units could also be matriarchal. The family form of these economic units could be both vertical (extending through generations) and horizontal or *frérèche* (siblings, from the French for brother) in structure and naturally came with all the stresses and strains that family groupings imply. Apart from husband and wife disputes (and divorce was common), Huebner suggested that one of the common areas of domestic conflict, given the demographics, would have been the mother-in-law/daughter-in-law

6 For instance, *P.Amh.* II 97 (AD 198) includes an oil press and *P.Wisc.* II 58 (AD 298) is a house that was previously a mill. There is also the house rental *P.Mich.* XIV 678 (AD 98), where the landlord allows a fuller to operate his trade in the gateway and on the roof of the house, which, given the smelly and unpleasant method of Roman fulling involving urine, would have had a big impact on the neighbourhood.

7 Alston calculated an average number of occupants per house of between 7 and 9 and an average number of people per family group or household at around 5.5, based on 11 texts mostly from the Arsinoite nome ranging in date from the first to the third centuries. Alston 2002: 70.

8 Huebner 2013: 33.

9 See Bagnall & Frier 2006: 65–6 for more detail on lodgers.

relationship. A second-century letter to a son from his mother seeking to sour the relationship with his wife ('Your wife says in fact "She does not trust you ..."') would back this up.[10] Evidence from the terms within financial contracts would also suggest that conflict within a family was expected and that intra-family goodwill was not always to be relied upon. 'Prenup' marital contracts were relatively common, protecting the dowry that the wife brought to the marriage.[11] When family members lent each other money, they could foresee heavy penalties protecting the lender from default, as happened when in AD 37 Tryphon lent a relatively small sum to his widowed mother Thamounis.[12] Another complication, or perhaps simplification, to family life was the frequency of incestuous marriages between brothers and sisters.[13]

Occasionally the documents provide more information on the personal circumstances of the individuals concerned. For instance, in *P.Oxy.* XIV 1648 (late second century), a mother bought a house for her daughter, and in *CPR* I 131 (first half of third century), the driver for one individual was his own geographical move to another city.

Property will have been acquired by purchase but also through inheritance. Partible inheritance was the norm, rather than all property passing to the first-born male (primogeniture), and whilst daughters were also entitled to inherit as well as sons there was not usually an equal distribution. I explore this further in Chapter 6. Therefore, real estate, including owned houses, would have been fragmented by inheritance and this might have acted as a stimulus to the marketplace. The frequency of sales where only a fraction of the whole building was sold reflects the partible inheritance system where multiple heirs would inherit a property. This system posed a problem when fractions of a house became too small to be marketable. If you were the inheritor of a fraction of a house you could possibly find a modus vivendi to share living space with other family members, but it might be difficult to define and thus commoditise a small fraction of a house for renting or selling to a third party. An example of this effect is given in *P.Mich.* V 276 from AD 47, when

> Didymos and Herodes and Herakleides and Maron and Herakleides, also called Louris, all five sons of Herakleides, acknowledge that we have sold

[10] *SB* III 6264 (second century). Huebner 2013: 142–9, although the evidence she presented on how frequently mothers-in-law and daughters-in-law cohabited would not support a case for this issue being the norm, as only 15 per cent of married women (n = 30/200) experienced this at any one time, based on census data.

[11] See *P.Mich.* II 121r IV i for an abstract of an example from AD 42.

[12] *SB* X 10238; see Rowlandson 1998: 116–17.

[13] Although Huebner 2013: 48 argued (against most other scholarship) that brother–sister marriage prevalence should be seen as reflecting a practice of adoption of a son-in-law.

> to Tamaron, daughter of Herakleides, from the present day, forever, the seventh share of the half of a house and yard and all the appurtenances, held in common and undivided by us and by Didymos, the brother of our dead father Herakleides.[14]

However, even after consolidation, Tamaron still only ended up with a fraction of a house and yard.

The nature of occupying a house also requires us to step back from our preconceptions. Hobson's view is worth quoting:

> The average Egyptian peasant was likely to share a house and its attached court/stable/kitchen with other branches of his family; he might also rent space in his house to non-relatives in order to generate some cash ... But he lived mostly out of doors, and his sense of place was not therefore bound by the confines of a single building ... When he identified himself for official purposes he might give his name, the names of his father and mother and paternal grandfather, but he did not refer to the house where he lived. ... An individual house might provide shelter for a household ... but it was a far cry from our idea of home.[15]

Buying or selling a house

House sales were recorded in contracts and most of the available contracts come from villages in the Arsinoite nome or from the city of Oxyrhynchus. There were few legal constraints on who could, or could not, own or rent a property and indeed the Roman state, by the establishment and maintenance of property registers and the *bibliotheke enkteseon*, would have encouraged the real estate sale markets through the exchange of information that confirmed ownership. A significant institutional constraint on real estate markets was, however, the level of taxes and other frictional costs, such as legal or registration fees. If these fees were too high they would dampen market activity and reduce turnover. The evidence for Roman Egypt suggests that the tax payable on transfers of houses was typically quite high from a modern Anglo-Saxon perspective, at 10 per cent of the purchase price or more.[16] However, the costs are of the same order as *notaire*/tax costs in modern France and thus whilst they may have reduced turnover they do not constitute an impenetrable barrier to the operation of a relatively efficient market driven by the pursuit of profit.

[14] See also Hoogendijk 2006: 203 for a good example of how house ownership became fragmented over two generations.

[15] Hobson 1985: 228–9.

[16] Wallace 1938: 227–9.

A set of transactions that could influence or bias my analysis are 'fiduciary' sales. These are sales where a sale document is concluded along with a loan and where the price of the house is the same as the amount of the loan. Such sales are generally regarded as a method for providing security to the lender rather than a genuine sale at market value, and as such I have not included them in the data I used to analyse prices.[17]

As noted above, ownership of a house was frequently fragmented and when looking at sales and purchases the data show that the smallest fraction of a house sold is 1/42nd, but houses were also often sold in their entirety.[18]

Real estate sale contracts were complex documents that contained clauses designed to protect both parties and we can compare a relatively complete example of a house sale (*P.Mich.* X 583 from AD 78) and a similarly complete land sale (*P.Oxy.* III 504 early second century) with the standard contract terms for a modern UK property sale (see Table 3).[19] It will be seen that the majority of the clauses in a modern contract are also replicated in the ancient ones and the care taken in drafting is obvious from this extract from the house sale that goes somewhat further than a modern one in the commitments of the seller.

> Maron and his representatives will guarantee to Hermas and his representatives the property sold in accordance with this sale with full guarantees for all time; and he will deliver the property unencumbered, unpledged, not offered as collateral, not alienated, and free from all debts, both public and private, and will see that it has been neither previously mortgaged nor previously sold to other persons, nor any part of it either, in any way whatsoever, and will see that no one hinders the purchaser, Hermas, or his heirs from exercising ownership and control over the purchases, as stated above, entering and departing, demolishing and constructing on the property however they choose, and furthermore, selling the property, mortgaging it to others, transferring it and using it in whatever way they choose, free from interference.

The fact that remedies are more often foreseen for buyers rather than sellers reflects the information deficit risk of the buyer, who will have had much less information on the purchased property than the seller. Such care and attention paid to mitigate the risks of buying show a very clear understanding of the risks, and the significant financial penalties payable

[17] Lerouxel 2015: 169.

[18] See *P.Lond.* II 334 (AD 166) for the small fraction sale. From the 275 house sales where we know the amount of fraction of the house sold, 116 were entire houses and 159 were fractions.

[19] The Law Society, 'Standard Conditions of Sale', 5th ed., 2018 rev. www.lawsociety.org.uk/topics/property/standard-conditions-of-sale (accessed 26 June 2021).

Table 3 Comparison of contract terms

UK property sale contract	Roman Egypt house sale	Roman Egypt land sale
Definition of parties	Yes	Yes
Joint parties	Yes	Yes
Tax included in price	Yes	Yes
Third party rights	Not in this case but see *P. Mich.* V 269 where the wife of the seller gives consent.	Yes, the adoptive mother of the seller gives consent.
Deposit	Not applicable in this case since full payment made.	Not applicable in this case since full payment made.
Property is free from incumbrances	Yes	No
Physical state	Yes	No, but see *P.Mil.Vogl.* I 26 where the nature of irrigation is described.
Leases affecting property	No	No
Proof of seller's title	Yes history of how acquired provided.	Yes, documents provided.
Timetable	Yes	Yes
Defining the property	Yes	Yes
Buyer's risk at exchange	No, but see *P.Hamb.* I 16 where buyer recognises his risk after purchase.	No
Insurance	No	No
Buyer's occupation	Yes	Yes
Apportionments	No	Yes, tax.
Payment	Yes	Yes
Remedies for buyer	Yes	Yes
Remedies for seller	No	No

further demonstrate the clear financial emphasis of both parties. These are transactions embedded in a (strikingly familiar to modern eyes) legal system that was based on financial rather than social concerns.

Turning to house prices, if all the prices (excluding outliers, including stone houses and fiduciary sales) are re-calibrated to 'real' values as at AD 150 then the distribution of prices is as shown in Figure 21. I would interpret this pattern of price distribution as indicating that there are two distinct groups of house prices and thus houses: those under 800 drachmas and those more expensive houses, which cost more than 1,000 drachmas.

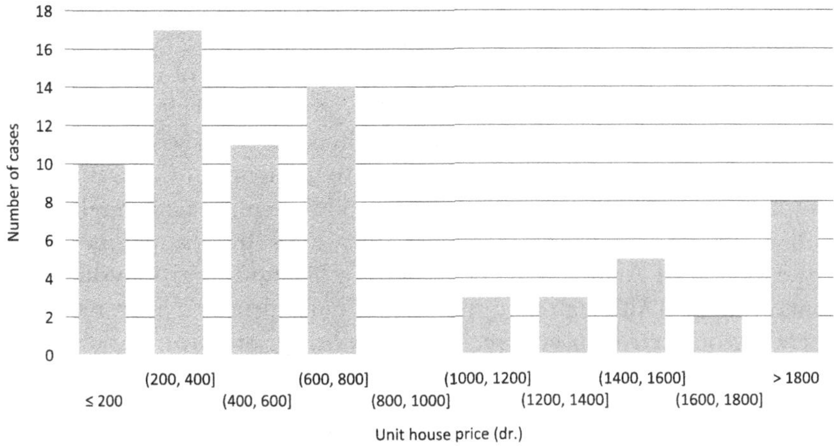

Figure 21 House prices, AD 1–270, recalibrated to AD 15 'real values'

As to the reason for this split distribution, it could relate to the typology of houses and it is tempting to relate this to the structure of the house, for instance the number of storeys, but I can identify no such relationship within the descriptions of the transactions.

There are two cases that are clearly outliers where the price paid is in excess of 20,000 drachmas. One of these, a sale of a house in Oxyrhynchus, *P.Oxy.* XIV 1634 (AD 222), is clearly exceptional since it is the only house with a known price that is explicitly stated to be stone built. The other case, *P.Gen.2* 44 (AD 260), from the Arsinoite nome, is also unusual in being the purchase of a 1/32nd share of two houses, one with two towers and a court, for in excess of 1,500 drachmas, which equates to a price per house of 24,800 drachmas. It would appear appropriate to exclude these atypical documents from the comparison but their presence should be noted as potentially meaning that in addition to the two price bands I identified above there may be a third band constituted by the houses of the rich at considerably higher prices, but for which we only have these two examples.

Both the city and village datasets show a gap in prices in the 800–1,000 drachmas bracket, with the bulk of houses selling for below 800 drachmas. There are 'expensive' houses in both city and village contexts but the key difference is that the distribution of house prices in cities peaks around 700 drachmas whilst house prices in villages are more typically around 300 drachmas.[20] Thus, as might be expected, prices for city houses were higher

[20] This pattern is reflected in the median prices of city and village prices, which are around 680 and 400 drachmas respectively. The overall median house price at AD 150 price levels is 600 drachmas.

than those in villages, but in both contexts relatively expensive houses could be found.[21]

This is perhaps the appropriate point to add a word of warning as to the term 'city' in the context of Roman Egypt. The principal cities where our data come from are Arsinoe and Oxyrhynchus, with some additional data from Antinoopolis and others. There are no significant data from the great city of Alexandria. These provincial 'cities' were, in reality, relatively small in modern terms, although certainly cities from a pre-industrial perspective, with Arsinoe having 20,000+ inhabitants and Oxyrhynchus around 15,000.[22] Although every reader will have their own interpretations depending on their own culture, from a British perspective I would tend to think of them as very large county towns, having the legal, religious and commercial institutions, such as courts, temples and physical markets, which served their surrounding hinterland rather than cities in the modern sense.

Transactions were normally done face to face between the principals, assisted in some cases by signatories and guardians. This can be seen in the ratio of 'closed' transactions, which are known to have occurred between people in the same location compared to the proportion of those 'open' transactions known to have been between people in different locations. This ratio is 3.7 for house sales, meaning that there were almost four times as many local transactions compared to ones involving people outside their immediate location. This is the highest ratio of any of the types of transactions dealt with in this book. The equivalent ratio for house leases is also higher than 1, at 1.9.

There is no evidence of auctions of private houses, or indeed of private land, although we do see auctions of confiscated property by the state. Only rarely were agents, managers or representatives used to substitute for, or assist, the principal buyer or vendor. I have identified only 14 agents, excluding guardians, within the sales. The face-to-face nature of the transaction means that counterparties were subject to geographical constraints and, as noted above, there is a very high proportion of counterparties who live in the same location. So deals were generally done between people who already knew each other and the market survived without the assistance of real estate agents/realtors. There was, however, the familiar stress of house hunting as evidenced by a letter from Diogenis to her brother 'about a house for us to move into: we found one which we will let go before we move over to Agathinos. The house is by the Ision, next to the house of Claudianus ... We are moving there in Phamenoth'.[23] Nevertheless, the

[21] Montevecchi 1941: 104–5 noted the low prices of village houses.

[22] Alston 2002: 333.

[23] *PSI* IX 1080 (third century?). Phamenoth is a month roughly equivalent to March.

tightly geographically constrained nature of the market will have reduced competition among buyers and sellers. House sales were also infrequent transactions, perhaps three or four times less likely to occur than buying or selling a piece of agricultural land.

Whilst the absolute level of prices and the way in which houses were sold provide valuable information on how the markets were structured, another source of information is the format used for prices. 'Prices' in this context does not only mean sale price but can be extended to include rents as the price of occupation. I would draw a distinction between 'conventional' and 'marginal' pricing. In conventional pricing, prices are rounded, which may reflect institutional constraints or market inefficiency. In marginal pricing, the number format is not rounded and this can be considered as evidence for negotiation and competition. Another associated aspect of prices is the degree to which they are variable, since, as Temin noted, 'variable prices then can be used as markers for the presence of market exchange'.[24] Certainly, a relatively small degree of variability in prices would be an indicator of the presence of market forces, but a very high degree of variability may indicate a failure in the pricing mechanism within the market, where participants lack the comparative data to make a rational decision.

Prices for sales of houses were very often rounded. The percentage of house sales between 100 drachmas and 1,000 drachmas that were rounded to the nearest 100 was 70 per cent. As a comparison to a competitive but by no means perfect market, recent equivalent figures for the housing market in England and Wales show that only 5 per cent of all sale prices between £100,000 and £1,000,000 were rounded to £100,000.[25] This shows that, given the relative infrequency of these transactions and the consequent lack of available information, meaningful, reasoned negotiation was very difficult. If neither side had sufficient data upon which to base their negotiating position, it is more likely that prices would have been rounded. 'Prices' that is to say rents, in leases were also rounded and we can see the inefficiency of the market in operation in an offer from a certain Chairemon to rent a confiscated house from the state, where he ups his offer from 8 drachmas a year to 20 drachmas.[26] The sudden jump in the offer

[24] Temin 2013: 8. See also Rathbone 2013: 136–7: 'the more expensive goods and those bought in quantity were subject to fluctuations in price which imply the operation of a free local market'. And, for an excellent summary of pricing theory in economics, see Weber 2012.

[25] See Kelly 2020: 155. Some 35 per cent of recent prices were rounded to a multiple of 10,000 or 100,000.

[26] Some 88 per cent of house rents were rounded to the nearest 4 drachmas; see Kelly 2020: 250. *SB* XX 14281 (AD 142).

suggests that there does not appear to have been a clear benchmark for both parties to use in their negotiation. It is also to be noted that prices in both sales and leases are highly variable (as well as highly rounded), that again would suggest that the market was not efficient.[27]

As to why people were buying and selling houses: people tended to buy and sell houses at relatively advanced ages. Most buyers were aged between 33 and 52 and the peak of activity as vendors was between 43 and 52 years of age. At first sight, the vendor activity would seem to be consistent with inheritance on the death of a father or his widow. However, in an age of high mortality, many people would have lost both their parents before they reached 30 years of age, and thus this is not the case.[28] A possible explanation for these relatively aged market participants may have been that transactions resulted not from inheritance, when as Huebner pointed out siblings may have stayed together, but from the subsequent re-organisation of domestic space as other members of the household died, children matured, married (and in the case of daughters generally left the household) and had children of their own.[29] The relatively high number of intra-family transactions (9 per cent, much higher than other transaction types) would also be an indicator that sales reflected a change in the needs and standing of the family members rather than any desire to make a profit.

Vacant lots

We have 88 cases of the private purchase or valuation of a vacant lot (*psilios topos*). The interpretation of the data is constrained by the fact that the measure of area most often cited in the documents for vacant lots, the *bikos*, does not have any generally agreed value. The data for vacant lots do not therefore provide much useable information as to values. However, as we might expect, a comparison of the median price of vacant lots with the median price of houses, without outliers and fiduciary sales, shows that, typically, vacant lots were considerably cheaper than houses. A median value of 202 drachmas for the price of a vacant lot compares to a median of 600 drachmas for a house, which included the land upon which the house was built.[30] This implies that despite the relatively simple construction techniques described above, the bulk of the value of the house was viewed to be in the physical building rather than the land upon which it was built, assuming that vacant lots were typically of a sufficient size to build at least one house. Also assuming one house per vacant lot, this one-third value

27 Kelly 2020: 250.

28 See Kelly 2020: Appendix C.

29 Huebner 2013: 55.

30 For vacant lots, n = 18. All figures re-calibrated to 'real' values at AD 150.

ratio is, perhaps by curious coincidence, exactly the same as the rule of thumb used in the UK residential building market for the price of land compared to the price of a completed house and its land.[31]

Whilst the purpose for which a vacant lot was purchased cannot be determined from the information available, it seems reasonable to suppose that these purchases could be considered as investments since capital or labour would need to be expended to make such a vacant lot useful, either by the construction of buildings or by its use in some agricultural or commercial fashion, such as a place to park your donkey. Finally, there is one point to be made in relation to these lots. These plots are described simply as empty lots and they will have been in a village or city. An empty lot could be used either for building or potentially for economic activities including gardening. However, the fact that we have no examples of the rental of a vacant lot would suggest that these are primarily building lots rather than that they were used for urban gardening or other economic activity since if the latter were the case some rental agreements would be expected to exist.

House rentals

We have fewer texts for house leases than for other transactions – only 97 documents, which contain 157 transactions. The Tebtunis *grapheion* (or village record office) archive alone accounts for 55 of these transactions. Apart from the ability or obligation to record rental agreements, there were no other institutional constraints as to who could rent housing. Their relative rarity is striking given Bagnall and Frier noted that, according to the census returns, just under one-sixth of families reside in houses they do not own, although renting was far more common in cities than in villages, with 30 per cent of city families renting.[32] It is also clear from the census declarations that it was common to take in lodgers, who might share an undefined space within the house, as opposed to tenants who enjoyed a defined fraction of a house, but this rental activity is not evident in our documents.[33] I believe that the relatively small number of recorded rental agreements when compared to the number of house sales and other documents, tells us that the vast majority of tenancy agreements were verbal and informal.

31 'The Value of Land' (4 June 2015). www.savills.co.uk/research_articles/229130/188996-0 (accessed 18 January 2021).

32 Bagnall & Frier 2006: 69; see also Hobson 1985: 224–5 on infrequency of house leases in villages.

33 Bagnall & Frier 2006: 65–6, 70.

Table 4 Contract comparison

Modern main terms for short term tenancies	*P.Oxy*. III 502
Defining the parties	Yes
Other occupiers	Yes – tenant can assign occupation to others.
Description of property and common parts	Yes
Term and expiry	Yes
The rent and its payment	Yes
Tax and utilities	Yes – the landlord is responsible for the police and brick-making tax.
Inventory and condition	Yes
Deposit	No – but landlord has right to 50 per cent increase in rent arrears and lien on tenant's assets.
Tenant's obligations including care of property	Yes tenant needs to return the property 'free from filth' and with a new rope for the well.
Landlord's obligations including right of tenant to quiet enjoyment of property and repair	Nothing as regards repairs but tenant has right to enjoy property 'without hindrance'.
Landlord's right of repossession	Yes – see terms on arrears.

Where we do have more formal contracts we can again compare them with the standard terms in use in the UK today in Table 4.[34] The Roman Egypt example comes from Oxyrhynchus, when in AD 98 Dionysa leased to Ptolema the house that she owns, which previously belonged to her second cousin. Once again we can see that the vast majority of risks to both parties have been foreseen in much the same way as in current contracts, reflecting a universality of concern and approach to a financial transaction. One area where there is a difference is the lack, in Roman Egypt, of a deposit approach to securing the financial risk for the landlord of damage or rent default, which is common in modern rentals. This approach could well have been adopted in Roman Egypt, since as we will see in Chapter 5 on the credit market, the concept and practice of giving a deposit was well advanced. Instead, the landlord would have to rely on the rule of law to

[34] From the UK government's 'Model Agreement for an Assured Shorthold Tenancy and Accompanying Guidance'. https://assets.publishing.service.gov.uk/government/uploads/system/uploads/attachment_data/file/955826/Model_agreement_for_a_shorthold_assured_tenancy_and_accompanying_guidance_2021.pdf (accessed 15 July 2021).

seek damages to recoup any failure by the tenant to meet their obligations. Although there are a number of reasons that might be advanced as to why this should have been the case, including a greater respect for the ability of the law to enforce contracts, I believe the most likely reason is that generally the housing rental market was a buyer's market in the sense that supply generally exceeded demand. As a result, landlords could not require a deposit that would have provided them with greater security than simply relying on the force of law. I will explore why we can categorise the rental market as a buyer's market later in this chapter.

The locations of the house rental agreements are broadly parallel to the distribution for house sales, with a predominance of Arsinoite village and Oxyrhynchus transactions. Turning to the duration of rental agreements, the median length of house leases, at three years, is somewhat longer than land leases, and the two months when the largest number of contracts were contracted, Mesore and Thoth, lie on either side of the end of the calendar year.[35] As might be expected, there is a great variability in the level of rents, which probably reflects the location, size and quality of the property, but may also reflect inefficiencies in the pricing mechanisms of the markets.

Generally, we have no useful information on the types of houses being let other than their location, but where we have information on the fraction of the house from rental agreements, renting of fractions of houses is relatively rare.[36] The comparable figures for house sales have more fractions of houses being sold than whole houses. I suspect that this pattern partly reflects the fact it was not economic, given the frictional costs, and not legally or practically necessary for either party, to record lodging agreements where a fraction of a house would be let out. However, it could also reflect the difficulties of reifying and commoditising ill-defined spaces expressed as fractions of a house, generally acquired through the system of partible inheritance, as discussed above.

There were two ways to rent housing in Roman Egypt: payment of a fixed rent or providing the landlord with an 'antichretic' loan, where in lieu of interest the lender had the right to inhabit all or part of a house. The number of antichretic loans declines sharply after the first century and they disappear in the later part of the period considered, to be replaced by simple rental agreements. As to why this happens, I would argue that loans were inefficient instruments in that the cost of recording them was disproportionate to the size of the transaction. The implicit annual interest on the loans, assuming the 'standard' rate of 12 per cent per annum,

[35] This is consistent with Haslam's editorial comment that 'most property leases take effect from the new year, whether the contract was drawn up before the period began ... or after': *P.Oxy.* XLIV 3200 (second to third centuries), n. to lines 6–7.

[36] Some 32 out of 44 rental agreements are for whole houses.

which represents the financial gain to the borrower or landlord, had a median value of 13 drachmas. The cost for the scribe for completing these agreements, as evidenced by the Tebtunis *grapheion* fees, was high, and ranged from 2 to 8 drachmas.[37] In addition, as seen in *SB* XXII 15850 (AD 126), antichretic loans also attracted taxes when first established and renewed. With these high frictional costs for loan documentation it may well have been more effective to record these arrangements informally, perhaps verbally, or to use a simple rental agreement that was less expensive to record and did not attract taxes.

The terms of the antichretic loans do provide some indication as to why individuals wanted to gain the right of occupation. In a number of cases, some individuals were definitely interested in becoming a 'professional' landlord, as is demonstrated when antichretic loans allow for sub-letting. Thus the person who was lending the money in an antichretic loan might not be doing so to obtain residence for their own immediate family but rather was looking to make a profit by sub-letting the residence rights received. In *P.Mich.* XII 635 (AD 71), the lender, Maron, obtains a commitment from the borrowers that 'they will see that no one hinders Maron or his representatives from living in this property, lodging others therein, collecting the rents, and using all the appurtenances of the house and courtyard in common'. Note the expectation that Maron will sub-let the property through an agent, which is unusual in property transactions.

As regards the cost (to a tenant) or return (to a landlord) from housing, the median figure for rents is 43 drachmas and that for loans is 13 drachmas. However, these figures are unadjusted for the size of the housing concerned. When the figures are adjusted to include only those transactions where we know the fraction of the house concerned and the rent or capital loaned, then the median income to the landlord from an antichretic loan would be 49 drachmas per house per annum (n = 19). The comparable median rent would be 44 drachmas per house (n = 24). The closeness of these two figures would suggest that antichretic loan amounts and rents were set within a similar value framework.

I noted above that there are two distinct groups of house prices and thus houses: those sold for under 800 drachmas and those more expensive houses that cost more than 1,000 drachmas. If we plot the house rents and income from antichretic loans we can see in Figure 22 a similar split in the distribution of these 'markets within markets'. There are many rents of less than 80 drachmas, but there are also a few where the annual landlord income of a house is above 140 drachmas.[38] The median rental income

[37] See *P.Mich.* II 123.

[38] The nine cases where landlord income exceeds 140 dr. per annum are (five rental agreements): *P.Worp.* 20, Antinoopolis (AD 155), a house with workshops; P.Yale. inv.

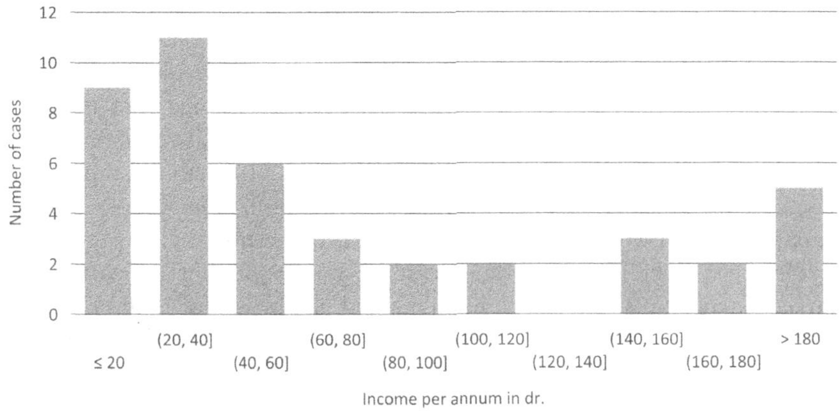

Figure 22 Landlord income

shows the same pattern as purchase price, with higher amounts in the cities compared to the villages.[39]

Assessing a landlord's rate of return and risk

Modelling the rates of return likely to be achieved in different transactions can shed important light on the drivers and motivations of individuals in the marketplace. If a transaction can be seen to provide an attractive return then this might point to the profit motive being a key driver, but it cannot, in itself, prove that this was the case. Leasing a room to a friend might well be profitable, but it could also be driven by emotional ties and prospective or retrospective reciprocity. However, if the likely return from an investment were to be unattractive or even negative, then profit-making would not have been the driver unless the individual had an unrealistic expectation of return.

To calculate the return on any investment type, the first step is to estimate the likely return from each specific transaction. Only transactions that pre-date AD 274 have been assessed since the jump in prices after that

685, Oxyrhynchus (AD 157–188), *P.Oxy.* III 502, Oxyrhynchus (AD 164); *BGU* XI 2034, Arsinoe (start of third century), which has an enormous monthly rent of 200–300 dr.; and *P.Turner* 37, Arsinoe (AD 270), which is a house with some commercial premises attached and (four antichretic loans): *P.Lond.* III 1168, Hermopolis (AD 44); *P.Mich.* XII 635, Bacchias (AD 71), *P.Mich.* X 585, Bacchias (AD 87) and *P.Hamb.* I 30, Philadelphia (AD 89).

39 The median rental income for village houses is 40 dr., where the median house price is 400 dr. The median rental income for city houses is 84 dr., where the median house price is 680 dr. For all houses, the median rental income is 49 dr., and the median house price is 600 dr. All figures have been re-calibrated to AD 150 levels.

date and the high inflation described in Chapter 2 make it very difficult to assess a real return for later periods. The return is estimated by dividing the likely annual financial gain by the amount of the capital employed. Thus, the return from a housing or land lease is equal to the net rent received divided by the value of the real estate, and that on a loan was equal to the net interest received divided by the amount of the loan. To enable comparison, these returns are expressed in percentages per annum, although of course a Roman Egyptian would not have thought in these terms.

However, I believe that there can be no doubt that at least some market participants had the mathematical skills to calculate a likely profit. There is a somewhat reductive debate on whether they had the accounting skills to manage complex transactions and investments. Finley asserted that 'Graeco-Roman bookkeeping was exceedingly rudimentary, essentially restricted to a listing of receipts and expenditures, from which it was impossible to determine the profitability or otherwise of any single activity'.[40] However, as Macve and Rathbone have shown, this position is difficult to maintain, given the evidence, including the Heroninos archive.[41] In any event, lack of knowledge of the peculiarities of modern accounting techniques is no barrier to the assessment of likely profits. As Morley noted, 'rules of thumb, tradition and experience, regarded by Finley as signs of economic primitivism, are instead valid tools in determining production strategies'.[42]

Many individuals were perfectly familiar with the details of calculating returns and were able to compare different transactions to see which were more (or less) favourable. The ability to compare the profitability of transactions of different terms, durations and amounts is a critical pre-condition for the exercise of financial rationality within a market. *P.Kellis* I 90 (fourth century), is a school exercise that I suspect would stump most modern adults, where the pupil is asked how much time is needed for the interest (at 72 per cent, reflecting the interest rates which we will see in Chapter 5 had become common by that date) on 10,000 talents of silver to amount to 1,200 talents.[43]

In another example, the student is asked to determine the amount of a missing feature of a loan if the other elements are known. 'The monthly interest on 100 drachmas is 2 drachmas 3 obols (2.5 drachmas). Let four months pass, and the principal be 200 drachmas. How much is the interest?'[44]

[40] Finley 1999: 181.

[41] Rathbone 1991: 331–86; Macve 2002. See Harris 1993: 25 for a supporting statement.

[42] See Morley 1996: 73–5.

[43] The answer, assuming simple interest, is two months.

[44] *P. Mich.* III 145 (early second century). The answer, by the way, is 20 drachmas, assuming simple interest.

Returning to the calculations I have made, given the difficulty caused by the data for sales and income being split into two groups and the inherent variability of prices and rents, I have had to calculate an expected return based on the median income divided by the median value. A more sophisticated approach is used in later chapters for the land and credit markets. I also need to allow for the chance that a house may not have been able to have been leased given lack of willing tenants, and also for the chance of the tenant defaulting on the rent. The risk of not finding tenants was a real one. In a town survey of AD 235, in a high-status quarter of Oxyrhynchus, we have the example of Alexander Serenus, who is the owner of four houses: two contiguous houses where he houses his family, another one blocked up and one uninhabited. And there are other similar cases, such as Theon, who also has four houses: two let out but two uninhabited.[45] We also see a number of house sales where the house has fallen down or is in poor repair, presumably after being left empty and unmaintained for a period.[46]

I have calculated the expected returns on the rental transactions where we know the fraction of the house concerned and the size of the rent or loan concerned as 8.2 per cent per annum based on the overall medians.[47] To reflect the risk of not being able to attract a tenant, I have had to make a central assumption as to the chance of a tenant not being able to be found, which is 10 per cent.[48] I have also assumed an 8 per cent chance of the tenant defaulting on the rent, which is consistent with the default assumption I use for land tenants in Chapter 4. This reduces the median return on a house investment to 6.8 per cent per annum, assuming no ongoing frictional costs to the landlord. But the landlord would in reality also face significant depreciation costs over time as the fabric of the building would need renewal.[49] Also the landlord could be subject to taxes even when the house was leased, as is the case in *P.Oxy.* III 502 (AD 164),

[45] *P.Oslo* III 111 (AD 235): Alexander Serenus l.169, 172 and 215 and Theon l.154, 156, 264 and 277.

[46] As in *P.Oxy.* XLI 2972 (AD 72), the sale of half a partially fallen-down house.

[47] The median income is 49 drachmas and the median house price is 600 drachmas (all figures recalibrated to AD 150 levels); see Kelly 2020: 165.

[48] The evidence from *P.Oslo* III 111 would suggest a much higher rate but we have too little data to corroborate a higher assumption. For reference, the percentage of houses empty in the UK was 2.7 per cent in 2019, but that is within a very liquid, information-rich market. See 'Empty Housing (England)', House of Commons Library Briefing Paper. https://researchbriefings.files.parliament.uk/documents/SN03012/SN03012.pdf (accessed 20 July 2021).

[49] Although tenants were sometimes required to ensure the house was in a clean state at the end of the lease as in *P.Erl.* 72 (fourth century), most houses were relatively insubstantial mud-brick constructions with a somewhat short lifetime.

when the police and brick taxes are still at the landlord's expense, or water tax, as appears to be the case in *P.Marm.* r (AD 190–191). However, whether a general tax applied to house ownership, or there was a tax on income on house leases, is currently unknown.[50] I will compare the return above with the returns available from other types of investment in Chapter 7.

Housing from a tenant's perspective

In a small number of cases, the personal circumstances of the individual show us the motivation for renting. These examples include a certain Terentianus who moved to a new village on retirement from military service in AD 135–136, or the need for a secondary pied-à-terre residence in Oxyrhynchus for Sarapion from Hermopolis, but the vast majority of house leases would simply relate to individuals who wanted a relatively cheap place to live.[51]

But how expensive was it to rent a house from the tenant's perspective? We can get a relative indication of the cost of housing for an individual by comparing the typical rent per person to their possible overall income. We have already seen above that the rental for a whole house averaged close to 50 drachmas a year (re-calibrated to AD 150 terms). Following Alston, the typical number of people occupying a house was around seven, so for a family of four who were renting half a house it might have cost them around 25 drachmas a year.[52] We can compare this to earnings in two different ways. First, typical unskilled casual male earnings were around 1 drachma per day. Assuming the family had a combined wage earning capacity of two males and could work for 250 days a year, then their gross earnings would have been around 500 drachmas a year, and the cost of housing would have been relatively small at 5 per cent of gross earnings (25 divided by 500). Another way to estimate the gross earnings is to consider the consumption baskets developed by Allen, where on a 'respectable' basis, where an individual could afford wine and some meat, he calculated the typical cost of living based on Diocletian's Price Edict. Scheidel then used Allen's figures to determine an estimate of the typical cost in the first century AD of between 209 and 312 or more drachmas a year for an individual male, without any allowance for housing.[53] Assuming the calorific and other needs of a family of four were equivalent to three men, then the total required

[50] Wallace 1938: 75–6.

[51] For the veteran, see *SB* VI 9636 (AD 135–136), and for the pied-à-terre, see *PSI* XVII 1699 (AD 174).

[52] Based on the median rent for a whole house of 49 drachmas a year; see Alston 2002: 70 for occupancy.

[53] Scheidel 2010: 430.

earnings for a 'respectable' standard of living would be, say 250 drachmas times 3, plus 25 drachmas for housing, or 775 drachmas. The relative cost of housing for this respectable family is even smaller than for the labouring family at around 3 per cent of gross earnings. Whilst this does not allow for taxation, with no direct income tax and a relatively low poll tax, it is clear that housing costs were very low as a percentage of net income/gross expenditure.[54] To provide a modern comparison, households renting in the Western world generally pay between 19 per cent and 33 per cent of gross income for rent.[55] We therefore need to take a very different view of the importance, or rather the lack of importance, of housing to family finances to that of our own experience. Housing was in no way central to family finances as it is to the modern developed world. In reality, the proportions of income paid in Roman Egypt are closer to modern estimated rents in Sub-Saharan Africa, which are typically 10 per cent or less of gross expenditure.[56]

But would the family have been better off buying a house? We have seen that the average cost of a house would have been around 600 drachmas so they would have needed around 300 drachmas to purchase half a house. If they were to borrow this amount and were paying the 'standard' interest rate of 12 per cent then their yearly interest cost would have been around 36 drachmas. We have no examples of individuals clearly borrowing to purchase houses on the security of a mortgage on the property itself. We do have, however, examples of mortgages on property already owned and here interest rates were generally lower, at around 6 per cent per year. If the family had the necessary connections and access to this mortgage market (I examine the likelihood of this being the case in Chapter 5) then the cost of borrowing would fall to around 18 drachmas. Overall, these costs are consistent with rental costs, but provide no substantial financial incentive for the family to purchase rather than rent.

But could the family have saved enough to purchase a house if they could not borrow the money? Using the model I detail in Chapter 4, I have estimated the chance of a farming tenant family saving 300 drachmas in surplus assets after a generation, which in Roman Egyptian terms is 15 years. Some 44 per cent of private tenant families, in these relatively

54 See Kelly forthcoming a for further information on the level of the taxation burden.

55 Carliner & Marya (2016): 17, although note that these rates include utilities. In Roman Egypt, householders may have also paid for 'utilities' in that there was a water tax.

56 Lozano-Gracia & Young (2014): Figure 16. Modern-day Egypt does not provide a good comparator, however, since, with substantial urbanization, relative costs are very high.

benign circumstances, would have saved enough to purchase half a house. This is consistent with Hobson's conclusion that 'the mere fact that state farmers, the lowest element on the social scale, were able to afford even a part of a house is in itself a testimony to the low value of ordinary real estate'.[57] However, they may well have preferred to use these excess assets in different ways, such as purchasing land, providing dowries or acquiring social capital.

Houses as investments?

Another key question is the extent to which houses were viewed as an investment to be leased out as a 'buy to let' that could provide financial gain through rental, or rather were considered as a necessary, depreciating, asset for family occupation. The details of the transactions rarely provide explicit information on the intentions of participants but my analysis can provide hints as to what drove individuals to engage in sales and purchases.

The frequent division, re-use and re-organisation of housing units meant there was a flexible housing structure that would, in theory, have been suitable for letting and sub-letting and thus capable of providing investment income. One indicator of an investment-driven transaction would be if the transaction involved a number of houses in different locations. It would be unlikely that the individual would have had a personal need for such a diverse portfolio and thus it might be expected that the purchaser was seeking to buy the houses as an investment. There are indeed a number of transactions where houses were sold as a portfolio in different locations that might indicate that the parties had or would in the future seek to create an income from renting.[58] The antichretic loans that specifically allowed for sub-letting are another indicator of such motivations.

The census records suggest that in a city context around 30 per cent of families rented housing from landlords, although the proportion in villages is much lower.[59] Such a large percentage would tend to support the proposition that city houses were indeed considered as an investment, since it is difficult to see how a large rental sector could have evolved and

[57] Hobson 1985: 228.

[58] These are *P.Ryl.* II 160d (AD 42), *P.Fay.* 31 (AD 125–130), *P.Bagnall* 31 (AD 138), *P.Stras.* VI 585 (AD 153), *P.Petaus* 13,14 and 16 (AD 182–187), confiscated houses, *SB* XXVI 16478 (first half of third century), *P.Oxy.* XLVII 3365 (AD 241), part of sale of a landed estate, *P.Gen.* II 116 (AD 247), with land, *P.Gen.2* 44 (AD 260).

[59] Bagnall & Frier 2006: 69. But note the evidence from *P.Oslo* III 111 (AD 235), which has lower proportions of rented houses. In the Western District of the Hermaion quarter of Oxyrhynchus, 14 per cent of houses are let out. However, the editor points out that there were many houses uninhabited, more than half in the same quarter.

been sustained without commercial renting. It also should be remembered that we lack information for Alexandria where different practices may have existed.

The cases noted above show that some market participants did view housing as an investment. However, in many cases the driver for the transaction will have been familial in nature and on balance these familial concerns show up more clearly within the corpus of house sales than for agricultural land sales. The ages of the market participants are not consistent with inheritance being a key trigger for sale and purchase but may indicate that family circumstances were driving some transactions as older participants bought and sold property to reflect their changing needs. The relatively large number of intra-family transactions would also indicate that practical personal housing considerations may have been stronger drivers than commercial ones.

The question of buyer motivations is important because it has a fundamental impact on the nature of the marketplace. Tenants would have been driven by the simple need to find somewhere to live but the behaviour of houseowners in their attitude to setting rent levels will have been influenced by how and why they had acquired the house in the first place. 'Accidental landlords' who had acquired housing from inheritance or those who were renting out a vacant portion of the family home would have different pricing strategies to those 'buy to let' landlords who had purchased a house or a portion thereof with a specific view to make a financial return. In behavioural finance terms, it may be proposed that the first group would be more willing to accept a 'satisficing' rent, whereas the second would be driven to maximise profit.

Another of my findings is that the typical monetary return to the landlord in cash by transaction is small. Letting houses is by definition constrained by the size of the family to whom a house is rented and to the size of housing stock.[60] The median annual gross income from house leasing per transaction is 49 drachmas, which is much smaller than that for the land leases I deal with in Chapter 4, which is 280 drachmas.[61] Thus to secure the same level of income, an investor would on average have to engage in five or more house leases for every land lease. This would be time-consuming and whilst a substantial investor could employ a manager or agent to act on his behalf, the costs of employing the agent would increase expenses. The second reason why housing may not have been attractive to an investor are the considerable expenses, maintenance/depreciation and frictional costs associated with housing stock that acted as a drag on returns

[60] Note Bagnall & Frier's suggestion that the larger the household, the lower the likelihood of renting compared to owner-occupation. Bagnall & Frier 2006: 69.

[61] Figures re-calibrated to AD 150 values.

on the investment, which even before these costs I have estimated to be only in the region of 6.8 per cent per annum. Also antichretic loans, with their very high frictional costs, cannot be considered as financially rational instruments.

It should also be remembered that owning houses for leasing had the risk of not finding tenants. Whilst a similar risk may apply to finding a tenant for land bought as an investment, there is always the alternative of farming the land yourself or with hired labour. Such an alternative does not apply to a vacant house that was not needed for owner occupation.

Another reason why, in my opinion, commercial, investment-driven house leasing was not common is that the absolute numbers of house leases that have survived compared to documents relating to other transactions is small. We only have 157 housing lease transactions compared to 1,273 land leases and 1,999 loans. The absence of house-leasing documents can be explained if, as I suggested above, the bulk of agreements were informal verbal leases of rooms that were surplus to the landlord's personal requirements. However, a commercial landlord seeking profit would surely have looked for similar levels of documentation and security for an investment in a house as he did for other transactions, and the paucity of the numbers of house leases is very telling. The ratio of the number of house leases compared to house sales at 0.4 is also very considerably less than the comparable ratio for land leases to land sales at 2.6.[62] The lower this ratio, the more likely is owner-occupation compared to leasing. I therefore believe that the balance of the evidence points clearly to only a limited involvement of commercial investment-driven activity in the housing market of the Arsinoite and Oxyrhynchite nomes.[63]

Conclusions

The first concluding point I would like to stress is the relative unimportance of housing from a financial perspective. As a percentage of income or expenditure, housing costs would have been very low. Space was not at a premium and we have few signs of housing being in strong demand; moreover, housing rents rose at rates that were at or below general price inflation.[64] Prices were heavily rounded and excessively variable, expenses of

[62] Some 157 house-leasing transactions compared to 368 house sales and 1,273 land leases compared to 482 land sales.

[63] In this I disagree with the latter part of Rathbone's statement that he believed 'that much elite wealth came from business, primarily lending, also leasing out residential property'. Rathbone 2009b: 225.

[64] Housing sale prices show increases somewhat higher than inflation in the latter part of the period under consideration, but the data are sparse.

doing business high and the returns on housing were poor when compared to other alternatives. Indeed, the rental market could be considered as a buyer's market, given the inability of the landlord to require a deposit to cover their risks, the seemingly habitual oversupply evidenced by the frequency of letting housing fall into disrepair and the evidence for vacant properties, the existence of accidental landlords willing to be satisfied with any reasonable offer, and finally the low cost to the tenant. All of these features point to a market where the balance of power lay in the tenant's rather than the landlord's hands.

These were local and, as we will see later, gendered markets, with deals made between principals on a face-to-face basis, and a relatively high proportion of deals being made between family members. The Roman Egyptians do not seem to have the need for realtors or estate agents. We have seen that there were indeed markets within these markets, given the limited but undeniable evidence for some investment-led decisions such as the purchase of multiple properties by one individual, in addition to individuals who were primarily concerned with a house as a space to live. Such markets within markets provide opportunities for arbitrage and speculation. Any market that contains buyers/sellers who would transact in any case with little regard to price provides an opportunity for profit for their counterparty. An example is today's currency exchange markets that contain both institutional buyers and sellers seeking to make a profit, commercial exporters and importers seeking to protect deals from currency fluctuations and individuals going on holiday who need foreign currency and would transact with little or no consideration of the value inherent in the trade. The presence of these forced buyers and sellers provides opportunities for others to make a profit by active trading. And we do have one example of speculation of this nature in the housing markets of Roman Egypt. In a banker's register of transactions of AD 212, one Cornelius sells half a house for 700 drachmas having purchased it for 600 drachmas a week previously, a healthy profit for no work.[65]

However, the majority of actors in the housing markets appear to me to have been driven by the simple needs of finding a place to live or making the most of housing that they had accidentally acquired that was surplus to their immediate needs.

[65] See *P.Lond.* III 1164c and 1164f (AD 212).

Chapter 4

Land

'Buy land, 'cause God ain't making any more of it.'

Tony Soprano, *The Sopranos* (after Mark Twain)

Ownership of agricultural land is a critical element of most ancient agrarian economies and the purpose of this chapter is to determine what patterns within the data can tell us about how the market in privately owned agricultural land functioned in Roman Egypt. In consequence of the importance of this subject within the economy, this is the longest chapter in the book.

Whilst many forms of land tenure have existed throughout history, the systems in operation in Roman Egypt were in essence relatively simple.[1] Title to land could be owned by institutions such as the state or temples, or by private individuals. These bodies and people could farm the land by their own or familial labour, by waged labour or by slaves. Alternatively, they could lease their land to others who in turn had the same options as to its exploitation. This chapter is mainly concerned with privately held land and the financial markets of sale/purchase and leasing that were used to help extract a return. As an exemplar of some of the features of the markets I will particularly reference a certain Aurelius Isidoros, a farmer from the village of Karanis, active at the end of the third and beginning of the fourth centuries who left behind an archive of documents that he and his family thought important and which appeared on the Egyptian antiquities market in the 1920s. With at least seven siblings who survived to adulthood from the marriage of his father Ptolemaios with his mother Herais, the Ptolemaios clan must have constituted a significant element of village society. Isidoros, who was born around AD 270, was, at one and the same time, a landlord and a tenant.[2] His archive shows an eventful and, at

1 Behind the simple overall structure there were many different legal categories of land. For a description of these categories, see Rowlandson 1996: 27–69.

2 *P.Cair.Isid.* 5 (AD 300–305), *P.Cair.Isid* 69 (AD 310), for land ownership, and *P.Cair. Isid.* 101 (AD 300), for an example of land tenancy.

times, stressful life. In his 20s and early 30s he is assaulted, has crops burnt, is burgled in the night and is the victim of a tax scam.[3] And, as we will see, things do not get much better as he ages.

The subject of the return that could be earned from land was, within a predominantly agrarian economy, of key interest to the elite in the Roman empire as evidenced by the consideration of the relative risks and returns from a landowner's perspective by Cato and Pliny the Younger.[4] Roman attitudes to agrarian investment have been the subject of a long-standing academic debate. The contrary positions are exemplified by these oppositional statements from Finley and Harris, respectively: 'Investment in land, in short, was never in antiquity a matter of systematic, calculated policy, of what Weber called economic rationality' contra 'Roman methods of calculating the profitability of an estate were as effective as those practised by a progressive landowner in the seventeenth century AD'.[5] Land brought with it both social prestige and attendant obligations and 'upper class Romans depended on their ability to achieve sufficient income from agriculture to maintain their social privileges'.[6] This chapter looks to see if that conclusion, which is specific to the class and place, can be extended further down the social chain and to a different locale or whether the other drivers I set out in Chapter 1 were more important.

Agricultural land sales

There were three principal areas capable of human exploitation by arable farming in Roman Egypt: the Nile valley, Arsinoite back water and the Nile Delta.[7] Methods of irrigation varied according to region, and particularly in the Arsinoite farmers were dependent on artificial irrigation and on a system of canals. Whatever the region, most agricultural land was planted in cereal crops, although farmers did diversify into other crops.[8] Where more intensive farming was used, the most common approaches based on

[3] See Boak & Youtie 1960.

[4] See, for instance, Cato, *De agricultura* 39.2 or Pliny, *Epistulæ* 9.37.

[5] Finley 1999: 116 and Harris 1993: 25.

[6] Kehoe 1997: 1. Note that social standing in Roman Egypt brought obligations in terms of civic duties but also some concrete economic benefits including tax exemptions; see Rowlandson 1996: 103–4.

[7] In passing, before starting to study Roman Egypt I had never made the connection between the Greek letter delta Δ and the shape of the delta of the Nile, which we see on maps of Egypt as an inverted Δ. Apart from illustrating my own stupidity, it also shows that the ancient peoples lacked our geospatial obsession with looking at maps from North to South. For them it was natural for them to go upriver to Upper Egypt and hence the delta of the Nile was not inverted.

[8] Bowman 2013: 234–9.

land lease requirements were vineyards and olive/date/palm groves.[9] We do have data from each of the three regions, but with a preponderance towards the Arsinoite and Nile valley areas.[10]

In contrast to vacant lots, agricultural land was generally priced for sale and rented per aroura, a measure that can be defined and that was equivalent to 2,760m^2.[11] Plot sizes were generally small and even larger estates had plots that were dispersed over wide areas.[12] The median sizes of plots sold or leased was 5 arouras, which is just under the area of two football pitches.

We should be aware that there were institutional constraints on sales and purchases. For instance, Rathbone believes that cessions of *catoecic* land may have been restricted to within the gymnasial social group, at least into the second century.[13] Any restriction on certain people from buying some types of land will have reduced competition and thus increased market inefficiency.[14] Turning to land taxes and charges, there were complex conveyancing charges that varied according to the gender and the status of the land or individual and that Yitfach described as 'potentially quite heavy', and this could well have acted as a brake, to some degree, on market activity.[15] It should be noted that joint-holders and then neighbours were in theory given prior rights by the state over other buyers when private property was put up for sale and were presumed to have a desire to purchase such property.[16] This would also have constrained market activity.

Land registers have been subject to considerable academic study.[17] However, the pattern of holdings to which they attest is the end result of a number of socio-economic factors that include inheritance, confiscation, marriage and market transactions. Since the purpose of this book is to examine the market, an analysis of sales rather than holdings is more

[9] Some 38 per cent of leases which were not for cereal crops were for vineyards, 31 per cent for groves, 17 per cent for gardens/vegetable plots, 13 per cent for flax and 1 per cent orchards (n = 173).

[10] For the Nile delta, see Blouin 2014 for a detailed study.

[11] See Rathbone 1991: xvi.

[12] The median sizes of plots sold or leased was 5 arouras (Kelly 2020: 78, 111). See Rathbone 1991: 23 for comment on large estates.

[13] Rathbone 2007b: 701n.14.

[14] For an example, see *SB* V 7599 (AD 95) in relation to a sale of land by the state.

[15] Yitfach 2015c: 146.

[16] See *P.Oxy.* XLI 2954 (third century) for a discussion of the Edict of Avidius Heliodorus. Another example of the interest of the state in land transactions is the requirement, attributed to a rescript of Diocletian, that land be sold at its true value. CJ 4.44.2.

[17] See Lerouxel 2016: 217–23 for a summary of available data and recent scholarship.

likely to provide relevant insights.[18] Sales have already been reviewed by Montevecchi who discussed their legal forms, Hobson who concentrated on gender issues and Rowlandson who examined the social context of sales in the Oxyrhynchite nome.[19] However, no up-to-date complete analysis of sales and purchases of agricultural land exists. I have therefore collected data directly from the primary sources using the methodology described previously.[20] The exact legal natures of the transactions are not analysed but this is an area to which considerable academic effort has already been devoted.[21] However, all the transactions concerned have one thing in common: they end with the land concerned becoming the property of a private individual or, more rarely, an institution. There are some 482 transactions represented within 381 documents in the available data for land sales.[22] For land leases we have even more data than sales. There are 847 documents that deal with land leasing and within these there are some 1,273 transactions involving 2,828 people.

The contractual terms for sales were complex as we saw in the previous chapter.[23] Leasing terms were equally complex but, unlike the other transactions we have examined, they differ considerably from modern terms in the UK that historically provided greater security of tenure to the tenant and that also foresee financial compensation, by law, for improvements made by the tenant to the land during their tenure. For leases of private cereal land, the tenant in Roman Egypt generally received no recompense for any improvements or any security of tenure beyond the period of the lease. These questions of security and incentivisation

18 Although, as Bowman 1985: 155 noted, comparisons of land registers from the same location at two different dates can provide some evidence as to market activity and turnover.

19 Montevecchi 1943; Hobson 1983; Rowlandson 1996.

20 That is a comprehensive search of the DDbDP, using descriptions and keywords, followed by an in-depth review of the relevant sources and cross-referencing against the previously compiled lists of relevant transactions. All transactions, other than gifts, dowries or loans associated with sales that involved the transfer of agricultural land between parties in return for a cash consideration are included, whether such transactions are technically considered as divisions of property, sales or cessions. Transactions which were of a mixed nature, where land was sold along with another asset – for instance, a slave in *CPR* VI 73 (AD 229) or a house in *P.Amh.* II 98 l.6–11 (second to third century), are included.

21 Nor do I attempt in this chapter to analyse the data by reference to legal or fiscal forms of private land such as 'catoecic'. Rowlandson 1996: 41–62 contains a clear description of the various categories of private land.

22 Although the details of many of the transactions are not complete, for instance if the document is damaged or is a register which only includes summaries of contracts. The list of these documents may be found in the website that accompanies this book.

23 See Table 2, above.

of tenants to maintain and improve land under their tenancy have been recurrent throughout history.[24]

We can, however, see this concern with the upkeep and investment in land in much greater transparency when we look at vineyard leases.[25] Vineyards are more complex agricultural undertakings than arable farms, requiring specialised labour, investment over time and a supporting infrastructure including a reed-bed to supply vine-props. Thus, in contrast to arable land leases, leases were sometimes not of the land itself but related to the labour concerned to produce the wine and maintain the vineyard, where the landlord paid a wage to the 'tenant' for specific tasks, thus ensuring in theory at least that the relevant work was completed. Where more traditional leases of land were adopted, the tenant was incentivised to maximise production by having their rent defined on a share-cropping basis or in kind.[26] That there was intended to be a true partnership and sharing of responsibilities can be seen in leases such as *P.Oxy.* IV 729 (AD 138), where the landlord provided free use of donkeys and an interest-free loan for the tenant of a new, partly productive, vineyard.

As stated above, whilst most arable leases did not make reference to investment, there are some exceptions. Take, for instance, our friend Isidoros. Around AD 291, he along with two co-tenants undertook to provide the investment needed to irrigate a plot of land and paid the rent for five years in advance.[27] This could reflect the exploitation of marginal land or the re-instatement of land that had fallen out of production. However, according to Kehoe, the rent concerned was considerably lower than the market.[28] Kehoe went on to state that given this 'buyers' market' favouring tenants, the reason why Isidoros, who was a landowner himself, had leased the land, and had left some land of his own uncultivated, was because 'he chose to cultivate only the best of his own land, and instead he applied his resources to leasing land of proven productivity'. This is an

[24] It has been a particularly contentious issue in Irish history, where the 'land question' lies at the heart of the political and social history of the nineteenth century. The 'Ulster custom', whereby tenants of that province enjoyed greater security than elsewhere and were compensated for their own investments on the expiry of the lease, contrasted with elsewhere on the island, and this contributed to political unrest and demand for land reforms. See Solow 1971: 11.

[25] See Rowlandson 1996: 228–36.

[26] Rowlandson 1996: 232.

[27] *P.Cair.Isid.* 98 (AD 291–292).

[28] See Kehoe 1992: 163: 'the landlord accepting a much reduced rent in exchange for concessions on the part of the lessee'. The rent, however, is not defined in the document. Another rationale for a five-year advanced payment, if it were in cash, would be that the landlord was concerned about the real value of money in an inflationary environment.

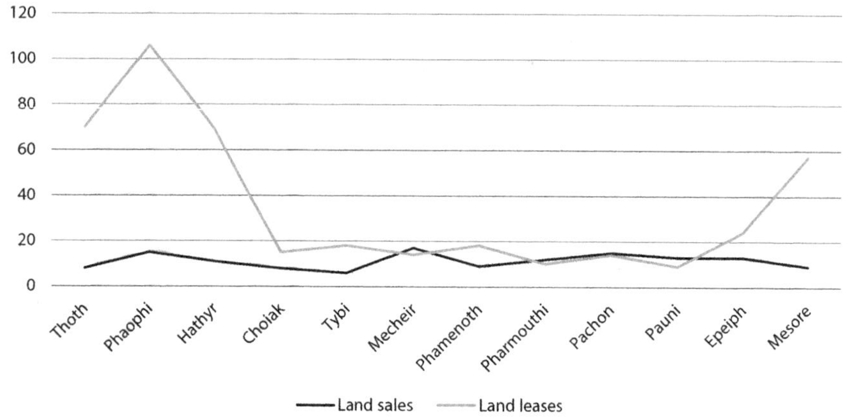

Figure 23 Number of transactions by month

attractive explanation and indicative of a degree of financial sophistication on the part of Isidoros, but it supposes that the end of the third century was a 'buyers' market' for tenants (and as we will see below I am not convinced by the evidence for this) and we should be aware that he was also paying taxes on the uncultivated land.[29]

Sales of land were generally randomly spread across the year, although there does appear to be a small peak in transactions in the month of Mecheir, which may not be dismissed as a random fluctuation with 95 per cent confidence.[30] The seemingly banal fact that the transactions are spread relatively evenly across the year has, I believe, an important significance. The implication is that for most market participants their financial means were disconnected from the annual cycles of the exploitation of the land. There was no peak in transactions at the beginning of the year, which might be expected if transactions were linked to the availability of cash (which might only be available after the harvest at the end of the previous year). Leases show a much stronger link to the yearly agricultural cycle, implying that the trigger for the transaction was the timing within the farming year to enable the necessary planting or sowing to be completed, as can be seen in Figure 23.[31] I believe this lack of a link to

[29] Karanis had certainly contracted in size by the end of the third century, but this does not in itself indicate that there was a shortage of people wanting to lease land.

[30] If the months of sale of arable land only are examined, a similar picture is seen. Note that this conclusion goes against Rowlandson's view, based on a very small sample, that there was a tendency to avoid sales between sowing and harvest from late Choiak to Pauni. Rowlandson 1996: 186.

[31] For sales n = 136 and for leases n = 424.

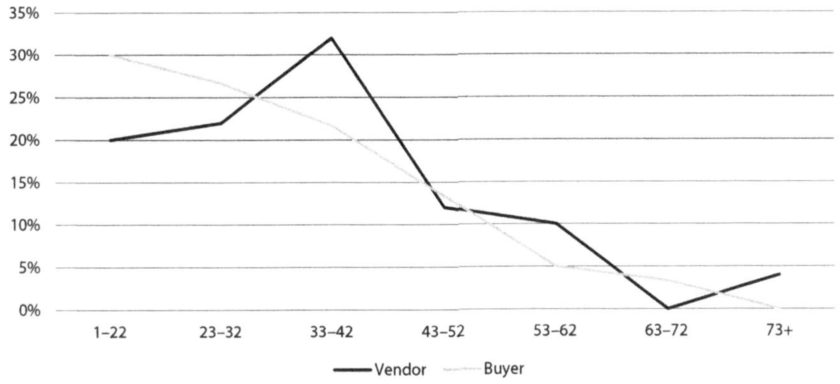

Figure 24 Land buyers and vendors, by age

the farming year for purchases implies that the cash used to settle these transactions was essentially surplus capital. From the perspective of the vendor, the timing evidence would not support any link between poor harvests and enforced sale.

Who bought and sold land?

Buyers were generally younger than vendors, with median ages of 30 and 37 respectively. The overall distribution of buyers and vendors by age is shown in Figure 24.[32] The first point to note is the very low incidence of young people selling in the market. The definition of financial minority is a grey area, but I have assumed in Figure 24 that all participants mentioned as minors in the data, but without a specific age, were under 23.[33]

The buyer market appears to follow broadly the population structure, but with an understandable lack of activity for minors who may not have been in a position to exercise agency and make proactive decisions. This lack of activity by minors is even more marked in the data for vendors. So despite the fragmentation of land holdings on partible inheritance, we can conclude that land, when inherited by individuals under 30, was rarely sold. Small parcels of land were still highly valued and could be farmed effectively under collective family ownership or leased. There also appears

[32] For vendors n = 50 and for buyers n = 82.

[33] According to Taubenschlag 1955: 102, there were different ages which constituted 'maturity' in Roman Egypt. In general, under local law, majority for sons occurred after their fourteenth year, and for daughters they ceased to be under their *patria potestas* on their marriage, but for 'Persians of the epigone' there was a special rule which fixed the age of majority at 20. Under Roman law, Romans were considered not to have reached adulthood until age 25, according to Taubenschlag 1955: 134.

to be a clear peak in vendor activity in those who were in their mid-30s to early 40s. This peak is consistent with the expected age distribution of children inheriting land from their parents.[34] We can see these patterns in practice in the case of Isidoros. When he was around 30 he owned some 35 arouras but this increases substantially to 140 arouras by the time he reaches 40, probably due to inheritance from his mother.[35] It then declines to 80 arouras by his mid-50s, presumably due to sales.

As I noted in Chapter 3, the nature of the economic and family units that underlie the named participants within the transactions is complicated by concepts of collective and individual ownership and control, household and family. People acted in common to buy and sell land, but there are also many examples where a patriarch signs on behalf of a broader family unit. These are most evident within family archives, including that of Isidoros, whose archive tells us that he operated in co-operation with some of his brothers and they signed on each other's behalf or farmed through an agricultural consortium known as a *pittakion*.[36] There are also hints that women's assets were 'hijacked' by male members of their broader family and I address this in Chapter 7. There was, however, only a limited prevalence of formalised inter-kin transactions and I can securely identify only 27 transactions between family members or around 6 per cent of all sale transactions.

When the locations of buyers and vendors are considered there are two features of the marketplace that I would highlight. First, there are no inter-village transactions involving a villager contracting with someone from a different village, even within the same nome. I suspect, but cannot prove, that many of the transactions from the Arsinoite nome in particular involved people from the same village, where there was no need to record residence since this was clear to all. The evidence from the villages suggests that the market was geographically constrained. This contrasts with sales of moveable goods such as donkeys where the parties are, on occasion, from different villages and nomes.[37]

Second, metropolite participants generally transacted with people from the same city and there are 42 cases where the transaction involved both

[34] The age at inheritance is assumed to occur when both father and mother have died. This is a simplification, since as Tacoma 2006: 215–16 notes, under the 'radical partible inheritance' system, inheritance could have occurred at multiple moments. Maternal and paternal inheritance could be separate events, although this was not always the case, and inheritance from siblings and other family members could also occur.

[35] *P.Cair.Isid.* 4, 5 (AD 299), *P.Cair. Isid.* 69 (AD 310).

[36] Boak & Youtie 1960: 5.

[37] See Claytor 2015 for a discussion of the donkey trade and in particular the role of markets such as Kerkesoucha.

buyer and vendor from the same city. There are only 25 cases where the metropolite participant transacted with a villager and I believe this feature is not a function of the provenance of the data or scribal preferences as to recording residence. Metropolite residents were more likely to contract with someone from their city than they were with an individual from a village where the land was located or someone from another city. Therefore this is evidence for a constrained geographical nature for the land market, despite the relative ease and rapidity of travel within and between nomes.[38] City dwellers largely bought and sold to others from their local social network in their own city, villagers to others in their own village. There was, however, a limited interaction between city-dwellers and villagers as their social networks overlapped.

Marketing and advertising

It is an archaeological and historical trope that absence of evidence is not evidence of absence, but the remarkable lack of any reference to auctions, marketing, advertising or competitive bidding in any of the hundreds of documents relating to private sales should be noted. It contrasts in particular with the relative frequency of references to the marketing of state land through public offers and counter bids in the much smaller group of state sales. I am aware of only one example of advertising private land for sale, *P.Tebt.* II 457 (second century), a simple papyrus presumably for public display, stating: 'Of Theogonis 1 aroura of reed land through Kronion. Who wants it, buy it'. However, there is some limited evidence for interactions within small social networks providing some impetus for competition in pricing. Consider the third-century letter written from Theomnestos to Apion Adonios advising him that a concubine of their acquaintance has put some land up for sale and that she should provide him with an option to make a bid, given that lots of parties were interested in the sale.[39] This example shows that financial and social circles were not necessarily distinct and that within both spheres word of mouth was a useful channel for the sales process, which may have led to some limited competitive pricing pressure.

Turning to sales of land by the state, typically these were of land that would have been unproductive at the date of sale. State ownership of

[38] Bagnall 1993b: 19.

[39] *SB* VI 9621, editor's translation: "Elle devrait donc te donner une option de vente, étant donné que beaucoup de personnes s'y intéressaient". Youtie 1967: 385–90 reviewed and contested the editor's translation without offering a direct alternative but there can be no doubt that the purpose of the letter was to bring the sale of the land to Apion Adonios's attention. Youtie drew comparisons with *PSI* XII 1259 from AD 120 to 225, which is a letter concerning a potential pre-emptive offer to purchase a house.

such land would often have resulted from confiscation where the previous owner had failed to meet liturgical or fiscal demands.[40] Such land, being normally in an unproductive state, would have required an investment in cash and labour in order to cultivate it, and was generally priced at a lower rate per aroura than privately owned land. Within the attested cases, there are four, which, because they relate to land that had recently been cultivated before confiscation, are unusually high in price.[41] Many of the prices concerned appear to be 'conventional' in that they are set in multiples of 4 drachmas. There are no examples of state land sales in the period from AD 275 to 350, although confiscations may be expected to have continued.

As noted above, in contrast to private sales, there is evidence for the 'marketing' of state land through auctions and 'advertising'. Consider, for instance, *P.Oxy.* XIV 1633 (AD 275), where bids for a plot of state land are 'publicly exposed', presumably to promote competition from different bidders and generate a higher price. Other documents concerning sales of state land show the bidding process in practice, such as *SB* I 5673 (AD 147) and *SB* X 10527 (AD 151–152), with individuals placing higher bids in an attempt to secure the land concerned. However, as with the housing example in the previous chapter, the bidding process was far from competitive in all cases. In *SB* I 5673, an individual offers double the previously agreed price for state land. This indicates that the state lacked any clear 'mark to market' mechanism when pricing land.

Land prices

When we look at prices for private land they varied according to the nature of the crops. There are 'cash crops' whose cultivation cannot, in isolation, feed a family unit. Gardens, vineyards, orchards, date palms and olive groves would all have produced such crops and required more intensive cultivation than arable land. The data from such transactions are not, however, easy to analyse. They rarely specify the area of the land sold, which makes them impossible to compare with other land categories. The remainder of this chapter therefore concentrates on arable land.

Some 374 out of the 482 land sales do not fall into the categories of state sales or land requiring intensive cultivation. The contracts often do not specify the type of land or the crops to be cultivated but it seems reasonable, given the general evidence that most cultivated land was under

[40] For example, *P.Oxy.* IV 721 (AD 13–14), where the land is specifically referred to as 'unproductive'.

[41] *P.Turner* 24 (AD 148–154), *SB* X 10527 (AD 151–152), *P.Oxy.* LXII 4337 (AD 178) and *BGU* I 156 (AD 201).

cereals, to assume that this land was arable.[42] Prices vary considerably, logically reflecting the heterogeneous nature of land itself. Of particular importance in Egypt was the means by which the land was irrigated, whether by the natural Nile flood or artificially, and the reliability of such irrigation, which will have varied by nome. It will be noted that 47 per cent of the land prices are rounded to the nearest 100 drachmas.[43] As with state land, this rounding may indicate a lack of competition between buyers, since if there was an active market more differentiated pricing might be expected.

The general shape of price trends over time is similar to prices more generally, being relatively steady from AD 50 to 150 and then picking up from AD 150 to 270.[44] The average rate of price increase is also similar to that for general goods. Oxyrhynchite prices seem to have been higher than those for other nomes, which may reflect, in some way, the essentially metropolite provenance of the data. One other point worth investigating is whether there is any relationship between the size of the transaction and the average per aroura price, but there is no evidence for differential pricing by size of deal, so there was no obvious advantage in bulk buying.

Motivations for buyers and sellers

Understanding the motivations for buyers and sellers within the market is key to understanding the institution of the market itself. The documents available rarely provide explicit information on the intentions of participants but it is possible to get some indications of their motivations through analysis of the data. To do so we need a conceptual framework within which such intentions can be placed.

One significant indicator of motivations of buyers is the way in which the land was to be exploited after purchase. These motivations can fall into two broad categories: "investment" purchases where the exploitation of the land was apparently not to be carried out by the immediate family of the party concerned (it would be leased or farmed by slave or waged labour) and "familial" purchases where the land was to be farmed by the immediate family members.[45]

42 Bowman 2013: 238–9.

43 As a percentage of all prices between 100 and 1,000 drachmas.

44 Note that I would therefore disagree with Scheidel's view that 'no clear change in nominal land prices – on the scale of a structural doubling or more – is visible in our samples' (2002: 102) and 'nominal cash rents and land prices failed to rise nearly as strongly as the prices of various consumer goods and the price of labour' (2002: 107).

45 For a discussion of the theoretical economic background to direct farming as opposed to leasing, see Currie 1981: 119.

Dealing first with investment transactions, there are some cases where the text of the source indicates that the transaction was of an investment nature:

- *P.Oxy.* XIV 1648, which can only be dated to AD 57–170, where the land concerned was associated with a commercial activity, in this case a dyeing works.
- *CPR* VI 73 (AD 222–235), where the land was sold with a mill and other accessories.
- *P.Mich.* V 259 (AD 33), which mentions that the land being purchased is of poor quality and in need of irrigation or other investment in order to bring it back into production.
- *P.Oxy.* XLII 3047 (AD 245), which records the history of purchases of a large estate then owned by Calpurnia Herkalia and includes ten transactions of smaller plots, some of which date back some 200 years but others with a more recent date of acquisition.[46]
- *SB* XVIII 13235 (AD 69–78), where the transaction was registered through a *phrontistes* (manager), thus implying that for at least one party the transaction was connected to a wider estate.
- *SB* X 10526 (AD 138–161), where the buyer was a serving soldier and unlikely to have been able to farm the land himself.
- *P.Oxy.* XIV 1636 (AD 249), which was identified by Rowlandson as showing indications of speculative activity given that the vendor, Aurelius Serenos alias Sarapion, had engaged in buying and selling activities not just in relation to the plot of land concerned in this papyrus, but also with regard to houses and slaves.[47]

The 58 state sales of land were typically at prices that reflected the poor state of the land, and in a number of cases it is explicitly mentioned that further investment would be needed to bring the land into production. Rowlandson describes these purchases as a 'very promising form of investment'.[48] Other investment transactions are the 50 cases of land producing cash crops requiring intensive cultivation such as vineyards, olive groves, orchards or gardens. Other cases that I would consider as being of an investment rather than a familial nature are the 40 transactions where the

[46] Line 25 of *P.Oxy.* XLII 3047 records an acquisition in the second year of Tiberius (AD 15–16) of 6 arouras, whilst line 33 shows an acquisition of 5 arouras dated to the reign of Alexander Severus (AD 233–234).

[47] Rowlandson 1996: 190–1.

[48] Rowlandson 1996: 189.

area being sold was greater than the size (12 arouras), which might typically have constituted an autarkic smallholding.[49] There are also 41 transactions relating to arable land where both buyer and seller are metropolites that were probably investments, since it seems unlikely that the land would have been worked personally by either party in the transaction or their immediate family.

Another 'marker' of investment-driven motivation would be evidence for borrowing or mortgaging in order to finance an acquisition, but, as will be shown in the chapter on loans, there is little or no evidence for financial gearing in this way.[50] An example of a clear investment motivation can, however, be seen in *P.Giss* 79 (c. AD 117), a letter from an agent to his principal. It is worth quoting since it also demonstrates an understanding of the laws of supply and demand, and a sensitivity as to purchase price likely to have been driven by a level of anticipated return on investment:

> Just now wine is selling at a very high price … So everybody wants to sell his vineyard. But if God grants a good yield of wine for the year, perhaps the owners will be less eager on account of the resulting cheapening of their properties. Therefore we will be able to purchase at a lower price in accordance with your desires.

Note that although this is a direct testimony of the thoughts of the investor, since no specific transaction can be associated with this letter, it is not included in the data analysed. Overall, therefore, there are a total of 205 transactions where at least one party was probably driven by investment considerations, which constitutes some 43 per cent of all transactions.[51] Allowing for the fact that within the remaining 57 per cent

49 A small family at subsistence level would have required at least 6 arouras of land simply to produce enough wheat to survive. But we have seen in the chapter on prices that even at a 'bare bones' level, goods other than wheat would be necessary to provide a minimal standard of living. Carrié 1997: 138. Assuming that half the production would need to have been sold to secure a total smallholding of perhaps 12 arouras, this might be used as an indicator of the size of farm necessary to be held by one such family in order to supply the necessary income to survive at a bare bones level (which is consistent with Bagnall's assessment of a minimum farm size of 10 arouras to provide bare bones subsistence for the average Karanis family. Bagnall 1993b: 117).

50 One of the few possible examples of financial gearing behaviour in Roman Egypt is the lease-sale of ships, which Rathbone interprets as being the 'long-term lease of a boat in return for a share in the operating profits'. Rathbone 2007a: 591.

51 The total of 205 consists of 16 with anecdotal evidence, 58 state sales, 50 cash crop sales, 40 large sales and 41 city-based sales. I thus disagree with Rowlandson, who, based on her view that land sales were determined by social relationships rather than the market, concluded that she doubted 'that there was ever an opportunity for widespread investment purchase of private land'. Rowlandson 1981: 378.

of transactions there will undoubtedly have been purchases driven by investment motivations that are simply not apparent to us, I would suggest that the majority of purchases of land were by investors rather than families seeking to farm the land themselves.

One other motivation that might be proposed, similar to that which we saw in the housing market, is a desire to consolidate land holdings by buying adjacent properties. However, the evidence for consolidation being a major driver of market activity seems weak and landowners appear to have preferred the benefits of diversification over consolidation.[52]

It is much more difficult, from a methodological perspective, to identify transactions driven by familial motivations than those driven by investment and I cannot securely identify any purchase or sale that would fall into this category. However, there were certainly gifts that did not involve any payment.[53] It is similarly difficult to identify transactions driven by reciprocity or acquisition of land simply to build social status. However, in the practice of *epibole*, the assignment by the state of a piece of marginal state land to a plot of private land, with the resultant obligation to pay rent, we can see redistribution in action, in Polanyi terms.

Land sales: conclusions

Comparative analysis of the land sale data with other financial transactions will shed further light on the nature of the market, but some features are already apparent. The first conclusion relates to the distribution of transactions over the calendar year. The level spread of transactions with no particular bias to any month indicates that the timing of transactions was independent of the agricultural year. Finley stated that the 'normal purchase of land in antiquity … was windfall purchase' – unplanned purchases when circumstances were propitious.[54] Finley defined 'windfall' by the reference to the price of land, as 'windfall land is visibly cheap or dear, as the case may be; no more sophisticated investigation is required than what I have already called crude empirical knowledge', rather than the circumstances that drove an individual to transact.[55] If Finley was correct, it might be expected that there would be a peak in transactions in the period after the harvest when such opportunities might arise given poor or excellent harvests. However, this is not the case. Buyers do not seem to have been dependent on the harvest to have had the necessary capital to make purchases. Neither were vendors typically driven by poor harvests

[52] Kelly 2020: 89–90.

[53] See, for instance, *P.Oxy.* II 273 (AD 95), where Julia Hereclea cedes arouras of her land to her underage unmarried daughter Gaia.

[54] Finley 1999: 119.

[55] Finley 1999: 120.

to sell. This suggests that buyers were using existing 'surplus' capital that was or had become available for investment to make their purchases. So whilst capital availability for purchases might have come from 'windfalls' in the day-to-day sense, possibly from inheritance, purchases were not solely driven by 'windfalls' in Finley's sense.

However, timing is only one element of the market. The modalities of sale in the sense of how the sale was transacted can also provide useful information. The lack of activity by agents and the pattern of residence of participants shows that the private market operated on a face-to-face basis, where people transacted with other people known to them or to their social circle. Villagers tended to contract with their own neighbours and there is no evidence for inter-village transactions. The same pattern is evident in the cities. As we will see in the chapter on gender, the impact of social networks can be seen in the fact that women preferred to transact with women and men with men. There were relatively few intra-family transactions and consolidation of property holdings does not appear to have been a major driver. Finally, more transactions were driven by people who were using surplus assets to make investments rather than by familial motivations. The relative infrequency of small familial purchases is an indication of low social mobility from the tenant to the land-owning classes.

Prices per aroura for arable land do not show any relationship between the size of the deal and the price, indicating that the market was not segmented by size and that market participants for larger or smaller transactions used the same pricing mechanisms. Prices are, however, volatile and rounded, which suggests that these pricing mechanism were not efficient. There is also a lack of evidence in private sales for many intermediaries acting in a broking or other fashion to facilitate the market. This would not have helped construct a market in a neoclassical economic sense, although it would mean that transaction costs were not inflated by middle-party costs.

Land leases

Within the 1,273 land lease transactions I have identified there are 173 related to land that may have required intensive cultivation, such as vineyards or orchards, but the bulk of the remainder are explicitly described as being arable land under cereal and fodder crops.[56] How the relative

[56] Leases of land owned by the state are not included in these numbers, but sub-leases of state land between private individuals are, as are sub-leases of private land. This section therefore does not include consideration of *pittakia*, which were collective agreements for joint exploitation of government land by groups of individuals. See France 1998: 143–4 for further discussion of *pittakia*. So-called 'leases of crops', the purchase of standing crops in the field to be harvested by the buyer, as, for example,

Table 5 Numbers of documents and percentage of all documentary papyri: leases and sales of agricultural land

	1st century	2nd century	3rd century	AD 300–350	All
Number of land leases	62	226	134	85	507
(%)	(2.5%)	(2.7%)	(2.4%)	(3.2%)	(2.7%)
Number of land sales	57	114	75	8	254
(%)	(2.3%)	(1.4%)	(1.3%)	(0.3%)	(1.3%)

number of land sales and leases changed over time is shown in Table 5.[57] One striking feature of Table 5 is the very high ratio of land lease documents compared to land sales in the first half of the fourth century.[58] The number of land leases as a proportion of all documentary papyri also holds up in the third and fourth centuries, and thus there is no indication of Kehoe's 'buyers' market' in leasing; but sales slump in the fourth century.[59] I would suggest that this reflects a real reduction in the number of sales since even if papyrological habits or practices changed it is difficult to see why such an important transaction as a land sale would not have been recorded when land leases continued to be recorded in line with previous practice. This sharp decline in land sales could reflect a strong preference to retain land at all costs in a time of great uncertainty.

In this context, Bagnall's view of the development of the prevalence of leasing into the fourth century is worth considering and quoting in full.

> I cannot offer firm figures from an earlier time, but it is my impression that in the second-century Fayum the percentage of land leased out was larger. The reduction in leasing is to my mind a symptom of decline, for it makes

that set out in *P.Fam.Tebt.* 5 (AD 98), have not been included since they fit better within the category of general commercial and labour contracts and lie outside my scope.

[57] Included in this table are only those documents which are sale or lease contracts or offers. Documents containing numerous transactions, such as contract registers or those which provide indirect evidence of a sale or lease, such as a letter, registration document or rent receipt have been excluded. These restrictions were undertaken since the purpose of this particular analysis is to assess the relative ratio of specific types of transactions. A more exact definition is thus preferable to avoid the distortion, for instance, of receipts of rent, whose inclusion in the relative frequency comparison would tend to bias any conclusion. Therefore, it will be noted that there are fewer documents in Table 5 than the total number of documents found.

[58] I have verified that this is not a feature due to bias to any particular archive materials; see Kelly 2020: 104–5.

[59] Kehoe 1992: 163.

> the opportunities available to an entrepreneurial peasant minimal, and it prevents significant economic mobility on the part of such entrepreneurs. We have evidence of the activities of rather prosperous farmers who were principally lessees in the first and second centuries, but those who do not already own land are squeezed out in the much tighter land picture of the fourth century.[60]

Leaving aside for the moment any bias in the equation of a reduction in entrepreneurial opportunities with a 'decline', my interpretation of the larger dataset, to which Bagnall did not have access, is that there was no decline in leasing but that the sales market did indeed 'tighten'.

Leases of private land were generally for short periods of up to a maximum of eight years and an average of 2.8 years, which contrasts with longer leases of state and temple land.[61] Whilst state tenants and their descendants were effectively tied to the land they were required to farm through the power of the state the same cannot be said of temple land. Connor suggested these long-term leases reflected a 'cautious management style focusing on risk-minimization' on the part of the temple's administrators but we should not assume that the length of a lease indicates a particular level of risk acceptance or aversion.[62] It is true that, as Connor stated, these long-term leases were consistent with the long-term focus of the temples themselves (or, in financial parlance, their 'investment horizon'), but longer-term transactions bring in themselves risks not present in shorter-term contracts. Rents expressed in cash for years some time in the future can lose their real value if inflation is high. Whilst inflationary risk may be limited if rents are defined in kind as opposed to cash terms, there are considerable human risks related to the tenant. The tenant may be incentivised to invest in time and money within the property by a long lease, but the landlord is also at greater risk of the land or irrigation falling into disrepair by the voluntary or involuntary (for instance, caused by illness) actions of the tenant. Shorter leases provide greater control for the landlord, but at the price of needing to find a new tenant at the end of each lease. An institution such as the state or a temple could take the risk of longer leases, but an individual landlord is likely to have been more acutely aware of shorter-term personal risks, which would require cash liquidity such as illness or a pressing personal need (such as the need for cash to fund a daughter's dowry). If the landlord needed to sell to raise cash, a plot of land without a long-term sitting tenant was considerably easier to sell than one with a semi-permanent tenant. In other words, an individual's investment

60 Bagnall 1985a: 307.

61 Kelly 2020: 116; Connor 2014: 231.

62 Connor 2014: 231.

horizon – that is the time when he may need to sell to realise cash from his asset – tends to be much shorter than an institution's. Similar concerns may also apply to the tenant. This is reflected in leases where the land required investment and we can see this in Isidoros's archive. In AD 300, he offered to lease an olive grove, where investment would be needed, and thus wanted a long lease, of five years.[63]

In behavioural finance terms, the duration of a lease is not therefore a direct indicator of risk-aversion or acceptance but rather of the parties' needs for liquidity and flexibility. The relative length of private land leases may thus give some indication of personal expectations of financial stability and confidence in the economy, since the greater the economic volatility the shorter the individual's investment horizon. There is a definite pattern to the lease duration in the data. The length of leases increases from the first century and then decreases substantially, and in a statistically significant way at a 95 per cent confidence level, from the second century to the first half of the fourth century.[64] I have verified that this is a diachronic rather than regional trend by checking that the data from both the Arsinoite and Oxyrhynchite nomes show the same pattern, and this would indicate a loss of financial confidence from the third century onwards. So, whilst the leasing market does not show any imbalance in buyers and sellers, we can see clear concerns as to social stability.

Who was renting land?

As with other types of transaction, land leases were largely contracted face to face by the principals. In the 507 leases noted above, only 89 individuals identified as agents, managers or other intermediaries, excluding guardians, are known to have been involved. Although this is a relatively small proportion, it is a higher percentage than any other type of transaction. The relatively large number of intermediaries reflects the more widely dispersed geographical distribution of counterparties for land leases compared to other transactions, as absentee landlords delegated the day-to-day management of their estates to *phrontistes* or other types of managers.

Of the 295 landlords in the extant leases where residence is known, 252 (85 per cent) were city-dwellers as opposed to villagers. The locations of landlords and tenants over the whole period were studied and these are presented in Table 6.[65] The vertical columns show the location of

63 *P.Col.* VII 179 (AD 300).

64 The median (average) lengths by century, excluding sub-leases, are first century 2 (2.4) n = 32, second century 4 (3.4) n = 112, third century 2 (2.4) n = 55, fourth century 1 (1.6) n = 24.

65 For an alternative schematic approach to land leasing relationships, for the Oxyrhynchite nome only, see Tacoma 2008: 102–3.

Table 6 Summary of locations of land lease counterparties

		Landlord		
		Cities	Serving military	Villages
Tenant	Cities	75	1	12
	Serving military	1	1	0
	Villages	112	4	16

the landlords, and the horizontal lines the corresponding tenants. So, for instance, there are 112 leases where the landlord is city-based and the tenant is a villager. The first point to note is the limited involvement of serving soldiers. There are a fair number of inter-location transactions, but these are largely within the same nome, with the exception of Alexandrian landlords in the Arsinoite nome. In the Oxyrhynchite nome, there are few examples of village-based landlords, although city-based tenants appear frequently. As Rowlandson noted, this is a distortion caused by the city find site of the Oxyrhynchite leases.[66]

Unlike the equivalent analysis for land sales and credit transactions, Table 6 hides a significant amount of inter-village activity. Of the 14 examples between villagers in the Arsinoite nome, nine involve landlords and tenants from different villages within the nome.[67] Only two of the inter-village transactions involve intensive production crops, so it is unlikely that the primary reason for inter-village activity was crop diversification. There is a higher than typical incidence of sub-leases and this is not surprising given the likelihood that outright ownership of land available for rent was concentrated in city-dwellers, so transactions between villagers are more likely to be further down the rental chain. The fact that the land concerned is more often in a different village to that where the tenant is resident might suggest that there was an imbalance in the local supply and demand of land available for rent, as Hobson suggests was the case for Soknopaiou Nesos, which lacked arable land in its own vicinity, and that in order to find suitable land for farming, a tenant would sometimes have to lease land away from their home and other obligations, with all the inconveniences that would imply.[68]

[66] Rowlandson 1999: 146.

[67] The one case where they come from the same village is *SB* XIV 11911, a garden lease from AD 224, but there are likely to have been other cases of this type when the location of the two individuals is not given because the individuals came from the same village and thus no location needed to be stated.

[68] See Hobson 1984a for a discussion of the somewhat atypical relationship of the village of Soknopaiou Nesos to other villages as regards agricultural land.

Unlike land sales and, to some degree, the credit transactions, which will be dealt with in the next chapter, land leases were often recurring, and were renewed between the same parties, which may have reduced the competitive nature of any negotiation. Land leases could also be inherited by tenants and passed down in the same family, providing stability to both parties. Isidoros, for example, had a 20-year relationship as a tenant with the absentee city-based lessor Aurelia Serenilla and her children.[69] These long-term relationships must have had symbiotic features where both parties valued the stability of the relationship compared to the risks of contracting with a new third party, and we can see this partnership in operation when Isidoros was allowed to stay in arrears for his rent.[70]

We should, however, recognise that the categories of 'landlord' and 'tenant' were not mutually exclusive social castes and, as Bagnall notes, an individual could be in both categories at the same time.[71] Nor should we assume a social or indeed wealth hierarchy within the landlord and tenant relationship. Consider again Isidoros, the farmer from Karanis. Whilst the relationship with the richer Serenilla may be considered one which exhibited the traditional roles of landlord and tenant, this was not always the case. Sometime prior to AD 316, he leased on a share-cropping basis some 25 arouras of land from two brothers.[72] The lease foresaw that although he was the tenant he supplied the oxen for ploughing and made a number of loans to the landlords. He was clearly in a financially stronger position than the lessors. Unfortunately, all did not go well and he had to petition on a number of occasions to try to recover what was owed to him by the landlords.

In many historical contexts we see a power imbalance (whether power is defined in social or wealth terms) between the principals (landlords and tenants). This power imbalance may, at an extreme, allow powerful landlords to set rents without reference to external market forces. However, the power imbalance in Roman Egypt is unlikely to have been as extreme as in societies where tenants were bound to a single landlord and dependent on him or her for not only the land they farmed but also the buildings in which they lived. In Roman Egypt, tenants generally rented small parcels of land, possibly from different landlords, and they might also be in possession of plots they owned personally. They usually lived in villages in houses that were not connected to the land leased. This was in no way a feudal society.

Turning to the age demographics of landlords and tenants, one point of interest is the relatively high number of young landlords.[73] This will reflect

69 Kehoe 1992: 160.

70 *P.Cair.Isid.* 114 (304).

71 Bagnall 1993b: 131.

72 *P.Mert.* II 91 (AD 316).

73 See Kelly 2020: 110.

their social or legal inability as 'minors' to mobilise the human resources to farm directly the land they own, which is likely to have been inherited. One attractive option for them would be to lease the land. Reflecting these young landlords to some extent, overall the median age of tenants at 37 is considerably higher than the median age of landlords at 30.5. However, as a percentage of their age group in the population, older individuals in their 40s are more likely to be tenants than younger adults. This reflects the likely ages of the leaders of the family-based economic unit seeking to rent the land.

How much land did they rent and what did they grow?

The overall sizes of land leased are similar to those for land sales with the same median size of land leased at 5 arouras. Leased plots were, in all nomes, typically of a size that could be farmed by a single family unit, although not enough to support them in itself. Van Minnen has suggested that the size of plots decreased 'significantly' in the third century and uses this feature as a support for his contention that the third century was a period of agricultural contraction.[74] The median size of plots in the third century is 5 arouras, a return to the median size that applied in the first century, and a small fall from the median size of 6 arouras in the second century. There is thus indeed a small decline in the median size of plots, but the decline is not as marked as van Minnen implies by his use of 'significantly'. Nor can we take the reduction in the absolute number of leased plots in the third century as an indication of contraction in the agricultural sector, since the proportion of leases within the documentary record remains relatively steady and the reduced number simply reflects the reduction in the number of published documentary papyri for this period.

On a shorter timescale, Duncan-Jones suggested that the size of land leased reduced considerably from the period of AD 140 to 165 compared to the period from AD 165 to 185, which he sees as an indicator of the impact of the Antonine Plague.[75] The number of surviving documents from the later period is small and the median plot sizes are similar for both periods. The proposition that there was a reduction in plot size from one period to the other cannot be considered proven with any strong statistical

[74] van Minnen 2000: 213. Van Minnen does not present or reference the data which support this suggestion.

[75] Duncan-Jones 1996: 121–2. Duncan-Jones worked from the existing collections of leases compiled by Drexhage and Hennig, which totalled 53 from the period AD 140–199, although the number of leases now available is higher, as seen above. It should be pointed out that I have excluded one document that would impact the data and that could fall in either period. This is *P.Stras.* VI 511, a petition dating from after February AD 169 in relation to an earlier large lease of 88 arouras.

confidence.[76] As such, the argument that this is evidence for the effect of the plague is not compelling.

Landlords took a particular interest in the crops that were to be planted or sown on their land during the tenancy. Crops that would exhaust the soil or were perhaps pernicious in some other way, such as being difficult to remove at the end of the lease, were sometimes explicitly stated to be avoided and leases often specifically forbade the tenant to sow crops such as woad or coriander, as in *P.Oxy.* I 101 (AD 142), or safflower, as in *P.Amh.* II 91 (AD 159). The simplest and most common way for a landlord to ensure that his land was not exhausted was to require that crops were rotated between demanding crops such as cereals, and rest crops such as hays or grass, typically called *chortos*, *chlora* or *aracus* (chickling), to be harvested for fodder or directly grazed.

Rotation of crops was required in roughly 60 per cent of the leases prior to AD 300 where we have information.[77] However, there was a difference by nome: 73 per cent of Oxyrhynchite leases require rotation but only 57 per cent of Arsinoite leases.[78] These figures should be regarded as being lower-end estimates of the proportion of land where crop rotation was undertaken, since it may well have been in the interests of a tenant, particularly one on a long lease, to rotate crops even if they were not obliged to under the terms of the lease. Given the predominance of second-century leases with data on rotation (85 out of 143) and the consequent relatively small number of leases from the first or third centuries, it is difficult to comment on diachronic trends, but I would note and support Rowlandson's conclusion that the crops to be grown became more diversified in the third century in the Oxyrhynchite nome.[79] Isidoros certainly understood the benefits of crop diversification, and apart from an interest in olives, he actively bought and sold, and probably had control of, bean crops.[80]

What did they pay in rent?

There were three different forms of rental payment: fixed payment leases where the rent was in cash; fixed payment leases where the rent was in kind, and share-cropping rents where the rent was payable as a proportion of the overall yield. Sometimes only one form of rent was used within a lease, but in the period up to AD 274, when prices were relatively stable, it was usually

[76] Using a Mann–Whitney U test the proposition cannot be proven from the data with a statistical confidence level of 80 per cent or more.

[77] Required in 89 out of 143 leases.

[78] In terms of statistical significance, it can be concluded with 95 per cent confidence that Oxyrhynchite leases more commonly required rotation than Arsinoite ones.

[79] Rowlandson 1996: 239–40.

[80] *P.Cair.Isid.* 87–91 (AD 308–309) provide examples of this trading.

the case that where cereal crops were to be sown the rent was set in kind, but that when land was under fodder it was set in cash. Share-cropping of arable land appears to be mostly a fourth-century practice and may reflect a preference for risk-sharing in an unstable period.[81] When share-cropping was adopted, the most common share of the output between landlord and tenant is 50:50, which is also the 'almost universally' adopted split in today's developing countries.[82] As a tenant, Isidoros accepted the proportion 50 per cent when he share-cropped in AD 316.

In a small number of leases, payment of the rent in advance for a number of years was required under the lease, as in *P.Oxy.* XXXI 2584 (AD 211), where an advance payment of the rent in cash for a lease of five years was required. Rowlandson saw this as a possible indicator of a reversal in the typical power imbalance between landlord and tenant, and that the landlord was in need of cash.[83] In the particular case of *P.Oxy.* XXXI 2584, the effective return to the landlord can be estimated at around 5.5 per cent per year, compared to the median sustainable return of 7.4 per cent for the Oxyrhynchite nome, which I calculate later in this chapter, and this relatively low return might indeed suggest the landowner was in need of cash and willing to strike a deal at poorer than normal rates of return as a result.[84] However, in times of high inflation, advance payment of rent would be an entirely rational approach from a landlord's perspective, and the advance payment that Isidoros of Karanis made in *P.Cair.Isid.* 98, which is another five-year lease, but from AD 291 to 292, may be explicable by this reasoning. However, this approach was obviously dependent on the ability of the tenants to lay their hands on substantial sums and cannot have been a realistic option for many of the leases where poorer tenants could not provide the rent until after the harvest.

With inflation averaging around 15 per cent per annum in the first half of the fourth century, which may disguise sharp increases in prices over the short term, it would have been risky to define fodder rents in cash because waiting a year for the cash payment could mean a significant reduction in its real purchasing power value. However, there are rational ways around this problem, such as expressing the rent for years when the land was under

[81] The earliest cereal share-cropping lease which can be securely dated is from AD 255–256: *P.Princ.* II 37, but the remainder all could lie within the fourth century. Van Minnen 2000: 212 suggested that Pliny the Younger's adoption of share-cropping was a last resort at a time of agricultural contraction (Pliny, *Epistulæ* 9.37), whereas Kehoe saw it as a rational response to changing circumstances (Kehoe 2007: 107).

[82] Otsuka et al. 1992: 1977n.10.

[83] Rowlandson 1996: 264.

[84] If we allow for the beneficial impact to the landowner of receiving the money in advance, the rate of return increases somewhat, but is still below the median for the nome.

fodder in non-cash terms. It is worth examining the forms of rent for leases of the period from AD 300 to 350, where land may have been expected to be under fodder, either because the lease is for longer than one year and crop rotation may be expected or because the crop is explicitly stated to be in fodder. We do see some different payment types arise in the period after AD 274. The ingenious variety of alternative payment forms include payments not only in fodder itself, but also in barley, lentils and wheat, which would have kept their 'real' value over time. Another equally rational approach was to require payment in 'Ptolemaic' coinage, as occurred in *P.Stras.* VI 557 (AD 291), but this was only an option when this type of coinage was available and limited in its effectiveness.[85]

Finally, there is one particularly strange feature of some of the leases within the Tebtunis *grapheion* register, *P.Mich.* II 121r (AD 42), which include leases where the rent is paid in advance for a lease that is to commence some years in the future: two years in the case of I xiv or II i and some five years in the case of III viii. This trust in the counterparty, or the ability of the state to enforce the legality of the lease, at a date in the relatively far future in an age of high mortality is striking. Perhaps these delayed leases reflect a certain desperation on the part of the landlords who may have required immediate cash, as was suggested above for simple advance rental payments, although an alternative suggestion is that these leases relate to abandoned land that would take some time to bring into production.[86] Unfortunately, we lack the data as to the amount of the rent. A low rent would have indicated a balance of power weighted towards the tenant rather than the landlord and support the forced nature of the transaction from the landlord's side. In the case of *P.Mich.* II 121r II i, however, the rent for land that was to be planted with wheat or barley was payable unusually in cash rather than kind, indicating a need from the landlord for cash. Furthermore, the lease in *P.Mich.* II.121r II i has as a tenant an independent woman, acting with her son as guardian. We will see in Chapter 6 that women rarely act as the tenant of land but are more often landlords. Thus, it would seem that from the point of view of the tenant, this deferred lease should be regarded as a rational medium-term 'investment' rather than a lease intended to provide subsistence or immediate income for the family

85 Note that the term 'ptolemaic' is not thought to mean literally coinage from that period, but is a conventional term intended to convey coinage of good quality. See Crawford, n. to lines 24–5, *P.Oxy.* XLI 2951. For a more recent full discussion, see Kruse & Woytek 2020.

86 For the abandoned land suggestion: Rathbone, personal communication. An analogy can certainly be made with *emphyteutic* leases of state land, where those who undertook to bring infertile state-owned land into cultivation were exempted from taxation, typically for a period of three years. See Bogaert 2000: 181–5 for a discussion of *emphyteutic* leases.

unit. It is likely the woman secured this lease with a view to sub-leasing or having it farmed by her family at a later date.

There are 90 sub-leases within the documents and these have some different features as to duration compared to the primary leases. In general, sub-leases are of shorter duration than the primary lease with a median duration of one year. However, most of the sub-leases in the data are for private land and when land owned by an institution such as the state is sub-leased then the duration can be indefinite or extremely long. For instance, *P.Bingen* 59 (AD 33) is a sub-lease of state land for a period of 93 years and is explicitly to be inherited by the heirs of the sub-tenant. This is essentially a transfer of responsibility for farming the land in perpetuity rather than a true sub-lease and the same applies to documents such as *BGU* II 661 (AD 140), where the sub-tenant takes on responsibility for as long as the main lease from the state remains in force.[87]

The seasonality of the date of agreement of the lease can also be analysed, noting that the date of the delivery of cereal rents in kind is invariably in or around Pauni, after the harvest. As may be expected, most leases (76 per cent) are concluded at the turn of the calendar and farming year between the months of Mesore and Hathyr, prior to sowing.[88] The typical rents paid vary according to nome, and the rates for land under fodder in the Arsinoite nome are considerably lower than elsewhere.[89] When I undertook my thesis, I could not suggest a plausible reason for this difference, but it occurs to me that irrigation practices may explain this feature. In the Arsinoite nome, where artificial irrigation was the norm, why waste a precious resource by watering land under fodder when water was needed for that portion of the land under cereals? In nomes like the Oxyrhynchite, lying in the valley of the Nile, land under fodder would have been flooded in any event, producing higher yields than unirrigated land and therefore being capable of demanding a higher rent.

Cereal rents are generally defined in numbers of artabas of barley or wheat. Within an individual lease rates may vary according to the quality of

87 On occasions it should be noted that sub-leases of public land do not involve any net remuneration to the sub-lessor, consisting only in the transfer of the obligation to farm the land and pay the taxes/rent to the sub-lessee. Morris 1975: 114–16.

88 Note that Browne 1968: 17 states that leases in the Oxyrhynchite nome are drawn up in the first four months of the year, from Thoth to Choiak, but only one lease dates from Choiak and the bulk are drawn from the first three months only. In contrast to Oxyrhynchite leases, where there is only one case in Mesore, in the Arsinoite nome a substantial number of leases were also agreed at the end of the previous year.

89 There are 61 fodder cases where the rent is expressed solely in drachmas within the 78 fodder cases in total, given that some rents are defined in kind terms. The median rates per nome re-calibrated to AD 150 prices are as follows: Arsinoite (n = 21) 10 dr., Oxyrhynchite (n = 25) 22 dr., other (n = 15) 19 dr.

the land concerned, which implies that rents were set not on a conventional basis but with due consideration of expected yields.[90] There is, however, relatively little variation in the median numbers of artabas by nome for wheat, with the overall median being 6.6 artabas per aroura.[91] The Oxyrhynchite wheat rate is a little lower than other nomes at 6.4 artabas, and it will also be noted that there was usually a specific rent relief clause in the Oxyrhynchite documents by which the rent is to be reduced if the land is left dry due to a failure of the Nile flood.[92] This is not present in the Arsinoite leases and the rents for land under cereals, although on average being similar to other nomes are much more variable.[93] As with fodder rents, irrigation may explain this feature. In the Oxyrhynchite nome, most land was in the Nile valley and largely irrigated by assisted inundation, whereas in the Arsinoite nome a greater variety of irrigation methods were used.[94] As Bagnall noted, much of the Arsinoite nome was exceptional in being dependent on canal irrigation, and in the peripheral villages of the nome, where our papyri generally come from, 'the supply was limited and the canal system long, complex, and vulnerable'.[95] With that greater variety of irrigation methods, there would also have been a concurrent variety in the quality of that irrigation, not only in the amount of water distributed, but also in the degree to which the water included sediment, which acted as a natural fertilizer of the land within the flood plain of the Nile or its branches.[96] This variability in the extent, reliability and quality of irrigation within the Arsinoite nome, together with a greater variability in crop rotation practices, may therefore explain the wider variability of rents in kind.[97]

Scheidel has argued that land rents in kind in Egypt 'dropped precipitously' in the third century and used this as evidence to support his views

[90] See, for instance, *PSI* IX 1072 (third century), where for two different wheat plots within the same lease, one is rented at 9.75 artabas per aroura and another at 6.5. I have found no examples of 'peppercorn' rents, where an artificially low rent was payable, as occurs in other historical contexts.

[91] Only rents which relate to land sown in cereals are included.

[92] For private leases, only those from the Oxyrhynchite nome contain a rent relief clause in the case of the land being left dry, although such clauses do exist elsewhere for state land leases, such as *P.Tebt.* II 374 from Tebtunis in the Arsinoite nome (AD 131).

[93] The wheat rates are consistent with Bagnall's finding that 'average lease yields from the Arsinoite Nome in the first and second centuries are not much different from those of the Oxyrhynchite and Hermopolite Nomes; but the range is rather wider, and the highest figures we have come from the Arsinoite'. Bagnall 1985a: 306.

[94] See Bonneau 1971: *Graphique* V for a schematic description of the assisted inundation method.

[95] Bagnall 1993b: 17.

[96] Lewis 1983: 109.

[97] For variability in crop rotation, see Kelly 2020: 113.

Table 7 Median wheat rents per nome and date in artabas per aroura (number of cases)

	1st century	2nd century	3rd century
Arsinoite	7.0 (13)	9.0 (19)	4.5 (6)
Other	9.5 (3)	6.6(18)	5.7 (4)
Oxyrhynchite	6.0 (5)	6.8 (12)	6.0 (14)
All	7.0 (21)	7.4 (49)	6.0 (24)

on how the economy was impacted by the Antonine Plague.[98] To test this I examined the data in more detail and the medians by nome and date are as shown in Table 7. At first sight, if there is a precipitous decline in rents in the third century it stems from the data from the Arsinoite nome. However, if we examine the geographical distribution of the Arsinoite data a different possible explanation emerges. If we define high rates for both barley and wheat as being those of 13 artabas or more, then all of the 18 examples where we know the land's location come from the area around Tebtunis in the south of the Polemon district of the Arsinoite nome. However, in the third century we have no examples from the Tebtunis area, and all of the third-century data come from the northern and central areas of the nome, where, given their position at the end of the irrigation system, rates may be expected to be lower.[99] I would suggest therefore that the sharp third-century decline in rent rates that Scheidel outlined cannot be an Egypt-wide effect given that the data from the Oxyrhynchite nome show no such sharp decline and that any apparent decline in the Arsinoite

[98] Scheidel 2002: 101. He used data largely from Drexhage to support his conclusion. Note that Scheidel's methodology and reliance on unadjusted data from Drexhage is criticised by Bagnall in that it does not allow for land being under fodder. Bagnall 2002: 119. I have followed an approach which ensures that the rent rates concerned are those when the land was actually under wheat or barley. Van Minnen 2000: 212 also suggests there was a sharp decline in agricultural yields in the third century and beyond but it is not clear to me whether his argument is that on average total agricultural yield fell along with population or whether his argument is that the yield for each farmed artaba fell. He updated his argument further in van Minnen 2008: 231–3. See also Hennig 1967: 26–8 and Drexhage 1991: 162–3 for further discussion of the proposition that there was a sharp decline in average rent levels in the Fayum after the second century.

[99] The locations of the land in the third-century leases from the Arsinoite nome are: *SB* XIV 12197 (AD 211), Hephaistias in the north of the Herakleides district, *SB* XVI 12323 (AD 218), Theadelphia, *BGU* XI 2040 (AD 223), Theadelphia, *BGU* IV 1018 (third century), Kerkesephis in the north of the Polemon district and *SB* XII 10982 (AD 288), Tanis. There is one example of a mono-culture rate in barley for the third century which does happen to come from Tebtunis, *P.Tebt.* II 377 (AD 210), but this is not particularly low at 6.20 artabas per aroura.

nome is more likely to be a geographical distortion in the underlying data caused by the wide variability within that nome rather than a valid diachronic trend.[100]

What did these rent levels imply for tenants?

But how much did the tenant farmer pay in rent in real terms? How secure was their tenancy and how likely were they to prosper or fail? We saw in the previous chapter that housing costs were very low as a percentage of income or expenditure, but what would the equivalent proportion for tenant farmers be? I have published a model that projected the financial position of a family in the Oxyrhynchite nome.[101] The results from this model, produced in the form of a probability distribution, allow us to move away from the 'binary' model of rich and poor outlined in previous scholarship, and critiqued by Harris.[102] The model thus builds upon, and is indebted to, earlier work modelling social resilience in ancient Greece and elsewhere and on the use of microsimulation techniques.[103]

The model looks at the finances of an economic unit that is a family that includes a young couple and two other adult family members. The model thus reflects the fact that, typically, young couples did not, at least immediately, separate themselves from parents and other family members and allows them to enjoy the support of other family members particularly *in extremis*.[104] The following simple equation is tracked:

Savings or debt at beginning of year,

plus

income less subsistence less discretionary spending less interest on any debt which is the net surplus or deficit over year,

equals

savings or debt at end of year.

[100] The data for nomes other than the Arsinoite and Oxyrhynchite are too sparse to come to any strong conclusions.

[101] See Kelly 2021b and Kelly forthcoming a.

[102] Harris 2011: 31–2.

[103] Foxhall 1990 for risks for tenant farmers; Gallant 1991 for ancient Greece; and Smith & Oeppen 1993 for microsimulation techniques.

[104] See Huebner 2013: 48, who suggests that it would be 'the death of the patriarch (sometimes the widow) which was the crucial factor for any realignment of residence patterns'. However, families/households do not always form simple collective economic units otherwise we would have no intra-family transactions, and Huebner noted that strong family ties could be outweighed by economic considerations for cohabitation, particularly fraternal competition. Huebner 2013: 57.

This savings/debt calculation is performed separately for wheat and cash, and, as a result, at the year end, the families may have a surplus or deficit in either category.

The detailed assumptions within the model and their derivation will be found in the Appendix and the papers concerned, but to answer the initial question of how much, in relative terms, a family unit who rented all their land would need to pay for rent, around 55 per cent of expenditure would relate to rental costs.[105] This is a very high level of expenditure when compared to the low percentages of expenditure on housing costs demonstrated in the previous chapter.

The model not only tracks prosperity but also allows for families to fail completely, and 'ruin' is defined as a family falling into debt of two times expected gross income. This is a level of debt when any family would not be able to continue to service the existing debt, the level of interest payable being greater than their expected surplus in a good year. Even allowing for mutual support from fellow villagers and an extended family network, this is a level of indebtedness where no one would, or was able to, lend money for a family to survive, and then the family would, in all likelihood, fall into ruin, leading to starvation, flight and penury.[106]

At the end of 15 years, which is a generation in Roman Egyptian terms, 4.7 per cent of tenant families would have been ruined, and 34 per cent would have been in debt. The model, however, is relatively benign and predicts that around 8 per cent of the families really prosper in that their savings are more than 3,000 drachmas, which would be enough to purchase a small plot of land of around 6 arouras. This would not be enough to support a family as a whole but does indicate a degree of prosperity and the ability of this family to help support the next generation, whilst continuing to operate as a family unit. However, the rates of ruin are much lower when other types of economic units are analysed. If we look at smallholders who owned enough land to support their family their chance of ruin drops to 2 per cent, while if you were a petty landlord who owned two plots, one of which you farmed and the other you rented out, the chance of ruin over a generation essentially drops to zero.[107]

The model is only plausible if it produces results that reflect the evidence for the society concerned. In the case of Roman Egypt, the second

[105] See also the Appendix. Assuming 5 arouras per person, 50/50 in wheat and fodder, rent (per aroura) of 6.4 artabas of wheat and 22 drachmas, makes a total rental cost of 183 dr. Other bare bones expenditure is estimated at 143 dr. per person.

[106] There are frequent references within the papyri to individuals who have fled their responsibilities. For a considered approach to the reasons for flight, see Blouin 2014: 243–66.

[107] Kelly forthcoming a.

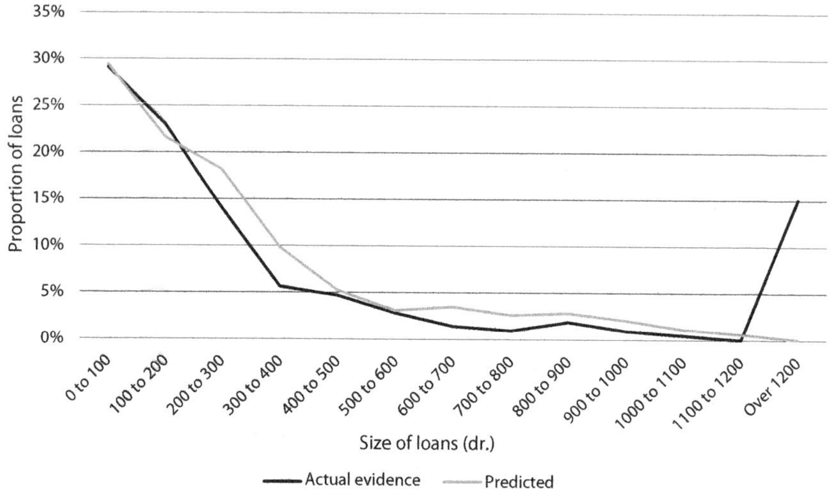

Figure 25 Predicted village loan size vs actual evidence

century period was one of comparative stability from both a climatic and a social perspective. The model needs therefore to produce results that show a society that is sustainable. The model is internally sustainable from a demographic perspective, producing results that support a stable or slightly increasing population. The model is also internally socially sustainable. Some 95 per cent of families do not fall into ruin by the end of the generation, and those who do are more than balanced by those who prosper and whose children would be well placed to become smallholders on their own account. Nevertheless, the model produces results that show the significant strains on the financial well-being of the tenant families and their wider families. There is a high chance of falling into debt, consistent with the levels found in nineteenth-century rural Egypt.[108] This was truly 'a world profoundly dependent on credit'.[109] One other way of testing whether the model outputs are plausible is to see if the projected typical size of borrowing required is reasonable compared to the actual evidence from the credit market of Roman Egypt. The median size of loan required for those borrowing in year 15 of the model is predicted at 195 drachmas. The median size of cash loans in a village context in Roman Egypt at the

[108] The model predicts that 34 per cent will have fallen into debt by year 15, although more will have fallen into debt and then recovered given good harvests. For comparison, 37 per cent of rural smallholder families in early twentieth-century Egypt were in debt according to Richards 1982: Figure 3.15.

[109] Harris 2006: 14.

same period is 168 drachmas.[110] The borrowing requirements predicted are thus consistent with the credit market evidence and this is confirmed in Figure 25, when the distribution of the amounts of the predicted and actual loans are compared, since both curves show a similar shape.[111] The model is, of course, incapable of predicting the larger loans that the richer village landowners contracted, since it deals only with tenants. Hence the presence in the actual data of loans of more than 1,200 drachmas, but otherwise the actual and predicted lines follow a very similar pattern.

I have also adapted the model to allow for the possibility of families to abandon newborn children as a last resort action due to unsustainable financial stress at the time of the child's birth.[112] The general evidence for the abandonment of newborns in the Roman Empire is clear. Even if we only look at the narrower case of exposure, Harris described the evidence for widespread adoption of this practice as 'nearly overwhelming'.[113] He concluded that Roman Egypt was a 'place where child-exposure was commonplace', although Frier demurred and stated that 'Egyptians did not use infanticide or exposure in order to limit their families', and exposure could, of course, have been driven by other considerations such as gender or deformity.[114] Depending on the level of existing debt that would have

110 Based on the author's doctoral research, n = 213. Lerouxel's data showed loans of a similar size, but with a smaller sample. He quoted a median cash loan size for the period from AD 70 to 170 for unsecured loans of 218 dr. (n = 32). Lerouxel 2016: 114.

111 The period selected is AD 70 to 170 to allow for any distortion from institutional changes; see Lerouxel 2016: 42.

112 It should be noted that the term 'abandonment', which includes the narrower cases of 'exposure' or 'infanticide', has been adopted. Whilst abandonment could take the form of exposure or killing the newborn, it could also involve selling the child to be brought up as a slave or giving it to a third party. Selling children was made legal by Constantine in AD 313 but undoubtedly will have occurred before this date. Harris, without citing much evidence, posits that perhaps the level of fatalities from child exposure in Egypt was less than in other provinces, given 'indigenous attitudes'. Harris 1994: 10.

113 Harris 1994: 1. This evidence comes from a variety of sources, including the well-known letter from an absent husband to his pregnant wife telling her to abandon the child if it is a girl (*P.Oxy.* IV 744), the frequency of wet nurse agreements combined with loans, which have been interpreted as a way of avoiding infanticide by effectively selling a newborn as a slave (see Montevecchi 1984), and finally the provisions under the law codes which dealt with the practice (see Taubenschlag 1955: 101). In addition, as regards the validity of considering the ***kopr-*** names as providing evidence for these individuals having been, or being the descendants of, infants abandoned on dung heaps, see Harris 1994: 8.

114 Harris 1994: 8; Frier 1994: 327n.28. I only estimated abandonment caused by financial necessity. Three of the four potential reasons identified by Harris for abandonment are thus not allowed for: illegitimacy, deformity, or evil omens/despair, including marriage break-up during pregnancy. Harris 1994: 11–12. Note the practice

triggered action by the family, ranging from 1 year's net income (200 dr.) to 2 years' rent, subsistence and seed (1,500 dr.), between 8 per cent and 24 per cent of tenant families would have had to abandon a newborn at least once during a 15-year period.[115] Child abandonment driven by excessive debt would therefore have been likely to have been a common experience among tenant families. Most people would have known neighbours or cousins who were forced to abandon a newborn and even if the vast majority of tenant families, perhaps around 90 per cent, would, in prosperous times, have avoided abandoning any of their children, they may have feared that it would happen to them. It would thus have been a social practice that would have been understood as a necessity by rural society. It was partially effective in reducing the risk of complete ruin for the family and saving the lives of the siblings to the abandoned child, but only if adopted early enough within the debt cycle. It had no impact, however, in helping a family to climb out of debt. In times of crisis, it would have immediately increased in frequency and persisted as a practice, and, inevitably, in those times, more of the abandoned newborns would have died.

The results fully reflect what Banerjee and Duflo described as the 'S-Shape Curve and the Poverty Trap'.[116] If income in the future is plotted against income in the past they proposed that the shape of the curve would be an elongated S-shape with lower incomes falling into a spiral of reducing income as expected income falls below current – hence the poverty trap. In our example, this happens when poor climatic conditions mean that harvest yields are lower and families fall into debt so that their net income falls as they now not only have to feed the family but also pay the interest on the debt. They can claw their way out of this poverty trap if they are lucky enough to have successive good harvests but not all families will be that fortunate.

One of the model's central conclusions is that the main risk to tenant farmers is weather variability rather than average expected yield. If the harvest variability assumption is increased just from a 20 per cent assumption to 25 per cent, the chance of ruin more than doubles.[117] This conclusion is validated when we look at the experience of poor farmers in modern-day India. Binswanger and Rosenzweig proposed that profit

of brother–sister marriages in Egypt is likely to have increased the chance of congenital birth defects. Nor does it allow for gender preferment or for abandonment due to the death of the mother in childbirth and a consequent inability to find or pay a wet nurse, curiously ignored by Harris. All of these reasons mean that my estimates of the levels of abandonment by tenant families are likely to be understated.

[115] See Kelly forthcoming a.

[116] Banerjee & Duflo 2011: 11.

[117] Kelly forthcoming a.

rates would increase substantially in areas where the rainfall pattern was very predictable.[118] They put this down to the ability of richer farmers to absorb risk and invest in an efficient way for the future. But even without specifically allowing for this effect, the model shows the significant impact of weather variability on financial outcomes and that it has a differential impact depending on initial wealth. For tenants, climate-related risks were certainly more important than the risk of having too many children, but a failure to save some of your surplus in good years was a sure path to financial ruin. Overall, tenants could have little expectation of escaping from the additional work they needed to perform, just to pay their rent, to save sufficiently to achieve the much more financially stable ideal of land ownership, which leads neatly into the next section.

How much did landlords make from leasing?

I have set out above the rents per aroura in kind and cash terms, but rents in artabas of wheat or drachmas provide little information in themselves. An example may assist. Imagine you owned a small plot of cereal land near Oxyrhynchus, the size of our proverbial football pitch (2.5 arouras), and you leased it out to be sown half in wheat and half in fodder. Your annual rental income would be some 90 drachmas, and even though you would be liable for tax on the land and other costs totalling around 25 drachmas, you would still clear some 65 drachmas a year – if the Nile flooded and the tenant paid his rent. That is the equivalent of a labourer's wages for perhaps three months, or you could spend your earnings on half a donkey, or it would pay for a couple of bottles of wine each week, although there was no way you could afford even a part share in a slave.

A more scientific way of assessing how much landlords made from leasing is to assess the rate of return, in percentage terms, that they earned. The return from a land lease was equal to the rent received less the landlord's frictional costs divided by the value of the real estate. The rent for each transaction is known from the documents themselves, whilst the value of the land can be estimated using the best-fit lines for land prices shown in Figure 9.[119] The missing data therefore are the frictional costs, and my assumptions as to these costs are outlined in the Appendix.

[118] Binswanger & Rosenzweig 1993: 75.

[119] Where rent is expressed in artabas of wheat or barley, these have been converted into drachma amounts using the best-fit lines shown in Figures 3 and 4. I noted above that arable land prices from the Oxyrhynchite nome had a higher level than those from the Arsinoite or other nomes. I have therefore adopted separate estimates of land prices depending on whether the land was in the Oxyrhynchite or another nome. I have avoided the temptation to try and second guess what categories of land may or may not be represented by different price levels, as was undertaken by Alston 1995: 108

To ensure readers are clear on the methodology, a worked example is provided below of the estimated return on investment for a lease of fodder. In *P.Sarap.* 26 (a lease from the Hermopolite nome, which dates from AD 125), 8 arouras are to be sown in *aracus* (fodder) for an annual rent of 26 drachmas per aroura, with no supplementary payments. The gross income to the landlord is thus 208 drachmas, and no frictional costs are attributed to the landlord, but he continues to be responsible for land tax, which is estimated at 1⅛ artabas of wheat for each of the 8 arouras. The price of wheat in AD 125 is estimated at 9.14 drachmas, from the best-fit line in Figure 3, so the value of the artaba tax is some 84 drachmas (8 × 8/7 × 9.14). The *naubion* tax is estimated at half a drachma per aroura and is thus 4 drachmas in total. Therefore, the net income to the landlord is 120 drachmas (208 − 84 − 4). The value of an aroura of land in the Hermopolite nome at AD 125 is estimated at 285 drachmas from the relevant best-fit line, and thus the effective capital employed in owning 8 arouras is estimated at 2,280 drachmas. The annual return is therefore 120 divided by 2,280, or 5.3 per cent. Whilst this gives an estimate of the return while the land was in fodder, a different calculation would be necessary when the land was under cereals, which, as we will see, generally produced a higher return.

Whilst returns calculated when the land was exclusively under fodder and cereals are of interest, they provide no direct information as to the level of sustainable term returns likely to be received by a landlord since it would not have been financially beneficial to leave land under fodder indefinitely and to have kept land under cereals over a number of years would have reduced the yield by exhausting the nutrients in the soil. The only approach that can provide us with reliable estimates is to use multiple year or mixed crop leases. We also need to take account of the risk of the tenant not being able to pay his rent, or, in the case of the Oxyrhynchite nome, the clause in the lease that states no rent is due when the Nile fails to flood. We can estimate the chance of this happening by examining historical records from Roman and later times as to how often the Nile flood failed.

We are fortunate to have good information on the Nile floods and that Bonneau has classified the level of the flood for each year where information is available for the period from AD 1 to 274 into a number of categories ranging from bad ('mauvaise') to strong ('forte').[120] The chance of the flood

and Scheidel 2002: 102, since I would agree with Bagnall as to the difficulties of such categorisations. Bagnall 2002: 116.

120 Bonneau 1971: 219. Although Bonneau's categorisations contain some inconsistencies, they are the best indicators currently available as to the likelihood of Nile flood failure. At a frequency of 8 per cent, this is consistent with an event which is not habitual but is foreseeable and which requires clauses within lease contracts that deal with its possible occurrence. Note that, according to Blouin 2014: 16n.22, Tristant calculated

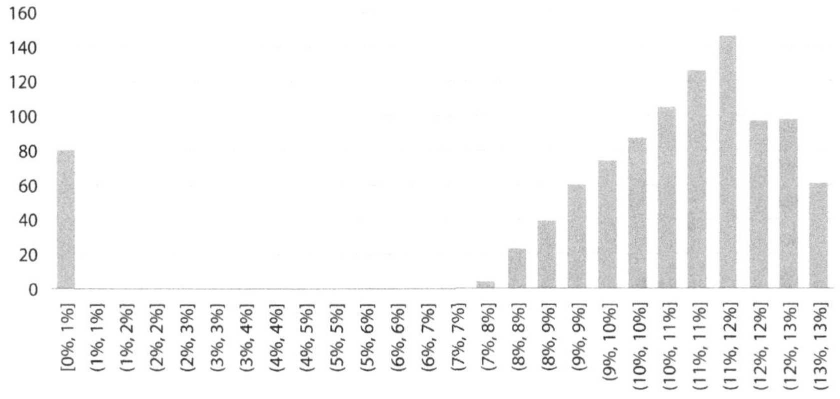

Figure 26 *SB* XVIII 13287

being in the bad category was 8 per cent, or roughly once in every 12 years. I have therefore made the assumption that the chance of a poor harvest that would not permit the payment of rent would be linked to the Nile flood and I have taken 8 per cent as the probability that the harvest failed or was so poor as to mean that the rent would not be paid.[121] If the flood was too great it would be likely that the harvest would be late or reduced in size, but it would be unlikely that it failed entirely and the rent could well have been paid. I have assumed that the chance of non-payment of rent is inversely correlated with the price of cereals, based on the logic that when harvests fail crop prices rise. I have also taken into account the fact that cereal prices will have had some intrinsic variability that is independent of the success of the harvest. The full list of assumptions is provided in the Appendix.

I modelled the possible returns by completing 1,000 simulations for each of the 105 individual leases, and Figure 26 shows the results for one lease. Note the 8 per cent chance of losing money for the landlord in years when the Nile does not flood and no rent is receivable. Figure 27 shows the aggregated results formed by adding together all the 105,000 results for the 105 available individual leases and Figure 28 and Table 8 summarise these results. The tighter and lower distribution of returns for the Oxyrhynchite nome compared to the Arsinoite nome is clear. In general, I believe that the Oxyrhynchite nome may be a better indicator of the return from leasing land in Roman Egypt than that derived from using the larger dataset from all nomes, for two reasons. First, the Oxyrhynchite nome lies in the Nile

that on the basis of data from the seventh to the fifteenth centuries, 7 per cent of Nile floods failed or were late.

[121] For a discussion of the theoretical background to this 'fluvial risk', see Blouin 2014: 15–18.

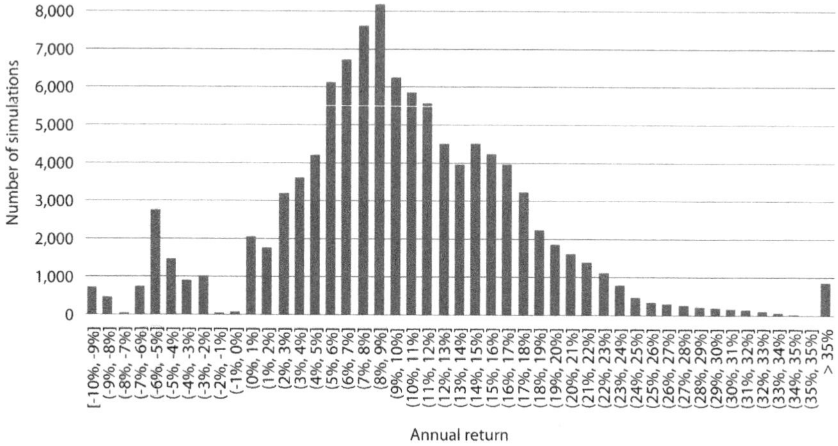

Figure 27 All land leases

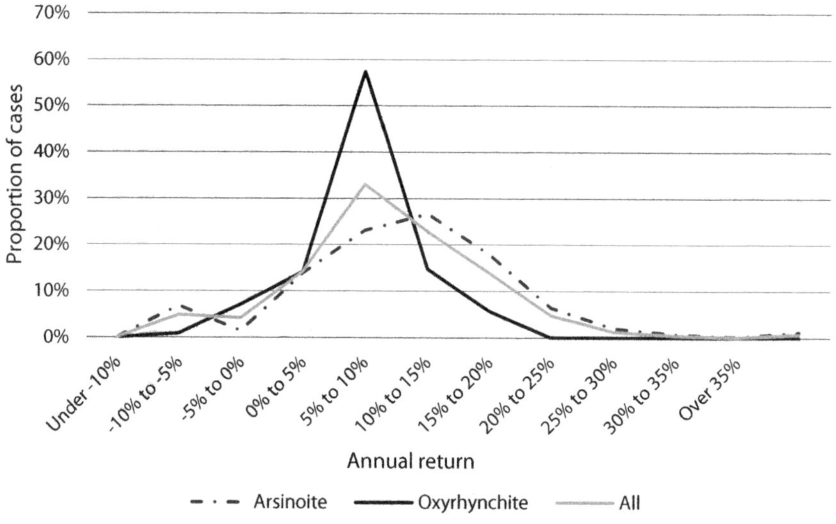

Figure 28 Land leasing (stochastic return distribution)

Table 8 Median and average stochastic returns per annum per nome

Nome	Median	Average
Arsinoite	11.0%	10.8%
Oxyrhynchite	7.4%	7.2%
All	8.9%	9.6%

valley itself, as does much of the exploitable land of Roman Egypt, and is therefore more typical than the Arsinoite nome with its peculiarities of geographical position and irrigation techniques. Second, I have made a necessary assumption that the price of land per aroura is the same within any particular nome at a given date. This is clearly untrue, since land prices are likely to have varied according to their quality, and although it might not impact significantly on the medians and averages, it will tend to widen the distribution of both deterministic and stochastic results. In the model, the lower the assumed value of land, the higher the calculated return. Thus, the return on fertile plots is exaggerated, since the value of land used is probably too low, and vice versa for poor-quality land. The greater the variability in the land in the nome concerned, the greater this effect. Land prices are less variable than in the Oxyrhynchite nome than elsewhere and thus the impact of this effect is less pronounced.[122] I will therefore generally use the Oxyrhynchite leasing results for comparison purposes from this point forward.

A by-product of the analysis above is that it allows an estimate to be made of the tax take by the state from landowners in Roman Egypt. The marginal tax rate on investment in land, without crown tax, had a median value of 25 per cent, and when crown tax became payable it was 41 per cent. This contrasts with a much lower tax rate for tenants where the tax rate as a percentage of income after rent is around 5 per cent. So, whatever the nature of the other features of the Roman imperial state apparatus, the taxation system may actually be considered as progressive rather than oppressive in that it extracted proportionately more from the wealthy than the poor.

But ownership of land did not only bring you economic benefits, it brought you social capital and all the attendant (and sometimes negative from a financial perspective) consequences. Let's go back to Isidoros, who, as he ages, faces increasing redistributive demands on his resources from the state. Although he was illiterate, Isidoros had to fulfil at least ten different liturgical or community functions, all of which would have been costly in either time or money. It is his landed wealth, in an age without income tax records and demands, which drew the attention of the local authorities to Isidoros's ability to fulfil the liturgies. Whilst some of the liturgies, such as acting as the sitologos (the official responsible for the village's state granary and for collection and reporting of taxes paid in kind), would have afforded Isidoros the ability to wield power locally and possibly use the process to his own advantage, others would have been less welcome. Indeed, in AD 319, Isidoros complains bitterly that as an aged man (he was then around 50) he

122 The R^2 coefficient for Oxyrhynchite nome prices (43 per cent) is much higher than elsewhere (8 per cent for Arsinoite and 15 per cent for other nomes), indicating that the typical price of land is more tightly distributed than elsewhere; see Kelly 2020: 94.

should be excused another liturgy.[123] As we have seen, owners of land would also be assigned *epibole*, poor state land that would have low yields. Thus, although land could generate attractive financial returns, it came with a price in social redistributive demands.

We can compare the median returns on Egyptian arable land calculated above, after taxes, with the previous attempts by scholars to calculate this return. Unfortunately, none of Kehoe, Rathbone and Rowlandson, who have provided the most comprehensive and thoughtful monographs on the agricultural economy of Roman Egypt, ventured to suggest a range of rates of return.[124] Carrié, however, addressed the question of returns from land leasing in Roman Egypt explicitly and arrived at a conclusion that in the first and second centuries the effective return on leased land varied between 11.7 per cent and 15.8 per cent, and for the third century between 7 per cent and 15.8 per cent.[125] He accepted that for the years when the land is under fodder the return will be less than when under cereals and made a rough adjustment for this effect. Carrié was working from best estimate ranges for the values of land and rent rates only in wheat. His results are necessarily vague and I would contend that my approach – which works from the primary sources taking full account of when land was sown in barley, fodder and wheat, non-payment of rent, and allows averages, medians and distributions to be calculated – is preferable.

The fact that landowners accepted very low returns when land was under fodder, even in 1-year leases when no direct compensation was available from higher returns in years when the land was sown in cereals within the same lease, shows financial rationality in their willingness to forego immediate returns on their capital in exchange for deferred gratification. A difference in returns between the Arsinoite and Oxyrhynchite nome has been noted. If the Egyptian market was fully integrated in a geographical sense, and landowners acted in a financially rational way, then differences in returns between nomes should be minimal, as capital was employed across the country, and rents and land prices produced similar levels of return through forces of market supply and demand. Certainly, most financial activity was within a nome rather than being inter-nome, with the exception of some landlords from Alexandria active in the Arsinoite nome, which would suggest that the leasing market was not geographically integrated. However, it should be remembered that differences in returns may reflect differences in the risks and variability in return from different types of land in different locations rather than any lack of market integration.

123 *P.Cair.Isid.* 138 (AD 319).

124 Kehoe 1992; Rathbone 1991; Rowlandson 1996.

125 Carrié 1997: 132.

Conclusion

I will summarise my view of the markets in Chapter 8, but the life of Isidoros has illustrated many of the themes of this chapter. The categories of landlord, smallholder and tenant were not mutually exclusive, and individuals could, at one and the same time, fall into any of the three categories. Isidoros fulfilled at least two of these roles as tenant and smallholder, making what look like financially rational decisions about which plots of land to farm and which to abandon. He leased land both from a city-based absentee landlord and from his neighbours, and cultivated these relationships, enjoying some flexibility to delay his rent. Although most of his land was sown with cereals, he diversified his agricultural activity with his interest in beans and olives. When he took on a risky lease he sought a longer duration to enable him to recoup any investment. However, the ownership of land provided both ongoing income and, perhaps more importantly, security against the vagaries of the Nile flood, illness and changing family needs, and would have been a primary concern. But note that Isidoros inherited much of his wealth and unfortunately for those without initial capital the chances of upward social mobility in wealth terms were very slim.

To exploit the land he banded together with his brothers and worked the land in common with them, illustrating the concept of family-based economic units. His land brought both benefits and disadvantages and also conflict. His petitions show frequent disputes with his neighbours mostly revolving around land and I suspect that Isidoros was not beyond responding in kind, coming from a family with military connections. With the built-in family gang of seven brothers and all their children he would have been dangerous to cross in a village of probably fewer than one thousand people at the time.[126] To this physical presence we can add the structural authority that came with state appointments for himself and his sons to oversee the granary and tax collections and the opportunities for corruption that these entailed. Isidoros was a man who wielded local petty power but who made enemies. His reliance on family, clashes with the tax man, love for land, wheeling and dealing in commodities and familiarity with violence, reminds me strongly of Tony Soprano, whose quote provides the epigraph to this chapter. But he did not get it all his own way. In one of the later documents of his archive his neighbours got their own back by breaking into his house while he was working in his fields and smashing up his furniture.[127]

[126] Isidoros's grandfather was a *speculator* (a spy or messenger) in the Roman army and his father continued to have strong military connections. His papers show him dealing with three different military men (see *P.Cair.Isid.* 109–10 (AD 279), *P.Cair.Isid.* 31 (AD 276) and *P.Cair.Isid.* 83 (second half, third century)). Boak 1955: 162 suggests a total of 142 landholders in Karanis in the early fourth century.

[127] *P.Cair.Isid.* 75 (AD 316).

Chapter 5

Usury or Solidarity?

Debt is a divisive subject in academia and in the public domain. It can be viewed as a positive force facilitating economic growth or a 'perversion of a promise', which results in the violent subordination of one person by another.[1] This chapter examines the credit market from the perspective of both the borrower and the lender. Were borrowers aided or hindered by the availability of credit? Were lenders seeking to maximise profit at all costs or lending within a societal framework that was based on reciprocity and redistribution or other institutional structures?

The types of transactions dealt with in this chapter are those where a debt is formalised in a deliberate manner by both principals. They include both deposits, where the lender may require the repayment of the loan at any time at their option, and loans, where lender and borrower agree on a fixed timing for repayment. Also considered as loans are mortgages, sales on credit, pledges related to debts, pawns, maritime loans and letters of credit.[2]

There is a much larger body of documents related to loans than to land or housing sales indicating that credit transactions were more common than real estate. This is despite the fact that the generally smaller size of the loan transactions would have made them less likely to be formalised in writing than real estate sales, which were generally

[1] Graeber 2014: 391.

[2] A number of other types of credit transactions have not been included in this chapter, either since they cannot be analysed in the same way or because they are substantially different from the loans and deposits I deal with. Advance sales, where a buyer of goods makes a payment in advance in return for a delivery of goods at some point in the future, can be considered as containing a loan from buyer to vendor of the purchase price. However, they do not lend themselves to financial analysis since they include not only the loan but also some potential adjustment to the price, and we lack the price data to identify the effective terms of the transaction. Similar considerations apply to 'the large-scale use of credit arrangements' within the accounts of large estates (see Rathbone 1991: 397). Finally, the body of loans on ostraca from Mons Claudianus have not been included in the quantitative analysis as these relate to a quite separate geographical and social context from the civilian, agrarian provenance of the bulk of the data.

larger in size. In total I have collected 1,229 documents containing 1,999 transactions involving more than 4,000 individuals. This is a larger body of data than the 432 transactions considered in Lerouxel's recent monograph on credit.[3]

Legal framework and institutional constraints

The *Gnomon of the Idios Logos*, an official document providing guidance as to fiscal practice in Roman Egypt, had a provision with regard to the maximum interest on cash loans that was legally allowable. This rate was 12 per cent and lower than the 24 per cent applicable in Ptolemaic Egypt.[4] This 12 per cent rate probably dates back to the later republic and the cap on interest rates evidenced by the decrees of the senate and the tribunes in 51 or 50 BC.[5] There was a long-standing concern of viewing usury at higher rates as undesirable, as evidenced in Cicero's prosecution of Verres.[6] In Roman Egypt, there was also a requirement that the total interest payable should not exceed the principal loaned, which is attested in a petition of AD 158–159, *P.Fouad* I 26, and in the reduction in interest payments, taken by the lender in *SB* VIII 9923 (AD 175–176) or *P.Tebt.* II 397 (AD 198), to ensure that the interest did not exceed the principal.[7] Modern governments were a little late in employing the same protections and the UK government only introduced this same principle in 2015 when the usurious interest rates on payday loans forced them into action. Measures that protected borrowers made sound economic sense from the perspective of the Roman state, since, as I will demonstrate below, excessive interest rates would typically result in more failures of smallholders and tenants and a consequent reduction in agricultural output and tax take. A similar rationale can apply to modern states. In Roman Egypt, however, there were no known restrictions on interest rates on loans in kind, which, we will also see below, frequently exceeded 12 per cent.

[3] Lerouxel 2016: 7. This is partly because more types of documents, including contract registers containing extracts or receipts for repayment, have been included, whereas Lerouxel's primary focus was on loan contracts themselves, although he does include consideration of other evidence within the body of his work. Lerouxel also includes documents only from selected locations and his date range only extends to AD 275.

[4] Taubenschlag 1955: 260. For a discussion of the evidence for Roman Italy, see Andreau 2000.

[5] See Cicero, *Letters to Atticus* 5.21 and Dio Cassius, *Roman History* 41: 37.2 for the evidence for the decrees. See Kay 2014: 114, 255–6, 260 for discussion of limits and usury.

[6] Cicero, *Against Verres* 3.70.

[7] See *SB* XX 14401 (AD 147) for further evidence of legal constraints.

Loans were generally simply structured, typically describing the amount borrowed, and either the interest rate applicable or the amount to be repaid, and the repayment date. The fixed date for repayment meant that both parties were clear from the outset as to the amounts concerned and there was no need for any complex mathematical skills. Generally, simple interest rather than compound interest applied and the interest was payable at the end of the term with the return of the principal, although, as we will see, there were exceptions.

A deposit, ***paratheke***, differed from a loan in that it generally did not have a set date for repayment, but rather was to be repaid at the demand of the lender. The ***paratheke*** in Roman Egypt had some similarities to the Latin ***depositum*** but it was a contractual formula rather than a contract purely for safekeeping and therefore it could be used in a wider set of circumstances.[8] Haklai and Roth both suggest that interest applied on deposits, but I would adopt a contrary view, more aligned with Tenger.[9] First there are no mentions of interest applying in deposit contracts. Second, interest cannot have been included up front since a deposit is repayable at the demand of the lender and thus if it were included and the lender demanded repayment immediately then the borrower would have made an immediate and irretrievable loss of the amount of the interest. Therefore, interest can only have been payable at the repayment of the deposit. But we have no examples of deposit repayment documents mentioning interest. Also, because the term is unknown, the financial liability in drachmas of the borrower is impossible to calculate at the outset, something which is always known for fixed-term loans. This open-ended liability, whose calculation may have been beyond the mathematical skills of the borrower (who would always know how much interest would need to be paid for a loan), would make accepting an interest-bearing deposit unattractive. For the above reasons I believe that deposits should be taken as they are recorded, a financial transaction where one party places a financial asset in the care of another without expectation of interest payments, but in substance quite similar to a loan of no fixed duration.

Credit transactions varied also as to the security that was provided to the lender in case of default by the borrower.[10] In simple loans, typically for small amounts, no security was specified within the loan document. However, it was common amongst loans of a more formal nature for the lender to have rights over the general assets of the borrower when seeking

[8] See Haklai 2020: 448.

[9] Haklai 2020: 451; Roth 1970: 53–6, contra Tenger 1993: 63–7.

[10] See Lerouxel 2016: 245–92 for a comparison of the guarantees which provided the lender with security in Roman Egypt and Campania.

to enforce a debt, and a term meaning 'as if by a court order' often provided the legal background to assist the lender. However, the strongest form of security, then as now, was to provide the lender with the rights to seize, or to keep in their possession, a specific asset. Portable items such as clothes or jewellery could be pawned, or fixed assets such as real estate could be pledged through some form of mortgage.

The formal legal structure of a mortgage, in the *hypotheke*, *hypallagma* or *mesiteia* forms, does not, as Lerouxel notes, appear within our transactions until around AD 69 when the *bibliotheke enkteseon*, or records office, was established and provided the necessary institutional structure to establish and monitor ownership of real estate.[11] Prior to this date, specific security was sometimes provided through simultaneous loans and fiduciary sales where in the event of default the lender had already established legal title over the real estate through the fiduciary sale. Lerouxel believed that the enhanced ability to monitor and prove real estate ownership provided by this new institution encouraged the use of secured loans and points to the increase in the median size of loans to support his proposition. This proposition is tested below.

One important structural feature of the credit market of Roman Egypt is that debts were inheritable as well as assets. Certainly not a case of 'he that dies pays all debts'.[12] Thus an individual with adult offspring or a partner was a better credit risk as a debtor than one without immediate family. This transferability of obligation means that to some extent loans became financial instruments capable of trading. This is shown in loans across the empire, from Alexandria, Dacia and London.[13] However, the vast majority of loans remained short-term arrangements between two sets of principals and were not traded to third parties.

Turning to financial institutions, the role of the banks seems to have been limited to reducing the information deficit between creditors and debtors, thus lowering search and information costs and risks. However, they did not generally use the money deposited with them to extend loans to third parties and thus 'the money supply remained largely limited to the stock

[11] Lerouxel 2016: 341–2; Lerouxel 2015: 171–2.

[12] Stephano in Shakespeare's *The Tempest*, Act 1, scene ii.

[13] In the Alexandrian case, a loan is specifically stated to be repayable to the creditor or their heirs or whoever the creditor mandates (*P. Fouad* I 45 AD 153). In the Dacian case, a loan is to be repaid to the lender or 'to whomever it might in the future concern'. Shelton 1998: 137 (CIL III 934 *c.*AD 162). The London case is more fragmentary, but the phrase 'or to whom the business will concern …' is interpreted to relate to a legal document, probably a loan-note. https://romaninscriptionsofbritain.org/inscriptions/TabLondBloomberg54 (accessed 1 September 2022): Tab.Lond.Bloomberg<WT54>. AD 65/70–80.

of metal currency'.[14] This has important structural economic consequences since the emergence of commercial banks with fractional reserving in the early modern era is generally credited with facilitating economic growth and increasing the money supply. Without these institutions providing ready credit to entrepreneurs, the Roman Egyptian economy was necessarily constrained.

What was borrowed and for how long?

Turning to the type of transactions: loans for a fixed term constitute 90 per cent of the 1,999 transactions. Deposits, where the term is not pre-determined, are 10 per cent of the data. Credit transactions, both loans and deposits, can be further subdivided according to the type of capital and the vast bulk of transactions: 83 per cent were in cash, with 11 per cent in kind and 6 per cent mixed. So cash loans of a fixed term are the most common type of credit transaction.

One question that arises is the degree to which the proportion of loans in cash and kind changed over time, particularly during the period of high inflation after AD 274. A preference for loans in kind, which would keep their 'real' value in times of high inflation as opposed to coins of dubious purchasing power when repaid, would be a financially rational approach for lenders. The percentage distribution between cash, kind and mixed transactions over time shows some changes in practice, with kind loans increasing in prevalence from 5 per cent in the first century to 13 per cent in the second, 15 per cent in the period from AD 200 to 273 and 20 per cent in the period AD 274–350.[15] There is indeed a possible increase in the prevalence of loans in kind rather than in cash but it pre-dates the Third-Century Crisis and the jump in prices in AD 274 and the high inflation period that followed as described in Chapter 2.[16]

It has also been proposed that during the Roman period there was a trend towards deposits rather than loans.[17] This proposition can be tested

[14] Verboven 2020: 412. See also Haklai 2020: 454.

[15] The total number of loans for each period is 567 for the first century, 774 for the second, 282 for the period from AD 200 to 273 and 160 for AD 274 to 350. In some cases the form of the capital cannot be determined and thus the total number of transactions is less than the total number of transactions of 1,999.

[16] A trend for repayment in total in kind, or 'sales on delivery', or for interest to be paid in kind on loans originally made in cash, largely post-dates the middle of the fourth century. The earliest dated example of a cash loan when interest is payable in kind is *SB* XIV 12088 from AD 346; see Blouin 2010: 101n.10. My findings only partially confirm Carrié's impression that there was a trend to kind rather than cash loans. Carrié 2003: 266. Note that Carrié's statement that in the Roman period 80 per cent of loans were in kind is clearly a simplification. Carrié 2003: 278.

[17] Haklai 2020: 450–1.

by considering the proportion of loans compared to deposits but my data show no clear trend.[18]

The median size of cash loans prior to AD 274, re-calibrated for general inflation to AD 150 prices, was 160 drachmas. To put this in context, this sum was a considerable one for an ordinary person in Roman Egypt as it represented more than half a year's wages for a labourer.[19] As can be seen in Table 9, Lerouxel's proposition that the size of loans increased after the establishment of the *bibliotheke enkteseon* is supported, but no causal link is proved. However, if loans became larger and more complex, there is no growth in the number of loan documents after the establishment of the *bibliotheke enkteseon*, and indeed the proportion of credit transactions within the normative database, and thus the likely number of transactions, declines from around AD 75.

This decline in the relative number of loan documents combined with the growth in the median size of transactions leads to the question of whether the total volume of the credit market was growing or decreasing. Howgego's statement in this regard that 'as there is no evidence on which to base quantification, it is difficult to trace changes in the level of monetary credit over time' is correct in that it is difficult to trace trends, but incorrect in stating that there is no evidence.[20] The total amount of loans cannot simply be added together for each time period since this is a function as much of the number of documents found and published as of the volume of business being transacted. Therefore we need to look at the development of both the typical size and relative number of loans over time and how this varied by location.

The loan sizes set out in Table 9 show a striking difference in the sizes of loans in cities compared to villages. Although overall the size of loans increased steadily over time, even after allowing for inflation, in reality this was a city-based phenomenon. A larger real loan size would be an indicator of a growth in the wealth of those transacting or of loans that were intended for investment purposes rather than consumption, or a consequence of institutional changes that assisted larger loans by allowing them to be secured against property. But there is no sign of any of these features in the village credit markets, where the villagers had no direct

18 The percentage of credit transactions represented by deposits is 18 per cent (n = 610) for the first century, 6 per cent (n = 893) for the second, 3 per cent (n = 318) for the period from AD 200 to 273 and 9 per cent (n = 178) for AD 274–350.

19 Based on the mid second-century AD modal average daily wages for rural casual work in the Fayum quoted in Rathbone 2009a: 316.

20 Howgego 1992: 15. Note that the use of documents rather than transactions as the basis for the relative number of loans reduces, but does not eliminate, the bias due to the prominence of certain archives although it does eliminate any bias caused by numerous transactions within a single document.

Table 9 Median cash transaction amounts in drachmas adjusted for inflation by provenance

Date	AD 1–70	AD 70–170	AD 170–273
City n = 313	200	415	517
Village n = 536	100	168	130
Total n = 1,111	102	200	304

Note: There are 395 transactions where the provenance cannot be attributed to either city or village and this explains why the numbers of city and village cases do not add up to the total.

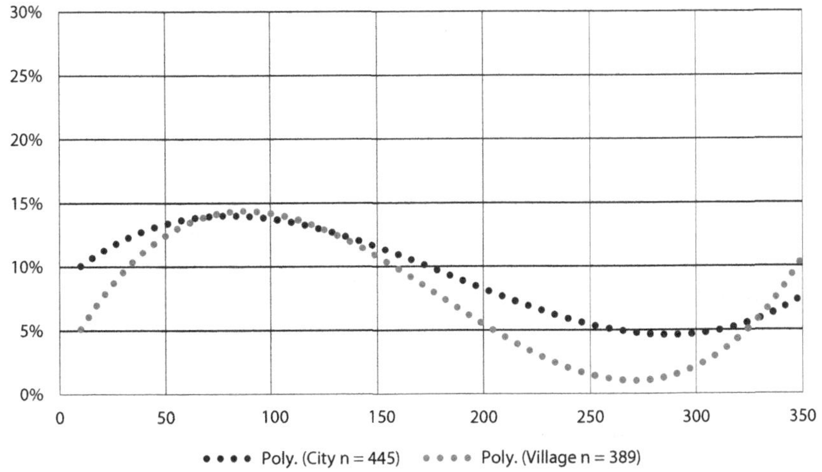

Figure 29 Proportion of documentary papyri which are credit transactions in cities, villages and overall

access to the city-based ***bibliotheke enkteseon***. The city-based principals could, however, access the records office, given their geographical proximity and the literacy that wealth allowed, and this facilitated their access to the mortgage market, which relied on the establishment of title to a plot of land to secure a loan. The mortgage market was thus a 'limited-access' market. Given, as we will see, we have very little evidence for loans for investment, the increase in loan sizes in the cities does I believe indicate a concentration of wealth there, possibly facilitated by the establishment of the records office.

The relative frequency of documents attesting loans can also be broken down by city and village provenance and the best-fit trendlines for relative frequency are shown in Figure 29. In the cities, the relative number of documents (and thus the likely number of transactions) falls but the increase in typical size more than makes up for this. Thus, overall credit activity in cities is likely to have increased over time when measured in total monetary terms. In the villages, the typical loan size is relatively stable, but the relative number of cases declines throughout the second century and the first half of the third century and collapses to almost zero, although it picks up in the fourth century. This collapse of the village credit market would have serious consequences for social stability in the third century, as we will see when the position of tenant farmers is modelled later in this chapter.

It would seem, in line with Lerouxel's proposition, that financial activity was drawn to the city-based markets.[21] We will also see below that the practice of city dwellers lending to villagers was largely a second- and third-century practice, which would also indicate a change in the credit market. Whatever the reason, it would appear that there was a concentration of financial activity and wealth in cities in the second and third centuries, but no substantial increase in credit activity overall.

From AD 274, as might be expected, after the jump in general prices and given the continued inflationary conditions in the fourth century, the size of cash loans increased. But it did not keep pace with inflation since the annual average increase of the trendline for the size of monetary loans from AD 275 to 350 is 9.6 per cent compared to 13.7 per cent for general inflation based on the blended index.

Turning to loans in kind, the median size of cereal loans was 8 artabas. These loans were generally in wheat and the equivalent median value in cash at AD 150 prices of, say, 12 drachmas per artaba would be 96 drachmas. The cash component of mixed loans prior to AD 274 had a median value of 81 drachmas after adjustment to AD 150 levels, and the kind component median was 7 artabas. Mixed loans therefore had a similar median value of around 165 drachmas to pure cash loans, whose median value was 160 drachmas. Where mixed loans varied from other loans was their provenance. Loans that were purely in kind or cash have a similar distribution: 50 per cent of kind loans and 56 per cent of cash loans come from villages. Mixed loans were, however, largely a village phenomenon, and 58 out of 69 cases, or 84 per cent, come from villages.

Whilst deposits were, by their nature, indefinite in term – as the lender or depositor had the right to call in the capital at any time – loans varied in their duration or term. Examining all transactions over the period from AD 1 to 350, loans were of a short duration and 90 per cent of all loans were for a duration one year or less.[22] However, the effective duration could

[21] Lerouxel 2008: 181.

[22] Some 9 per cent were for a period of between 1 and 5 years and only 1 per cent were originally contracted for a duration of more than 5 years. Note that the date of repayment referred to is that originally intended in the loan document where available. In ignoring durations calculated from loan repayment receipts I follow Lerouxel's

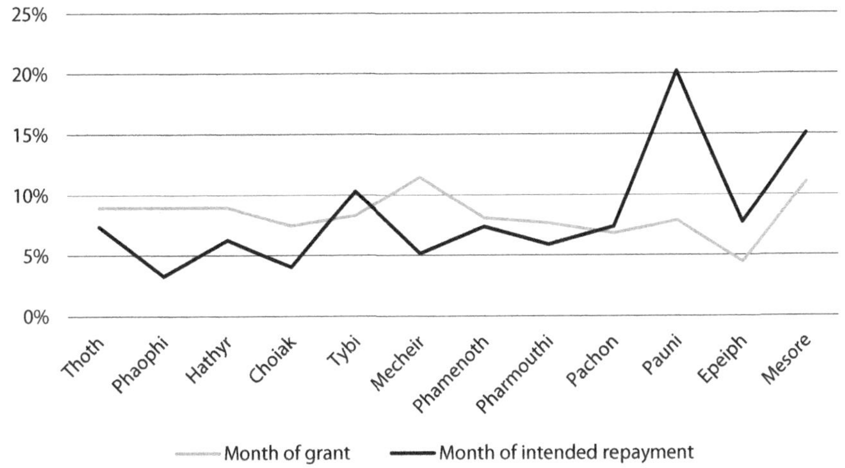

Figure 30 Cash loan seasonality

be longer if the borrower did not repay on time. In one extreme case (*P.Tebt. Wall* 6), a loan originally contracted in AD 84–85 was only repaid in the reign of Hadrian (AD 117–138). The short-term duration of the loans is a curious feature of the market, which contrasts with all credit markets from the early modern period onwards, where both short- and long-term loans are common. As we have seen, the land lease market has a much longer term than the credit market and leases of up to five years are relatively common, so there was no structural barrier in Roman Egypt to financial deals of a longer duration. Longer loans would have facilitated investment and economic and social stability, but why are they so rare? The answer, I believe, lies in the reasons why the loans were sought, and the seasonality (when in the year they were granted and repaid) of loans gives us a clue.

Figure 30 summarises the data for months of grant and intended repayment for all cash loans, excluding deposits, where some 470 transactions have a date of grant and 272 transactions have an intended date for repayment.[23] The months of grant are fairly evenly spread across

approach contra Tenger, although perhaps for different reasons. I have excluded these primarily because I am interested in the reasoning and intention of both parties when the loan was made rather than the actual duration, which is a function of subsequent circumstances. Lerouxel 2016: 53–4 stated his view that the durations within loan reimbursements should be ignored since reimbursement receipts are made only in 'exceptional circumstances'. I can see no reason why reimbursement receipts should not have been made in the common course of events, although the alternative approach of marking the original loan document as crossed out to signify that the loan had been repaid was certainly used on occasion as, for instance, in P.Duk. inv. 7 (AD 6).

[23] In practice, there are too few months of grant for deposits for these to be analysed.

the year, other than small but statistically significant peaks, at a 95 per cent confidence level, in Mecheir and Mesore, and a corresponding lower than average dip in Epeiph. There are, however, much clearer peaks, both statistically significant at a 95 per cent confidence level, in repayment date in Pauni after the main harvest and in Mesore at the end of the calendar year. The peak in Pauni suggests that for many borrowers repayment could only be made after the harvest. This has important ramifications for the risks that a lender faced. Not only was the lender dependent on the honesty and good faith of the borrower but he or she was also dependent on the quality of the harvest. The repayment peak in Mesore is of interest but, other than noting that it may reflect a preference for loans repayable within the calendar year, I cannot provide an explanation.[24]

The pattern of dates within the data for loans in kind, where there are 59 months of grant and 64 months of repayment, can also be examined and here the vast bulk of loans, more than 95 per cent, are due to be repaid in Pauni or Epeiph, after the harvest, as would be expected. The month of grant peaks in Hathyr, when planting of cereal crops was at its height, and the majority of loan grants are between Hathyr and Tybi, and this suggests that these loans were more often needed by the borrower as seed rather than for personal consumption when baked as bread.[25] The contrast with cash loans, which show no similar patterns in months of grant, and hence potential borrower motivation, is of interest.[26]

What interest was paid?

Loans varied in the interest rate payable to the lender and included: nil interest, interest as cash expressed as a fraction of the capital, interest in kind, services or work in lieu of interest (referred to as *paramone* loans) and the use of real estate or other fixed assets in lieu of interest (referred to as 'antichretic' loans, which I dealt with in the earlier chapter on housing, since the most common form of antichretic loan was to grant the lender the right to inhabit a house in lieu of interest).

Interest rates were defined in monthly terms and, as will be seen, the most commonly cited interest rate is 1 drachma per mina per month (or

[24] It would be tempting to link the peak in activity in Mesore to the need to borrow to meet cash tax payment obligations due at the end or beginning of the calendar year. However, Wallace does not note any concentration of cash tax payments at the end or start of the calendar year. Wallace 1938: 296n.62.

[25] See Bagnall 1993b: 21 and Rathbone 1991: 260–2 for descriptions of the agricultural year.

[26] Mixed loans show a similar pattern to loans purely in kind and presumably reflect the same motivations.

12 per cent), which was a simple formula that everyone could understand.[27] However, many individuals were perfectly familiar with the details of calculating interest at different rates and were able to compare different loans to see which were more, or less, favourable, as we saw in Chapter 3. The concept of compound interest is not mentioned explicitly in the loans, but some individuals were aware of the impact on risk and return when interest is payable only on repayment. Examples include *P.Oxy.* III 506 (AD 143), where a relatively long-term loan includes the provision that interest is payable at the end of each year, and *O.Stras.* II 902 (AD 205), where there are recalculations of interest and principal when partial repayments are made, ensuring that the interest is fair for both parties. Another example is *P.Genova* II 62 (AD 98), where the lender insists on repayment of interest but not capital on a monthly basis broadly achieving the same financial result as charging compound interest, assuming interest is reinvested, and with a lower risk as to default. We also have examples of loans being 'rolled over' at the end of a term where the new capital includes the interest accrued – for instance, *P.Sarap.* 14 (AD 103) – where 107 drachmas is the amount of the new loan that is rolled over from an original loan documented in *P.Sarap.* 13 (AD 102) of 100 drachmas some months previously.[28] By rolling over loans into a new transaction rather than simply extending the original loan, the lender achieves some of the benefits of compound interest. At 12 per cent, this would mean in this example 1.07 drachmas of interest for each month rather than 1 drachma, as per the original loan if it had simply been extended.

The amount of interest payable, before and after the key date of AD 274 when confidence in coinage collapsed and high inflation started, is shown in Table 10. Before AD 274, 12 per cent is the dominant known rate of interest, although there are many zero or low interest rate loans. In addition to varying over time, interest rates varied according to the amount of the loan, and larger loans attracted lower interest rates.[29] At first sight this seems illogical – surely the higher the loan the higher the

[27] Note that 1 drachma per mina per month is not exactly equivalent to 12 per cent when the term is not exactly a year, but, for the sake of simplicity, all loans which have interest payable at 1 drachma per mina per month are treated as being at 12 per cent, irrespective of the term, and a similar approach is taken for loans at other rates of interest. See Cuomo 2001: 143–91 for a general discussion of the level of sophistication of Graeco-Roman mathematics.

[28] See Rathbone & Temin 2008: 377 for evidence of this practice in the wider Roman world.

[29] For pre-AD 274 loans, the median loan size (re-calibrated for inflation to AD 150) for loans at less than 12 per cent was 1,547 dr. (n = 34), 12 per cent 274 dr. (n = 162) and over 12 per cent 111dr. (n = 24). The numbers of cases are less than quoted earlier since sometimes we know the interest rate but not the amount.

Table 10 Number of cash loans by interest rate, AD 1–350

Interest rate	Pre AD 274	Post AD 274	Total
0%	71	19	90
6% or less	16	1	17
6% to 12%	21	0	21
12%	194	4	198
Above 12%	25	6	31
Bearing interest at unknown rate	268	23	291

risk and the higher the interest rate that should be charged? However, the reason for this feature relates to the nature of the loans at low and higher rates. The low rates reflect the city-based mortgage market where land was offered as security, whilst the higher rates reflect the moneylenders/pawnbrokers market where small loans were granted on the security of portable objects.

When we look at the period after the jump in prices in AD 274 it is clear that interest rates in the fourth century increased substantially as inflation increased (as did the amounts of the loans themselves).[30] Low interest rate loans disappear, and a relative increase in the proportion of seemingly zero interest loans could indicate an increased tendency to disguise interest rates that were above the legal maximum of 12 per cent by deducting interest up front (see more on this below). The last firmly dated loan at 12 per cent comes from AD 286 to 287, which might suggest that individuals took some time to adjust to the new financial realities of high inflation, or that there was a brief period of price stability.[31] In the first half of the fourth century we have only three cash loans with specified interest rates, which vary from 20 per cent to 97 per cent per annum, and there is an increased prevalence of zero interest loans, which could hide higher interest rates. The fourth-century school exercise, *P.Kellis.* I 90, mentioned previously, uses an interest rate of 72 per cent, which compares with the equivalent early second-century exercise, *P.Mich.* III 145, when lower interest rates were being modelled. Economic conditions had moved on and so had practice, and even though we have relatively few examples of interest rates they clearly show a substantial and financially rational change in practice reflecting inflationary conditions.

30 I have not included the interest rates deduced by Worp in the introduction to *P.Kellis* 40–47 since the methodology is highly questionable as it is based on a number of debatable assumptions, one of which is that the interest was deducted from the initial amount in all cases.

31 *P.Vind.Bosw.* 12 (AD 286–287).

As to why 12 per cent was the dominant rate in the earlier period, there are two clear reasons. First, it was the highest legal rate possible, and we will see below that with likely default rates it is a minimum rate for unsecured loans where a lender might expect to make a small profit. Second, it was a remarkably easy mathematical formula for people to understand and check. Borrow 100 drachmas for a year and pay 1 drachma per month interest, so after 12 months you have paid 12 or, in modern terms, 12 per cent. Twelve is also a much handier number than the apparently similar alternative of 10. Twelve is divisible by 2, 3, 4 and 6 compared to only 2 and 5 if a decimal base had been used. This is one of the reasons that for most of history in the UK we used the pre-decimal 12 pence in the shilling before decimalisation in 1971, and that in the rest of Europe decimalisation was brought in only from the French Revolution. The Roman Egyptians followed a similar practice and typically had 6 obols to the drachma. And, of course, the UK's pounds, shillings and pence, or l.s.d. for short, derives directly from the Roman 'librum, solidus and denarius'. In short, a system based on 12 was a lot easier on mental arithmetic than a system based on 10.

It may be reasonable to assume, as Lerouxel did for certain periods, that 12 per cent was the rate applying to those loans (where we have the complete text) that are explicitly stated as being *entokou*, or 'interest bearing', even though there is no rate given, as for example in *BGU* XI 2045 (AD 215), since the relatively commonplace rate of 12 per cent would be understood by all parties to apply. This was described by Pestman as the 'customary' rate of interest.[32] However, there is no certainty that 12 per cent always applied to these cases. In this context, it does not appear reasonable to me to suppose, as did Schwartz for *P.Sarap.* 13–21, that in all cases where there is no interest stated that interest at 12 per cent was deducted at the outset.[33] And it does not seem reasonable to assume, as did Claytor, that when the word *entokou* appears in an entry in *abstracts* of contracts in an official register, not the full document, that 12 per cent is likely to apply.[34] Indeed, in the case that Claytor analysed, *P.Fay.* 344 (second century), we have six examples where the loan is described as *entokou* but only one where a 12 per cent interest rate is explicitly cited and the fact that this loan was differentiated from the others would suggest that the 12 per cent rate did not apply to the other six. There is also a tendency amongst scholars to overstate the prevalence of the 12 per cent rate.[35] For instance, Nelson stated that 12 per cent 'is the regular rate of interest, as

[32] Lerouxel 2012a: 171; Pestman 1971: 16.

[33] Schwartz 1961: 52.

[34] Claytor 2013: 84.

[35] Most recently, Lerouxel viewed the absence of variation in interest rates as one of the major features of the credit market in Roman Egypt. Lerouxel 2016: 340.

specified in paragraph 15 of the *Gnomon of the Idios Logos* and as attested in hundreds of loan agreements'.[36] The 'regular' rate of interest in the *Gnomon* is not 12 per cent but the maximum rate above which legal penalties would apply, and there are fewer than 200 cash loans where a 12 per cent rate is stated.[37] In A.H.M. Jones's view, the chief evidential value of a law is proving 'that the abuses which they were intended to remove were known to the central government'.[38] In this context it would imply that rates were above 12 per cent for a considerable time, since this law appears to have been in place throughout the first 300 years of Roman rule in Egypt.

Finally, even given the relative ease of use of a 12 per cent interest rate, it will be noted that the application of a 12 per cent interest rate to small amounts of money would have been impossible in practice. Consider *P.Fay.* 344g, a loan of 12 drachmas, where the interest rate is unknown, and a duration from Tybi to Pauni – a period of five months. Using percentages and decimals it is relatively easy for us to calculate the amount payable, assuming simple interest, at Pauni as 12 + 5 × 12/100 = 12.6, but there was no equivalent to 12.6 in the fractional world of drachmas, obols (where there were 6 or 7 to the drachma) and chalci (where there were 8 to an obol). There is no mathematical way of paying the interest – 0.6 drachmas – using obols and chalci, and thus the rate for this and similar loans cannot have been exactly 12 per cent, although an approximate payment can, of course, be made. In summary, 12 per cent is certainly the most common cash rate we can identify, but its ubiquity has been overstated.

Loans with no interest?

Loans with apparently no interest applying can be subdivided into those that genuinely had no interest payable and those that had interest that was hidden. The clearest reason to hide the real interest rate was because it was at a higher rate than the 12 per cent allowed by law. People were not totally averse to recording illegal practices on papyri, otherwise we would have no examples of high interest rates, but it would clearly have been better to avoid doing so.[39] The easiest way to disguise an illegally high interest rate was for the amount stated as lent to be smaller than the loan actually provided, the

36 Nelson 1999: 19.
37 Homer 1977: 51.
38 Jones 1964: I.viii.
39 For a blatant example of a willingness to record an illegal act within a contract, see *P.Oxy.* LXXIX 5209 (AD 267), where a father agrees that his son will deliberately lose a wrestling match in return for a bribe. A contract with illegal clauses may not have been enforceable under the rule of law, but it could be used to blackmail the defaulter or used to back up a moral right within the local community to any outstanding amount.

difference being the interest charged. So, for instance, if you borrowed 100 drachmas 'at 20 per cent interest', the document you signed as the borrower says that you received 100 drachmas, which you will repay in a year's time with no interest, but in practice you only actually receive 80.[40]

Occasionally, interest is stated to be included in the amount lent – for example in *P.Oslo* II 39 (AD 146) – or the opposite is explicitly noted to be the case by use of the phrase 'nothing has been added' to the capital – as in *P.Ups.Frid.* 3 (AD 122). I would take this phrase to refer to the fact that the amount of the loan stated in the document was equal to that actually provided and no interest figure had been added to the stated loan amount.[41] The fact that the scribe sometimes felt it necessary to state that nothing was added at source lends weight to the view that the deduction of interest at the outset was a well-known practice.

Dealing with loans where it is explicitly stated that there is no interest applying by inclusion of the term *atokou*, or without interest, Pestman has examined loans from the Ptolemaic period for evidence of goodwill but concluded that the data are 'too light in weight to give credence to the view that all ἀ̣τόκου loans were always made out of goodwill'.[42] Whether in the Ptolemaic or Roman period, there are, however, many reasons why a loan with no interest should have been made for goodwill purposes, and it should be noted that 'goodwill' in modern accounting terms is an intangible, often substantial, asset within corporate accounts. A loan at zero interest may have been made not only because of family or friendship ties but also because of other past or future mutual obligations, including those related to social or prestige capital, or in expectation of a reciprocal action. In general, I would agree with Andreau that there is no need to assume that all zero interest loans hid high interest rates, although as noted above this practice may have been more common after AD 274.[43]

It is worth looking in a little more detail at the nature of the 0 per cent loans and deposits in comparison with those loans where we know interest rates applied. The pre-AD 274 distributions by loan size, with loan amounts re-calibrated to AD 150 values, are shown in Figures 31 and 32. The first figure compares the distribution of 0 per cent loans and deposits and they have a very similar distribution, which would support a proposition that

[40] Actually, since the interest is deducted in advance, the actual rate of interest is higher at 25 per cent.

[41] I am not convinced by Lerouxel's arguments that loans which state that nothing has been added and where there is no interest mentioned should be considered as loans with interest. Lerouxel 2012a: 167–8.

[42] Pestman 1971: 21.

[43] Andreau 1999: 98 when discussing loans in Roman Egypt but within the wider context of the empire as a whole.

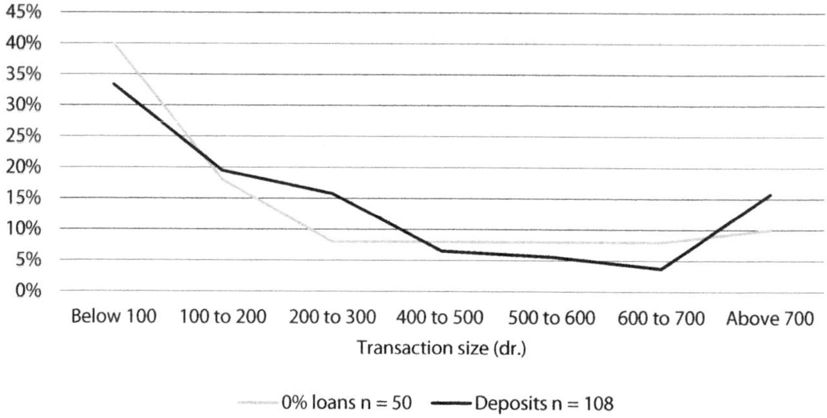

Figure 31 0% loans and deposits

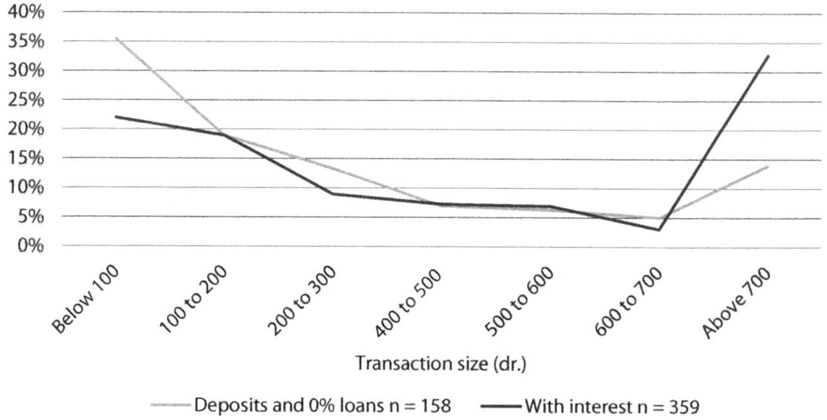

Figure 32 Transactions with and without interest

they had common features, especially when the distribution of loans that do bear interest shows such a different distribution in Figure 32. Zero interest transactions, whether loans or deposits, are mostly of a small size (under 250 drachmas with many under 100 drachmas). However, as Figure 32 demonstrates, the peak in loans that we know include interest is in large loans above 700 drachmas. In short, 0 per cent transactions, whether loans or deposits, constitute a fundamentally different typology of transaction and thus probably serve a different purpose than those which have an interest rate.

Loans with nuanced interest rates

In general, loans where the interest rate is not either 0 per cent or 12 per cent (that is loans where a pricing decision as to the rate was made within some form of financial market) show a concentration of transactions in cities rather than villages. Some 37 loans with interest rates of less than 12 per cent can be identified in the period up to AD 274 but only two can be given a secure village provenance, which is particularly striking given that most of our dataset is from villages rather than cities. This, combined with the data on relative sizes of loans, would suggest that financial transactions of a market nature, which did not rely on the conventional rate of 12 per cent, were concentrated in the cities rather than the villages. We do have five examples of nuanced higher interest rates from villages. However, three of the cases are from the early first century, at 18 per cent. Those below are likely simply to be 'hangovers' from Ptolemaic practice when the maximum legal interest rate was 24 per cent.[44]

When we look at the largely city-based high interest loans prior to AD 274, excluding the hangovers, the details are as follows:

- *P.Oxy.* LXXV 5052 (AD 86–87), which is a loan of 40 drachmas for 2 years at 15 per cent.
- *P.Sarap.* 13 (AD 102), a loan of 100 drachmas where the editor assumes that this loan is at 12 per cent, but since the loan rolls over into a new loan of 107 drachmas in *P.Sarap.* 14 (AD 103), the interest payable is 7 drachmas for a period of around five and a half months, which equates to an interest rate of 15 per cent.
- *P.Lond.* II 202 (AD 98–117), which is a moneylender's account with details of three loans: 1,500 drachmas at 12 per cent, 1,000 drachmas at 18 per cent and 260 drachmas at 22 per cent.
- *P.Mil.Vogl.* III 188 (AD 125?), which is an account of priests' expenses where the editor states that the interest is 3 per cent or 'half the normal'. However, in lines 20–21, the text reads that the interest for three months on 300 drachmas is 6 drachmas per month, which is 18 drachmas in total. This would imply that the interest rate is 24 per cent.
- *PSI* XVII 1689 (second century), a petition including evidence for lending at 36 per cent.
- *SB* XVI 12421 (second century), which is a pawnbroker's account with a number of entries and where the interest rate on two of the loans can be identified: 40 per cent on a loan of 8 drachmas for three months in line

[44] See Finckh 1962: 28–9. *SB* I 5243 (AD 7), *BGU* I 189 (AD 7), *P.Corn.* 6 (AD 17), *P.Mich.* V 336 (AD 27), *P.Lond.* III 1273 (AD 28–29) are the loans concerned.

20, and 22 per cent on a loan of 11 drachmas for an unknown period in lines 22 and 27. A further interest rate of 19 per cent is possible if the payment of 8 obols in relation to a period of three months in line 15 is interpreted as concerning a previously mentioned loan of 28 drachmas.

- *P.Fouad* I 26 (AD 158–159), where a moneylender provides at least two loans at 48 per cent.
- *P.Oxy.* VIII 1132 (c.AD 162), which relates to a loan of 600 drachmas at 24 per cent being paid off in advance of its original term.[45]
- *P.Mert.* I 23 (late second century), a letter which mentions a loan of 500 drachmas at 48 per cent in a transaction connected to the sale of two arouras of land.
- *P.Oxy.* I 114 (second or third century), a letter which mentions a loan of 200 drachmas from a pawnbroker at a rate of a 'stater', or 48 per cent.
- *P.Prag.* III 214 (second or third century), a moneylender's account where one of the loans is for 40 drachmas at an interest rate of 45 per cent.
- *PSI* XVII 1707 (third century), a pawnbroker's accounts where the editor identifies interest rates for four loans: line 7 (28 drachmas at 24.5 per cent), line 8 (40 drachmas at 21.4 per cent or 42.9 per cent), line 16 (100 drachmas at 13.7 per cent) and line 19 (40 drachmas at 35.7 per cent). The fractional and varied nature of the interest rates from one lender is striking, but the uncertainty of the estimates due to the fragmentary nature of the text should be borne in mind.

Another document that implies the existence of higher interest loans is *P.Mich.* III 145 (early second century), which is a school exercise involving interest at 30 per cent. As noted above, it is probable that there were other loans where interest at rates above 12 per cent was deducted from the original capital, given the illegality of the rate charged, but the highest visible interest rates seem to be associated with pawnbroker or moneylender activity, although stated interest rates between individuals do occasionally exceed 12 per cent. Evidence for moneylender activity can also be seen within *SB* XX 14401, a petition from AD 147, where Ptolemaios complains about the illegal activities of his namesake.

> Ptolemaios, son of a certain Pappus ex-gymnasiarch, from the same Arsinoite nome, reckless in his conduct and violent, leading the life of a moneylender and committing every impious and forbidden act, by

[45] Note that Bogaert stated that given the interest rate this loan would originally have been for a short duration, but there is no direct evidence on loan durations by interest rate to support this conclusion. Bogaert 2000: 210.

> demanding interest at the rate of a stater per mina per month by virtue of the power he has in the nome, in disregard of the prefects' decisions and the ordinances of the emperors … by descending into the villages with a gang and committing very many acts of outrage against those he lights upon … if ever we want to make an approach to the strategus about his violence, up until now he has been dragging the present matters before the office of the strategus and it is they who sit in council with the judge. As a result of this we are not getting legal satisfaction. And I shall lay evidence how having made a loan in one village, by successively getting 3½ obols as interest at a stater per mina per month, he is collecting annually half as much again. You will also find from others that he has got eight times the capital from someone else in a few years, although it is forbidden for anyone to exact more interest than the sum of the capital over the whole period of the loan.

Ptolemaios requests the Epistrategus to whom the petition is addressed,

> that you may order written instructions to be sent to the strategus of the meris of Heracleides so that I may be kept free from threats and acts of outrage by Ptolemaios, and that the interest (which) I have paid in excess of a drachma per mina per month be credited for me against the principal, and if it is apparent that I owe him anything after this, I shall undertake to repay him in a reasonable manner.

Whilst the figures in the petition above may be unreliable in that the petitioner is making the strongest case he can, this petition shows that high interest moneylending existed and that it was also possible to seek legal redress even against those of relatively high local social status. Other than pawnbroker loans, where portable items came into possession of the lender as security, there are no high interest loans where real estate is provided as a specific security or mortgage. The high interest loans are spread fairly evenly over the period and among the Arsinoite, Oxyrhynchite and other nomes and thus this seems to be a limited but widespread practice in Roman Egypt.

I will discuss the pawnbroker and moneylender market in greater detail in the next chapter on women, since this was clearly a gendered market, but the interest rates charged of around 40 per cent are consistent with (although a little lower than) the evidence from elsewhere in the Roman world and with modern traditional pawnbrokers of around 50 per cent to 75 per cent (as opposed to the truly exorbitant rates charged by online moneylenders). In Pompei we have evidence from graffiti that interest rates charged there were similar – around 40 per cent to 45 per cent in simple interest terms.[46]

[46] See CIL IV 4528 and CIL IV 8203. Note that both the pawnbroker and her client are women.

When looking at the loans at rates above 12 per cent across the Empire, Andreau states, and Temin supports him, that 'one hardly ever comes across loans at 15, 16 or 18 ... If the rate rose above 12 ... it soared straight to 24, 48 or even 60 percent'.[47] However, when we move away from the elite sources relied upon by Andreau, we find more loans at between 12 per cent and 23 per cent than at 24 per cent. In both high and low interest loans, although there is a preference for multiples of 12 and simple fractions – e.g., 6 per cent, 8 per cent, 18 per cent, 24 per cent – we also find more nuanced rates such as 3 per cent (*P.Oxy.* I 98), 7 per cent (*P.IFAO* I 12) and 22 per cent (*P.Lond.* II 202).

Loans at low interest rates share some characteristics. The median size of all pre-AD 274 loans is 160 drachmas, compared to a much higher median of 1,547 drachmas for low interest rate loans.[48] Six of the 17 transactions where the duration is known, or around 35 per cent, have durations of greater than one year, compared to the overall proportion of longer loans, which is 9 per cent.[49] The bulk of the low interest loans where we know whether or not security was provided are secured against specific property: 77 per cent, or 17 out of 22. This was achieved either through the pawning of relatively valuable portable goods or through the pledging or mortgaging of real estate. This proportion is somewhat higher than the proportion of all loans where we know the interest rate and which are secured against specific property, which is 58 per cent. The final feature of these loans is that they are almost universally contracted in cities. Of the 20 loans where the location of the principals can be deduced, either since it is explicitly stated or because of the provenance of the document, 17 solely involve individuals from cities, one is a loan from someone resident in Oxyrhynchus to a villager, one is a pawnbroker loan from Philadelphia at just below 12 per cent and the last is between two military colleagues.[50] So, low interest rate loans tend to be for large amounts, secured against specific property, for a longer than typical duration, and are a phenomenon of the city not the village.

Lewis has claimed that the lower interest rate, generally 6 per cent to 8 per cent, that I have identified for larger amount city-based loans, may be considered as 'an accommodation between friends'.[51] Contracting with a known counter-party for a long period, with specific security and for a large amount is an attractive financial proposition. When compared to

47 Andreau 1999: 94; Temin 2001: 15.

48 See Kelly 2020: subsection 5.1.4.

49 See Kelly 2020: subsection 5.1.5.

50 *P.Oxy.* III 506 (AD 143), *SB* VIII 9834 (AD 200–229) and *C.Ep.Lat.* 13 (AD 27) respectively.

51 Lewis 1983: 45.

placing numerous small unsecured, short-term loans with possibly distant, village-based, unknown counterparties a lender may well have been happy to sacrifice some interest to obtain a more secure and stable return, making a rational decision based on risk awareness. The features identified for these loans are consistent with the conclusion that they were commercial arrangements within a relatively sophisticated financial market, and an argument against Lewis's proposal is that 'favours' between friends would not require specific security. I believe therefore that, on the contrary, the contractual terms and other features of these typically mortgage-backed loans indicate that the lower interest rates result from the operation of market forces of supply and demand. Overall, given the number of loans that are not at 12 per cent, I cannot therefore agree with Lerouxel that up until AD 275 the interest rate almost never varied and was 12 per cent.[52]

One further question that can be asked is whether interest rates varied according to the duration of the loan. Worp posed a specific question in 1995: '[N]owadays short term loans for, e.g., bridging finance are usually at a higher % annualised than long term loans. Was the same practised in Antiquity?'[53] In asking this question he conflated the duration of a loan and its relative security. At the beginning of the year when this question was posed, US treasury yields were 5.95 per cent over three months, 7.91 per cent over five years and 8.07 per cent over 20 years.[54] This increasing 'yield curve' relationship is still the norm applicable today in modern economies: the longer the duration of the loan, the higher the rate of interest. For a borrower of the same reliability, who provides the same security, lenders acting as investors typically demand a higher interest rate for tying up their money for a longer period.[55] However, in the Egyptian data there is no evidence that higher interest rates were demanded for longer loans; indeed, it is the loans with low interest rates that tend to be of a longer duration.

When goods such as cereals were lent, rather than cash, the interest rates were considerably higher.[56] But loans in kind without interest did

[52] Lerouxel 2012b: 949.

[53] *P.Kellis* I 40: 120.

[54] US Treasury Department. www.treasury.gov/resource-center/data-chart-center/interest-rates/Pages/TextView.aspx?data=yieldYear&year=1995 (accessed 19 November 2018).

[55] Although this is by no means an immutable law, and the yield curve can invert, dependent on economic conditions and expectations. See Homer 1977: 386, Chart 41 for US yield curves over the first 70 years of the twentieth century.

[56] There is a difficulty of interpretation for loans in kind that is related to how the interest, which is typically defined as being part of the capital lent, is described, and scholars have differed in their interpretation of the description. Sometimes interest is described as 'the extra half' and sometimes 'the extra third'. In the first case, this could

exist and the same issues as to the real nature of zero interest loans apply.[57] Interest rates over the duration of the loan have a median rate of 50 per cent, with 17 of the 26 loans being at 50 per cent, and 8 at 33 per cent. Since loans were almost universally repayable after the harvest it would appear likely that for any available capital in kind a lender would only have one opportunity to make a loan in kind per year. Therefore these interest rates can be regarded as annual rates when any comparison is made with other opportunities to obtain a return on capital employed.[58] Pestman, in what may have been an attempt at simplification to suit his 'primer' audience, states that 'Interest on loan in kind is always 50 per cent',[59] but this is not always the case. Lerouxel adopts a contrary position and states that it is not possible to define a 'standard' rate of interest. I believe that the reality lies somewhere between these two extremes but that typically the effective annual interest rate on loans in kind was either 33 per cent or 50 per cent.

The higher rate of interest payable on loans in kind compared to cash reflects the risk that the lender is taking when he lends what is typically seed to provide the next year's harvest and the repayment of the loan. There is a significant likelihood that the harvest will fail and the borrower will be unable to repay the loan, and this concentrated risk, linked to a specific event, makes the requirement to pay a higher interest rate than on general cash loans perfectly rational.[60] However, we cannot assess whether it is a 'better' investment to lend kind rather than cash without numerically assessing the risks concerned and this is done in Chapter 7. Over time,

be interpreted as that the interest is half of the capital lent; for instance, if 4 artabas are lent, then the 'extra half' is 2 and thus 6 artabas are the stated amount of the loan and the amount to be repaid, and thus the interest rate is 50 per cent. It could, however, also be considered that the 'extra half' relates to the amount repaid and that thus if the amount repaid is 6 artabas, the interest is 3 artabas and the interest rate in the case above is thus 100 per cent. Luckily, we have a number of cases where the scribe has been specific in identifying the proportion and the actual amount of the interest element of the loan. Where the amount of the loan is not explicit or cannot be deduced from the context of the loan, as in *P.Lond.* III 1215, I have adopted the first approach, interpreting 'extra half' as 50 per cent and 'extra third' as 33 per cent since this seems more consistent with the evidence from those loans where the amount lent and repaid is explicitly stated. See Kelly 2020: Appendix 5.2.3 for the data on loans in kind.

57 See Foraboschi & Gara 1981: 336 and Lerouxel 2016: 303.

58 Contra Lerouxel, who preferred not to speak of interest rates on loans in kind but rather of supplements. Lerouxel 2016: 302.

59 Pestman 1994: 120.

60 The risk may be mitigated if the state of the Nile flood is known at the time of the loan. From the borrower's perspective, the high interest rate payable is affordable if the harvest is good, and repayment is probably irrelevant if the harvest fails since the farmer will struggle to feed their family. See Kelly 2021b for suggested surplus harvests for tenant farmers and the affordability of any seed loans.

the proportion of loans in kind as a share of all loans increases somewhat; however, I can see no particular trend as to the level of interest rates. Finally, we have too few mixed loans to analyse these in any detail, but the different elements of the loans seem generally to attract the same interest rates as in separate cash and kind loans.

Paramone loans were generally framed as a loan of a sum of money together with a contract of employment made on the same day between the same parties. The lender was the employer and the borrower was the employee or a relative who was obliged to remain in service of the employer for a set period. Some of these loans are related to apprenticeship contracts and others are associated with wet-nursing or nursing, which have somewhat different characteristics from other *paramones* since the employment concerned may not be full-time in nature and does not require the physical presence of the nurse at the lender's premises.[61] Overall, these loans range in size from 12 to 654 drachmas, with a median size, re-calibrated to AD 150 terms, of 100 drachmas. On a 100 drachma loan the financial benefit to the borrower at 12 per cent per annum is around one-quarter of a drachma per week. This can be compared with the typical unskilled male earnings at AD 150 prices of around 5 drachmas per week.[62] For those contracts related to apprenticeships, this may not be an entirely unreasonable benefit allowing for the fact that the apprentice would be learning a trade. However, even allowing that some employments such as wet-nursing might allow other employment or tasks to be undertaken, the financial benefit from the perspective of the employee/borrower seems very low. It may well be that some of these loans should be understood to be salary advances even though this is not stated in the documentation.

Turning to the effective financial gain from the lender's perspective, if these truly were loans rather than salary advances, then, in contrast, the effective gain appears to be considerable. For instance, the net financial benefit for a lender who took an abandoned infant and had it reared by a wet nurse would be a slave of some value. In one case, a slave aged around three years is sold for 300 drachmas, which is an amount roughly equivalent to a manual worker's wages for a year.[63] Lerouxel saw the proportion of *paramone* loans decreasing over time and viewed this as a sign of increasing monetisation, particularly in the villages.[64] The data from my database would not support this conclusion since although there are relatively few *paramone* loans overall, and if the exceptionally large number

[61] The standard work on these nursing contracts is Montevecchi 1984, but also see Lerouxel 2016: 61–3 and Ratzan 2015: 203–8.

[62] See Scheidel 2008: 5.

[63] *BGU* III 859 (AD 161–163).

[64] Lerouxel 2016: 59.

of nursing loans of the Tebtunis *grapheion* are not included, they continue to appear with similar frequency throughout the period from AD 1 to 350.

Who was active in the market?

An analysis of the gender of borrowers and lenders will be dealt with in the next chapter, but in general men are much more present in the market than women. But when in their lifetime did people generally need to borrow money? There are more borrowers' ages than lenders' partly due to the fact that generally there are more multiple borrowers than lenders within the transactions, but also because it was more common to include a description, including age, of the borrower than the lender.[65] This preference reflects the fact that it was the lender who was at risk from default and the age of the borrower was an important part of the description that would enable the lender to identify and take action against a defaulting borrower. The distribution of ages of borrowers and lenders are similar, but overall the median age of lenders, at 35, is lower than the median age of borrowers at 38.[66] In general, the number of borrowers is relatively constant as a proportion of the population after age 30, but there are relatively few borrowers (or lenders) in the earlier age brackets when compared to the population. In societies where individuals accumulate cash wealth over their lifetime one might expect lenders to be older than borrowers, but this does not appear to be the case in Roman Egypt. It is consistent, however, with Caldwell's proposition that in ancient societies cash flows were generally from the younger generation to the older one.[67] I believe, however, that we need to draw a distinction between assets and cash. The older generation was probably 'asset rich' but 'cash poor', explaining their continued need to borrow in their role as the head of the family's economic unit.

The median amount of money borrowed for those age brackets with a sufficient number of cases appears to increase with the age of the borrower, which contrasts strongly with typical modern-day patterns in, say, the UK, where median personal debt peaks in an individual's 30s and declines slowly thereafter.[68] So not only did older people have to borrow just as often as younger people, but they also had to borrow larger amounts. These two

65 We have 207 ages for lenders and 371 for borrowers.

66 Note that despite the relatively large data samples the difference in means/medians cannot be stated as significant, with 95 per cent confidence using a Mann–Whitney U test.

67 Caldwell 2005: 735.

68 ONS 2016: Table 8. The median amount of debt by age group, re-calibrated to AD 150 levels, is 76 dr. for ages 23–32 (n = 17), 82 dr. for ages 33–42 (n = 21), 174 dr. for ages 43–52 (n = 22) and 300 dr.(n = 9) for ages 53–62.

Table 11 Lenders' and borrowers' location summary

		Lender		
		Cities	Serving military	Villages
Borrower	Cities	167	1	10
	Serving military	1	13	0
	Villages	69	4	47

features reinforce the need to remove ourselves from our modern preconceptions of personal credit debt when seeking to understand the motivations that drove individuals to borrow and lend money in Roman Egypt.

Turning to geographical locations, in 312 cases we know where the lenders or borrowers lived. The pattern of the number of lenders and borrowers is shown in Table 11. There was very little inter-city or inter-village lending and more frequently city dwellers lent to village dwellers.[69] At first sight there seems to be a particular concentration of lending activity within Oxyrhynchus as opposed to Arsinoe, Hermopolis or other cities, but this is largely due to the overall number of documents with an Oxyrhynchite provenance. The market for loans was more localised than the land leasing market, for instance. Unlike other types of financial transactions, where serving military personnel appear rarely (although veterans are more common), there are a number of loans involving the serving military; however, most of these are internal to the army and do not involve civilians.

Trends over time need to be examined, and Lerouxel believed that, in the period before the establishment of the *bibliotheke enkteseon* (30 BC to AD 68–72), credit markets were 'closed', meaning that the principals did business mainly in the area where they lived, but that in the period after the establishment of this institution, markets became more open, particularly in the Arsinoite nome.[70] I can only test this proposition for the period from AD 1 to 70 and AD 71 to 170, since I have not collected the data for the

[69] This feature has been noted by a number of scholars, including Bagnall 1993b: 140; Schubert 2007: 15; and Temin 2013: 171. Lerouxel 2016: 341 suggested that this trend for villagers to borrow from city dwellers dates from AD 69 with the establishment of the *bibliotheke enkteseon* and that the sums available in this fashion were larger than would have been available in the village itself. Of the 69 transactions where a villager borrows from a city dweller, all indeed do postdate AD mid-60s but the median date of such loans is AD 221 and these are largely second- and third-century loans, so there is little evidence that the *bibliotheke enkteseon* innovation caused an immediate impact. The typical size of city to village loans prior to AD 274, adjusted for inflation, is 275 drachmas, which, as Lerouxel suggested, is higher than the usual village loan, which has a median size of 120 drachmas.

[70] Lerouxel 2012b: 961–2.

first 30 years of Roman rule. But if the proportion of 'open' transactions is compared for the two periods for all Egypt, there is no significant increase in the proportion of these transactions overall, being only 3 per cent of all transactions in both periods.[71] I cannot therefore see evidence to support Lerouxel's proposition that the establishment of the *bibliotheke enkteseon* provided a structural boost to the economy in the way he suggested.

Why were people borrowing?

There are a number of scholars of the ancient world who have made the distinction between 'loans for consumption' and 'loans for production' and discussed their likely proportions.[72] This is a key distinction since the two different types of loans had different impacts on the economy and the nature of the financial market. The greater the proportion of productive loans, the greater the likely positive effect on the development of the economy. The greater the number of consumption loans, the greater the likely power imbalance between borrowers who had urgent needs and lenders with capital to invest, and this would be reflected in the nature of the market. The following paragraphs therefore seek to determine what drove borrowers to transact and the extent to which consumption and production loans can be identified.

One marker of consumption loans within the data analysed is that on at least nine occasions a phrase is used in a document meaning the borrower had 'fallen into need', or a similar formulation relating to personal or private and immediate need is used to indicate the reason for the borrower to seek a loan.[73] These phrases only appear to come into use in papyri

[71] If the Arsinoite nome is looked at in isolation, the number of 'open' transactions increases from 1 to 14 in the two periods, but the proportion of all transactions only increases from 1.3 per cent to 2.7 per cent. The one 'open' transaction in the Arsinoite nome, outside the Tebtunis *grapheion* register, in the period AD 1–70, is *BGU* XIII 2337. The 14 'open' transactions in the period AD 71–170 are *BGU* III 888, *BGU* XI 2122, *P.Fam.Tebt.* 38, *P.Fam.Tebt.* 43, *P.Heid.* VII 399, *P.Louvre* II 110, *P.Oxf.* 11, *P.Stras.* V 437, *PSI* VIII 9211 l.10–3, *SB* VI 9247, *SB* X 10538, *SB* XII 10786, *SB* XII 10787 and *SB* XX 14970.

[72] Finley 1999: 198. Finley's position is 'almost wholly negative' on the role of moneylending in production and economic growth within the ancient economy. For an alternative view, see Millett 1991: 229–32.

[73] *P.Hamb.* IV 270 – not a loan contract as such (second to third centuries?), *P.Kellis* I 49 (AD 304), a loan of oil for personal needs, *P.Kellis* I 40 (AD 306–7), *P.Cair.Isid.* 76 (AD 318), *P.Col.* VII 169 (AD 318), *SB* VI 9270 (AD 337), *P.Kellis* I 18 (c.AD 350), *P.Fouad* I 53 (fourth century), a standard formula to acknowledge receipt of a cash loan and thus indicating the expected common reason for seeking a loan, and *P.Leid. Inst.* 17 (fourth century).

contracts in the fourth century, for whatever reason. However, outside the body of data analysed quantitatively, more information as to the rationale for the borrower is provided within the ostraca found at Mons Claudianus. These date to the start of the second century and two different motivations are noted: 'pressing need', and more directly, the need to eat.[74] Despite these regionally and temporally isolated instances, for the vast bulk of the transactions there are no explanations offered as to why the borrower needed the cash or goods.

In other cases, the rationale for borrowing may be deduced from the context or contents of the papyrus and places the transaction within the consumption category. There are two cases in military contexts of 'payday' loans where the loan was to be repaid at the next receipt of pay.[75] Such loans may reasonably, I believe, reflect the need of the borrower to meet short-term consumption demands or liabilities rather than suggest that the money was to be invested in some productive exercise. There are some 63 *paramone* loans that can be considered as advance wages, and three documents that are explicitly stated to be advance wages are also likely to have been for consumption rather than productive in nature. Very-short-term loans, which would presumably also have been required to meet some pressing need, may also be considered as relating to consumption. There are some 72 loans of three months or less that would fall into this category. A period of three months or less could not cover the planting, growing and harvesting seasons and thus these loans are unlikely to have been directly productive in an agricultural sense. There are 12 loans made to scribes to cover short-term expenses in P.Mich. II 123 (AD 45–46) and 65 loans where personal items were pawned, a number of which were at high interest rates that would have made them unsuitable transactions to fund a productive exercise. There are seven documents where the purpose is specifically stated to relate to consumption such as expenses, pre-existing debts or taxes falling due.[76]

In total, therefore, more than 230 loans can be identified as being likely to have been for consumption rather than production, which is around 12 per cent of the total number of transactions. Whilst a significant percentage of loans can thus be identified as being for consumption, it is

[74] For a list of the motives used in the Mons Claudianus ostraca, see *O.Claud.* 2000: 84.

[75] *C.Ep.Lat.* 13 (AD 27) and *C.Ep.Lat.* 154 (AD 140).

[76] *P.Oxy.* III 511 (AD 103), a loan to meet the tax on an earlier mortgage, *P.Mil. Vogl.* III 188 (AD 125?), where advanced expenses are charged interest, *P.Princ.* II 33 (AD 126), a loan between brothers to allow brother to pay land tax, *P.Oxy.* III 530 (second century), borrowing to pay off an existing debt, *P.Harr.* II 227 (AD 221), where the loan relates to shared expenses, *P.Tebt.* II 418 (third century), where a man borrows money from a friend to meet his wife's travel expenses and *P.Lond.* VI 1915 (c.AD 330–340), where the borrower needs to meet tax demands.

certainly the case that there are many more consumption loans where the motivation of the borrower is not visible. The lack of any pattern to cash loan grant timing during the year would suggest that the bulk of cash loans would not be of a productive agricultural nature since there is no peak in the year at planting time, as seen in kind loans, but of course non-agricultural productive loans would not necessarily have been driven by the rhythms of the farming year. Overall, the large number of consumption loans is consistent with an agrarian economy where peasant debt was endemic, and this was certainly the case in later periods in Egypt.

There are a number of types of loan that cannot, with confidence, be placed into either category of consumption or production. Some loans will have been driven by familial considerations but there are only 58 cases within the 1,999 transactions where the lender and borrower are clearly connected by familial ties. However, the rationale for borrowing the money cannot be determined simply from the presence of family relationships. The money or goods being borrowed from a family member could have been used for productive or consumption purposes. Monies received on deposit also pose a problem, given that if the borrower tied up the money in a productive enterprise or spent it on consumption it would not be available for repayment that was at the demand of the lender. Perhaps 'borrowers' in deposit transactions are best considered as deposit-takers who possibly, in turn, provided some non-financial benefit to the lender.

Large loans, beyond the immediate personal needs of an individual or family, could have been driven by the borrower's desire to invest, but they could equally have been required by the borrower in order to meet financial or other obligations, such as tax demands, arrears of rent or in order to provide funds for dowries or divorce settlements. So no direct correlation between a large loan size and an investment motivation can be inferred.

Turning to productive borrowing, Finley took the view that a mortgage was a short-term personal loan occasioned by personal disaster and certainly not a 'deliberate device for raising money at a low rate in order to invest at a higher rate'.[77] There are indeed no loans that demonstrate explicit interest rate 'arbitrage' or 'gearing', and this would support Finley's supposition. However, loans where the money was to be invested in productive exercises do exist. The clearest examples are the two maritime loans.[78] There are also loans from landlord to tenant, which are embedded within, or connected to, leasing contracts for land and which presumably provided the seed capital in cash and kind to enable the tenant to farm the land and to allow both

77 Finley 1999: 117.

78 The two maritime loans are *SB* XIV 11850 (AD 149?) and *SB* XVIII 13167 (mid-second century).

parties to recoup their investment in time. *P.Oxy.* III 507 (AD 146) also explicitly states that the borrower was using the money to invest in hay, which in turn was used as security against the loan. Another rare example of a loan associated with an investment is from *P.Gen.* II 100 (before AD 128), where a loan is directly associated with a land transaction on the same day.

We have almost no examples of people borrowing to finance small businesses but there is one delightful third-century Arsinoite case where a father, Sempronius, loans 320 drachmas in cash to his son Cephalon to assist in his son's shipping business. The father obviously has little faith in his son's business acumen since he opens his letter with 'to my mind you're not the man your father was …' and continues to berate him throughout the letter in what I hope is a light-hearted manner.[79] Cephalon has, in turn, lent wheat to an employee of theirs in whom his father has even less faith than in his son, and Sempronius suggests that Cephalon retains the loan from the employee's salary, writing, 'No, if something's owing to you, grab it and take your due – bearing in mind that you too are repaying the 320 drachmas you owe me'. This is a clear example of loans oiling the wheels of the Roman economy: by loaning the money, the father ensures that the son can run his business; by loaning the employee wheat, the son keeps the employee alive, and the net result is reduced frictional costs within the economy by the maintenance of a shipping business aiding other market participants to speed up the exchange of goods.

Whilst we have very little evidence for commercial borrowing, contrary to Morley's view, 'bills of exchange' (which can alternatively be referred to as 'letters of credit'), where an individual is able to obtain credit when away from their normal place of residence through the use of a document stating that they had the funds at their disposal at home, did exist.[80] These would have been helpful in conducting commerce, but perhaps could also be seen as a form of travellers' cheques. As we have seen, loans could also become tradeable securities in that they could be exchanged and sold on to a third party.[81]

There is also a category of loan where the item being borrowed cannot be consumed by the individual concerned and which can therefore be placed into the productive category. *P.Mich.* II 128 (AD 46) is a loan of

[79] Parsons 1969: 320.

[80] Morley 2007: 587: 'Romans lacked … bills of exchange'. For counter examples, consider *P.Oxy.Hels.* 48 (second to third centuries), where a letter of credit would have facilitated the purchase of wool, or *P.Oxy.* XLIII 3146 (AD 347), which is an advance from imperial funds, made in Oxyrhynchus but to be repaid in Alexandria.

[81] For instance, see *SB* XVIII 13858 (AD 211–217), where a mortgage is ceded to another party, or *P.Oxy.* III 508 (AD 102), where a loan is sold on.

reeds, which were presumably to be put to some productive purpose, or *BGU* I 77 (AD 169–175), which is a loan of a very large amount of grain. However, the largest category that can be assigned for productive purposes are the loans in kind and mixed (both kind and cash), which as has been demonstrated above were largely granted prior to planting and repaid after the harvest. There are 305 kind or mixed loans in the data, and typically around half of these loans were granted in the three months close to the season for cereal planting near Hathyr, so perhaps around 150 of these loans can be expected to have been of a productive nature.

One feature that may reflect the purposes they served and shed light on productive loans is the relative numbers of lenders and borrowers. In general, it is rare (in only 3 per cent of transactions) for there to be more lenders than borrowers. Most loans (73 per cent) have the same number of lenders and borrowers and 24 per cent have more borrowers than lenders. This pattern could be explained by the cooperative needs of individuals. Whilst some of the multiple lenders or borrowers are related by marriage or blood ties, there are also unrelated individuals who either loan or borrow in a communal way. Coming together to borrow money or kind could potentially relate to individuals who need, literally, 'seed' capital to farm the land or set up some form of productive exercise. It is unlikely to be a consumption loan since each individual would have their own specific needs.

Overall, therefore, borrowers' motivations, in the limited number of cases where they can be inferred, are balanced between consumption and production, but we have no significant evidence for long-term investment or indeed for loans that finance non-agricultural commercial activity.

Why were they lending?

Lender motivations also need to be examined. Rather than identifying productive or consumption loans, which are concepts appropriate for the borrower, we can seek to split the loans between those where the lender was seeking to gain financial profit and those where the lender had other motives.

Turning to the loans where the lender appears explicitly to have been driven by the profit motive, the *paramone* loans, where the loan allowed services to be provided to the lender and loans where usufruct of land or another commercial asset such as a loom were granted to the borrower in lieu of interest, can be assumed to indicate that the lender was commercially driven to seek financial profit even if it was not directly in cash.

Loans with interest payments would also indicate a profit motivation, and there were just over 600 transactions where an interest rate is explicitly charged (although we should also be aware of a reciprocal motivation). Another category of loan that has elements of reciprocity and profit-seeking is that from landlords to tenants. A loan by a landlord to a tenant could tide the tenant over to the next harvest and help ensure the next rent was paid. It could even be a loan of the seed, without which no crop would be sown and no rent paid. We do have evidence from leases of these types of loans, but not as often as might be expected.

There are, however, some categories of loan where the motivation to lend may reasonably be assumed not to have been directly related to maximising profit but reflected familial concerns, reciprocity or, more unlikely in this context, institutional constraints. There are 40 antichretic loans where the lender received accommodation of some form, and which might reasonably be assumed to be driven by familial concerns – that is finding a place to live. As noted above, it is my belief that most deposits were non-interest-bearing and if this is accepted, it appears reasonable to assume that deposits were made to provide security or for some other form of social or reciprocal benefit to the depositor/lender rather than direct financial gain. There are 192 deposit transactions within the data that might reasonably be assigned to reciprocity drivers. There are many zero interest loans, and some may well have been for mutual assistance/reciprocity, but, as noted above, we cannot be sure these do not hide an interest payment. Thus, in total, there are at least 230 transactions (even excluding all familial loans) that may not have been profit-driven (or around 12 per cent of the transactions). This is thus a substantial body of loans where profit is unlikely to have been the main driver for the lender, and this will have had a significant impact on the mechanics of the market.[82] Although strictly speaking outside the body of evidence that I have examined, in that the sources date from the late first century BC, there is explicit evidence for lending for mutual support from Alexandrian documents relating to loan clubs.[83] In *BGU* IV 1133, for instance, an arrangement similar to that of a modern Credit Union can be seen to operate, where members receive small loans to be repaid to the club in instalments.[84]

One final point concerning lender motivations relates to the practicalities involved in placing substantial sums into the credit market. The median size of land purchases, adjusted for inflation, was 600 drachmas,

[82] Although many familial loans may well have been made on preferential terms, familial ties did not on occasion stop very formal loan contracting being used, and of the 27 familial loans where it is stated whether interest applied, 13 require interest payments, generally at 12 per cent, although there is one, *P.Flor.* I 48 (AD 222), at a lower rate of 6 per cent. Loans between family members are listed in Kelly 2020: Appendix 5.1.3.

[83] See *BGU* IV 1133 to 1137, all late first century BC.

[84] For an excellent summary of the equivalent modern-day institutions (Rotating Savings and Credit Associations or 'roscas') and the necessary situational pre-conditions for their existence, see Biggart 2001.

compared to the median loan size of 160 drachmas. If an individual was seeking to invest a substantial sum of, say, in excess of 500 drachmas, then, given the loan sizes, they would probably either have to build a portfolio of village loans and effectively become a moneylender or seek a single counterparty in a city, possibly using a bank as an intermediary. Overall, I believe that the motivations of lenders were heavily dependent upon the segment of the credit markets in which they were operating and that this situational influence was the main driver as to behaviours.

How profitable was it to be a lender?

It might seem simple to calculate the effective profit a lender made from a loan, but we need to take into account the chance that the borrower would default on the loan and refuse to pay back the capital and the interest. In the previous chapter, I assumed that the chance of default on rent payments due to failure from the Nile flood was around 8 per cent, and using this same assumption for loan default (and we have seen above from the seasonality data how dependent loan repayments were on the harvest) I can provide a simple illustration of this effect.[85] Say you gave one hundred unsecured loans of 100 drachmas at 12 per cent, and 8 per cent of the borrowers defaulted. Your total investment would be 100 × 100 drachmas (10,000 drachmas). Your total return, allowing for the eight who defaulted on both your loan and its interest, would be 92 × (100 + 12 as interest) (10,304 drachmas), or a return of just over 3 per cent compared to your headline rate of 12 per cent, not even allowing for any expenses of drawing up the loan contract. We will see in Chapter 7 that this is a poor return relative to alternatives. If you were generous and charged headline rates of less than 9 per cent you were likely to lose money.

To move from this example to more general conclusions we need to do some modelling to allow not only for default but also frictional costs and for loans made in kind for commodity prices. Modelling of financial outcomes for cash loans is only reasonably secure for the period prior to AD 274, when prices are relatively stable. We are also constrained by the availability of data and by the uncertainty of the actual interest rates potentially hidden within loans seemingly at zero interest, or where the interest rate is not specified. There are three types of loan where we know both the amount and where the interest rate is explicitly stated and is not zero that are capable of being modelled: cash mortgages, unsecured cash loans and loans in kind. One other category of loan that could be modelled is loans

[85] As a comparison with modern developing nation village-based informal loan default rates in Nigeria, Udry reported a default rate of around 10 per cent. Udry 1994: 515.

backed by fiduciary sales, but the uncertainty as regards the applicability of sales tax of 10 per cent and who would be responsible for any such tax payments is too great to come to firm conclusions.[86]

Modelling requires assumptions and, as with land leasing, some of the most important sets of assumptions for all types of transaction are frictional transaction costs. The assumptions I have made are outlined in the Appendix. Since I have only modelled transactions where the interest rate is known, no assumption needs to be made for this or other known elements, such as the level of security provided and the amount of the loan.[87] In most cases, we also know the term of the transaction.[88]

It should be noted that in cash mortgages the lender is protected from adverse default costs by his right to seize the property concerned and there are many examples in the papyri of lenders exercising this right. When the right was exercised it may be that the property provided as security would have been of higher value than the loan made, as in the case of *P.Ryl.* II 119 (AD 62–66), which describes a dispute between the principals where the creditor refuses to give up the highly profitable usufruct of some mortgaged land despite the offer of repayment of the capital by the debtors. In view of the enforceable and potentially profitable ability to seize the mortgaged property, I have assumed that in case of default the lender was able to recoup both principal and interest payments from the property concerned.

The interest and capital gain/loss in a loan in kind is a function of the price of the commodity, and this is an important element of the likely return in cash terms. Therefore, assumptions need to be made as to the price, and the variability of that price, for barley and wheat, and I have adopted the same assumptions as in the chapter on prices. I have also assumed that the price of cereals is inversely proportional to the quality of the harvest. That is, in good years, when the harvest was plentiful, prices would be lower than normal, and the inverse applies in bad years.[89]

As with land leases, 1,000 simulations have been undertaken for each of the individual transactions concerned. These were then added together to produce the likely distribution of the return for each type of investment. So, for instance, 66,000 simulations were undertaken to determine the

[86] Johnson 1936: 558. The sales tax issue is of considerably greater importance than when assessing returns on real estate investment since there is no ability to amortise these costs over a significant period.

[87] Where we know the interest rate but not the amount loaned I have assumed that the small frictional costs would reduce the return by 1 per cent per annum.

[88] Where the interest rate and amount are known but the term is unknown, I have assumed it is one year. Where the term is known to be under a year but where the exact number of months is unknown, I have assumed six months.

[89] The full list of assumptions is given in the Appendix.

distribution of return overall for loaning cash on an unsecured basis: that is 66 individual transactions, each with 1,000 simulations.

The median return to the lender is 9.7 per cent but the average is only 0.2 per cent per annum, reflecting the risk of default. No default simulations for the mortgages were necessary, but the distribution of returns based on the 67 mortgages, after taxes and costs, has a median of 8 per cent and an average of 7.3 per cent. Turning to loans in kind, the median return is 28.7 per cent and the average is 24.4 per cent. A loan in kind is clearly a transaction where the average return is attractive, but this return has a price in the risk taken, since not only is there an 8 per cent chance of losing the whole amount loaned, but also a further 16 per cent chance of losing money on the deal because of the risk of reductions in the market price of barley or wheat.

Comparing these options, Bagnall posed the question: 'Why should one lend money at 12 per cent when one could buy wheat and lend it at 50 per cent?'[90] This is still a valid question even after adjustment of the rates for risk and costs. I address this in Chapter 7 where I will also consider how returns from the credit markets compare to investment in real estate.

How important was credit to the rural economy?

I have noted above that there seems to have been an almost complete collapse in the village loan market in the period leading up to AD 274. What would the effect of this have been on ordinary people?

I have modelled the effect of such a collapse in the monetised economy by considering how the tenant family's fortunes would have been impacted by an inability to borrow cash at traditionally low rates of 12 per cent. If people had no trust in the real value of money then they should have demanded higher interest rates if they lent money at all. I have therefore reworked the model to simulate a collapse in the rural credit market, assuming first that the only cash credit available was at rates equivalent to those from moneylenders (40 per cent). Under the original scenario, 4 per cent of tenant families would have been ruined after a generation. In the new model, the percentage of tenant families facing ruin nearly quadruples to 15 per cent, illustrating just how dependent the typical family was on the mutually beneficial local credit market.

Conclusions

The discussion above has shown that there were a number of different credit sub-sectors that overlapped. There were significant numbers of 'distressed'

[90] Bagnall 1977: 94.

borrowers seeking consumption loans to meet pressing personal needs, and lenders who were not driven by a pure profit motive. As with other types of financial transactions, there were relatively low levels of intermediation by agents and no evidence for commercial broking of transactions, although banks often did facilitate loans even if they did not generally act as principals. Whilst most market participants were private individuals, there were professional principals in the marketplace, namely moneylenders and pawnbrokers. The marketplace was largely dominated by men, and borrowers were, on average, somewhat older than lenders.

As Lerouxel noted, one innovation of the Roman system was the introduction of institutions designed to keep records of real estate, which facilitated lending secured by specific assets. This would have assisted the market to develop in sophistication by providing greater security to lenders and improving the information available to a lender. The market was, however, heavily localised, with little inter-village or inter-city activity. The localised nature of the market may have inhibited market competition and geographical integration but would have improved the information exchange between lender and borrower since they may well have known each other personally or have been part of the same social network. City to village lending only developed strongly from the second century onwards when the size of loans in the cities increased considerably compared to those in villages. Although the typical size of loans increased in the second and third centuries, there was no substantial overall increase in the size of the credit market as the number of transactions decreased, particularly in the villages. If Lerouxel is correct in suggesting that the efficiency of the market improved with the introduction of institutions that reduced the information deficit in the credit market, it was the cities that prospered at the expense of the villages, and no significant increase in productivity can be inferred. In the period after the jump in prices in AD 274 through to AD 350, cash loan sizes also increased, and cash loans continued to dominate the market even if there was a general increase of the proportion of loans in kind throughout the period from the first century to AD 350.

I hope I have demonstrated, through the modelling of family finances, the importance of reciprocal credit for social stability and family resilience. Given the pressures on tenant farmers, the existence of the local village credit market was key to their survival, and when that disappeared in the third century a key support to social cohesion was lost.

Turning to interest rates, we have seen in this chapter that, despite the lack of clarity caused by potentially hidden interest payments in zero interest loans, an interest rate of 12 per cent seems to have acted as a handy, conventional, easily understood, largely affordable 'standard' for most loans. However, the frequent statements as to the ubiquity of a 12 per cent rate understate the subtlety of the marketplace and the financial sophistication of some of its participants even within the essentially agrarian economy of rural Roman Egypt.

A hierarchy of interest rates existed that was based on the circumstances of the transactions. Whilst the 12 per cent interest rate was certainly the 'standard' rate for cash payments, there were circumstances where judgement was exercised. Rates could vary according to individual circumstances, with very high rates being charged to distressed borrowers by pawnbrokers and moneylenders. At the other extreme, a market existed for larger loans, where interest rates also varied according to circumstances. Consider a second-century loan document, *P.Erl.* 94, where we have secured loans between the same parties but at different rates at different times. Initially, there was a loan of 10,400 drachmas, with an additional mortgage of 3,400 drachmas, making a total of 13,800 drachmas, which was concluded at an interest rate of 10 per cent. When another secured loan for 7,200 drachmas between the same parties was concluded shortly thereafter, the existing loans still not yet repaid, the interest rate charged increased to 12 per cent. This change in interest rate shows the action of the market and presumably reflects either changes in the level of supply and demand within this market or changes in the individual circumstances and risk assessment of the principals.[91] Interest rates that were lower than 12 per cent were generally only available to city borrowers who were able to offer security and where the term was generally longer than normal and the size of the loan was larger. The acceptance of a lower headline rate of return by investors in exchange for greater security and stability of return is entirely rational.

Returning to the question posed at the beginning of this chapter, was usury or solidarity more prevalent? The small loan village market appears to me to have all the indicators of a market driven by solidarity rather than the pure pursuit of profit. If we take the dictionary definition of usury as lending at unreasonably high interest rates, there is actually relatively little evidence for it at work. Even the pawnbroker rates are at the lower end of historical interest rates for this activity.

However, the most obvious feature of the credit markets is that there are three clearly delineated sub-sectors. There was a village market where a 12 per cent interest rate would have meant that lenders on average just about recouped their loan. Another village-based market was that of loans

91 This is directly comparable to the interest rate change identified by Bransbourg within the Sulpicii archives, which he describes as being potentially the only example of a primary source from Graeco-Roman history which shows that an individual's actions reflected sensitivity to financial risk. In the case identified by Bransbourg, the interest rates between the same parties increase from between 7 per cent and 7.5 per cent to between 9 per cent and 10 per cent. Bransbourg 2014: 133.

in kind. Finally, there was a city market for the local elite where interest rates were low but loans were secured on mortgages on property. This mortgage market was clearly a limited-access institution, demarcated by geography, landed wealth, status and education, and essentially inaccessible to a tenant. There was some interaction between these markets but this was a one-way street. Villagers might receive loans in times of distress from city-based lenders but had no access to the mortgage market. And it was not just villagers who had restricted access to the low interest market, but also women, as we will see in the next chapter.

Chapter 6

Women and the Financial Markets

This chapter deals with how women interacted with the financial markets, but the first question we need to ask is which women?

Which women?

In Bagnall and Cribiore's words, 'It has become customary, even obligatory, in recent scholarship to point out that "women" do not form a self-explanatory category'.[1] That is, that women do not all share a particular set of experiences or exhibit the same set of behaviours. They concluded in their review of letters written by women that most of the letters collected are from the upper strata of society. I am, however, working with a different database, composed generally of somewhat dryer, more formulaic, legal documents. In accordance with the conclusions in my introductory chapter about men, many of the people concerned would have been ordinary women who worked the land. Also, whereas Bagnall and Cribiore's women are generally active subjects (writing or dictating their letters), the women in my database are both active subjects and unempowered parties in the transactions examined. I should also state at this point that I have tried not to assume any inherent sexism within my conceptual framework, but rather let the evidence tell the story of gender roles and discrimination.

Limited access and financial empowerment

I start, however, with a consideration of the theories behind limited-access institutions within society and the ongoing debate on female financial empowerment within agrarian economies, before considering whether institutional constraints would have aided or hindered the ability of the Roman Egyptian woman to act within the financial markets.

Ogilvie explained the concept of limited-access institutions as follows:

> The pre-industrial economy in particular was characterized by 'limited-access' institutions that coercively limited economic entry … Limiting

[1] Bagnall & Cribiore 2015: 8.

> access not only affects distribution. It also affects efficiency, because it creates incentives for the excluded to violate institutional rules by moving into the informal sector. Informal economic activity is better than none at all, but typically imposes higher costs and risks than if the same agents could do the same things through formal institutions.[2]

We have already seen that the mortgage market was a limited-access institution for villagers, but this chapter will address whether women were directly or indirectly denied access to other markets.

Turning to financial, or economic, empowerment, Kabeer saw empowerment as containing three required dimensions: resources, agency and achievements.[3] Resources for Kabeer include not only physical resources such as capital, but also authoritative resources such as the power to implement decisions as the head of an economic unit. Agency is the ability to define goals and to act upon them, whilst achievements are the outcomes of the process. Financial empowerment of women is seen in the modern world as socially positive. Positive outcomes claimed for women's empowerment include family welfare, intrahousehold equity and economic growth, particularly in its ability to reduce market distortions, labour supply inflexibilities and perverse allocative behaviour.[4] In this chapter, I will particularly explore the distortions in the financial markets that resulted from lack of female empowerment and the potential implications.

First, the specific legal aspects that may have constrained or aided women to act within the financial markets, including the dowry and inheritance laws and practices of Roman Egypt, need to be addressed. Typically, family groups formed an economic unit that shared resources, headed by a patriarchal or, on occasions, matriarchal figure. Around a quarter of the households reporting census data were headed by a woman, which gives some indication of how common a matriarchal head of a family economic unit would have been.[5] Indeed, 'the unrestricted right of females to inherit and to own property' should be noted.[6] This was a significant societal feature, and to put this in context, it was only in 1882 that married women in the UK were allowed to have complete control over all their property, by an extension of the limited provisions of the Married Women's Property Act of 1870. And it is less than 100 years since women in the UK were granted the right to hold and dispose of property on the same terms as men. Women in Roman Egypt, inside or outside of marriage, did not

2 Ogilvie 2007: 671.
3 Kabeer 1999: 3.
4 Kabeer 1999: 1.
5 Huebner 2013: 130.
6 Rowlandson 1996: 150.

enjoy full financial freedom, but in some ways were advantaged compared to their mid-Victorian UK counterparts.

However, although the inheritance system was partible rather than primogeniture in nature, daughters were still generally discriminated against, since sons, particularly eldest sons, tended to be favoured within wills.[7] Widows were also not always well treated by the inheritance system, and in general there would have been many widows, given the commonly higher age at marriage of men over women. Typically, on the death of a patriarch, it was his children or blood relatives who were his heirs, not his wife. She could, however, continue to exercise control of the economic unit constituted by the man's estate and have use (usufruct) of that estate for the ultimate benefit of any children.[8] This option was unlikely to have been available to the widow of a younger man who had not yet become head of a household, who was more likely to have returned to her parents' family, leaving her children behind.[9] Such a situation happened to the high-status Alexandrian widow Apollorion, who left her only child with her deceased husband's relatives in Oxyrhynchus, but her family did recover her gold, jewellery, cash, clothing, slaves and other goods which was her dowry on marriage.[10]

Some formal legal discrimination against women was present in financial dealings in Roman Egypt. For instance, women paid conveyancing fees for some types of land of two or three times the rates that men paid.[11] Such conveyancing fees could be payable on sale, mortgage or inheritance of land. Women were also to some extent disadvantaged by the need to act with a guardian in financial matters, typically a husband or other male relative, who was therefore aware of and could influence the transaction concerned.[12] Overall, however, women had most of the legal support, in both resources and agency, to allow them to trade effectively in the financial markets. But what happened in practice?

How did women acquire capital?

Women acquired capital, taken in the largest financial sense as including chattels, money and real estate, like men, primarily through inheritance. As I noted earlier, disincentives existed to treat men and women equally,

7 Huebner 2013: 50–1.
8 Yitfach 2006: 164.
9 Huebner 2013: 102.
10 *P.Coll.Youtie* II 67 (AD 260/1).
11 Yitfach 2015c: 140–1.
12 A woman could invoke the *ius trium liberorum* to act without a guardian when she was subject to Roman law and could show she had had three children.

because of social norms or heavier conveyancing fees. But, given the ages at marriage, women were more likely to be an inheritor than men. Another way that women, and on occasions, men, could acquire capital were parental gifts during the lifetime of the donor. Huebner has suggested that these lifetime gifts could have been used for the avoidance of inheritance taxes, which has parallels with modern-day financial wealth planning.[13]

Whilst inheritance and parental gifts were the key ways of acquiring capital, it could also be gained by work or trade and from dowries. We have seen, however, through my modelling in previous chapters, that for ordinary people, women or men, the chances of acquiring capital through saving from earned income were low. Women might be thought to have been provided with an advantage by the practice of the family of a bride giving a dowry on marriage that was to be used to her benefit and returned to the woman or her family in the event of the death of the husband or their divorce.[14] Such dowries were generally formed of portable valuables such as cash and jewellery. Hopkins expressed surprise at what he regarded as the low median size of dowries recorded in the Tebtunis record office in AD 42–46 at 80 drachmas.[15] But 80 drachmas would have been enough money to provide wheat seed for 10 arouras of land, which was enough for the young couple to support themselves within a wider family economic unit and it was thus not insubstantial.

As Tacoma noted, it seems likely that the dowry would have reduced the share due to the daughter of the inheritance on the parents' demise. Since dowries were rarely in the form of land, Tacoma made the point that 'this placed woman at a disadvantage ... they were likely to end up with less land, fewer houses, fewer slaves'.[16] Tacoma may, however, be overstating the case by including slaves, which could certainly be included in a dowry.[17]

How did women lose capital?

Both genders would have lost effective control of their own inherited or earned capital in the normal course of events through bad luck with harvests, poor investments or gifts made to family members. There is no evidence to suggest that women were more or less at risk than men in these respects. But they were also at risk from enforced gender-based loss. This

[13] Huebner 2013: 138–9.

[14] Rowlandson 1996: 155–6. A man would typically not directly receive any assets on marriage but would generally need to wait for the death of a relative to inherit significant capital.

[15] Hopkins 1980: 342.

[16] Tacoma 2006: 220.

[17] See *P.Coll.Youtie* II 67 (AD 260/1) for a dowry which includes slaves.

could arise on divorce, when the woman would not only risk losing her children but also would not be provided with any of the goods or earnings that she had contributed during the marriage. Typically, she could in theory retrieve her dowry, but if children stayed with their father, and she returned to her parents' home, then in some cases the ex-husband could retain some of the ex-wife's dowry to use for child maintenance.[18]

A woman's dowry was also at risk from the actions of her husband during marriage or, given its generally portable nature, from theft. In Oxyrhynchus, Syra complained to the local chief justice that her husband Sarapion, 'having squandered my dowry as he pleased, continually ill-treated me, using violence towards me, and depriving me of the necessities of life; finally he deserted me leaving me in a state of destitution'. She asked the justice for the return of her dowry of 200 drachmas increased by another 100. Whether she was successful is unknown.[19] This violence against women has echoes with modern-day Southern Asia and the current frequency of dowry-related deaths may give some insight into how common it was in the past. In India in 2013 more than 8,000 women died as a result of dowry-related violence, typically by burning or poisoning, despite laws that prohibit the giving or receiving of dowries.[20]

But theft from third parties was also a risk. A visit to the village baths by Aplounous and her mother Thermis ended with them being beaten up by another group, including women, and the loss of jewellery and a brass bowl.[21] In the same village (Euhemeria), Orsenouphis employed builders to work on his house, and, when demolishing a wall, the workmen allegedly found a box where Orsenouphis's mother had hidden her dowry goods some 40 years previously. Although the builders claimed the box was empty, Orsenouphis petitioned the chief of police to have the goods (jewellery and cash) returned.[22]

Marriage also brought with it risks for a woman's own assets other than her dowry. A husband could sell off assets that perhaps his wife had originally brought to the marriage. However, it was relatively common for wives to be consulted and to provide consent in land sales.[23] But whatever

[18] See Huebner 2013: 78–9.

[19] *P.Oxy.* II 281(AD 20–50). It was not always women complaining about marital theft; see *P.Oxy.* II 282 (AD 30–35), where Tryphon complains that his wife Demetrous has absconded with some of his own valuable property.

[20] Gondal 2015: 38.

[21] *P.Ryl.* II 124 (first century).

[22] *P.Ryl.* II 125 (AD 28–29). It seems a little odd that Orsenouphis or his mother (if still alive – he was 50 at the time) would have forgotten where the box was and let the builders demolish its hiding place.

[23] Note that Yitfach proposed that this requirement to obtain the permission of the wife is embedded in Egyptian marriage agreements where the wife was provided with

the legal constraints and rights accorded to women, within a marriage there was likely to be a power imbalance given the relative ages of man and wife, and coercion of the wife would have been a frequent occurrence. Husbands were on average 7½ years older than their wives. Girls as young as 12 were married and most women were married by age 20.[24] Whilst the Western mind rightly recoils against the concept of child marriage, we should remember that it is only a relatively short time since this was banned in the UK, for instance. When my mother was born in 1924, the minimum age for a girl to marry in the UK was 12, and for a boy 14.[25]

But women were not only at risk from older husbands. Take for instance the case of Dionysia who was in dispute with her father Chaeremon in AD 186 over a substantial mortgaged piece of land. Chaeremon even goes so far as to invoke Egyptian law and seek to 'take her away against her will from her husband's house' in order to obtain control over the assets in question.[26] However, Dionysia had Roman law on her side, and sought to refuse such coercion. Frustratingly, as in so many of the court cases of Roman Egypt, we do not know who won, and what happened to Dionysia, but the editors conclude that if the judge took Roman jurisprudence into account she would probably have been successful.[27]

The housing markets

In many house sales, the gender of the participants is in the document concerned.[28] Males are generally more involved in buying and selling than females, forming around 60 per cent of all market principals. Hobson speculated that women appear more often as vendors than buyers for economic reasons: 'this disparity indicates that women operate more conservatively on the property market than men; they may sell property which they have inherited, but they are less likely than men to invest

liens on the husband's property, but I suspect that in practice this could also relate to when the wife's property was sold by the husband. Yitfach 2015b: 123. Note that it was only in 1976 that Irish women received a similar right to be consulted on the sale of the family home.

24 Bagnall & Frier 2006: 112–13, 118.

25 The Act of Marriage Act of 1929 raised the minimum age to 16 for both sexes.

26 *P. Oxy.* II 237 (AD 186).

27 *P.Oxy.* II page 151. The editors (Grenfell and Hunt) show an empathy for Dionysia in their commentary, but they were scholars within their own imperial late nineteenth-century context and were not entirely politically correct, referring to an argument that contained an intrinsic logical inconsistency as being of a 'somewhat Hibernian fashion'. *P.Oxy.* II page 148.

28 There are 185 male buyers compared to 108 females and 203 male vendors and 135 females.

in new properties'.[29] However, my larger dataset shows no trend in this regard in that males and females form similar proportions of buyers and vendors.[30] Although there are more female vendors than buyers, 135 to 108, this simply reflects that there are generally more vendors than buyers, 338 to 293, which in turn reflects the partible inheritance system and shows that transactions tended to consolidate holdings irrespective of gender.

There is some evidence for a preference among both genders for transactions with their own gender. The total percentage of female participants is 39 per cent and if women were as likely to contract with men as counterparties as with other women, then it would be expected that 39 per cent of their counterparties would be other women. However, some 45 per cent of the counterparties where we can identify their gender were other women, which means that women were more likely to contract with other women.[31] A similar pattern appears for males, with 66 per cent of their counterparties being male compared to an 'expected' proportion of 61 per cent, and this also means that we can be confident that a preference for men to contract with other men existed. The size of this preference is, however, relatively small for both sexes, although more marked for women than men.

As regards the participants in vacant lot sales, this is a much more male-dominated domain than the markets for either houses or agricultural land. Only 25 per cent of all participants are female, compared to around 40 per cent for other real estate sales.[32] This may perhaps reflect social constraints on women mobilising the tradesmen and other resources necessary to exploit a vacant lot. Women appear more frequently as vendors rather than buyers, but this is not a statistically significant conclusion, with 95 per cent confidence.

Land sales

We have the genders of more than 600 people involved in land sales and the proportion of men and women acting in the market is roughly 60:40,

[29] Hobson 1983: 316. Hobson bases this view on house sales in Soknopaiou Nesos.

[30] Although there are more female vendors than buyers (135 to 108), this simply reflects that there are generally more vendors than buyers (338 to 293), which in turn reflects the partible inheritance system and shows that transactions tended to consolidate holdings irrespective of gender.

[31] If we examine the actions of adult women acting in a sole legal capacity only, a similar pattern emerges but it is not statistically significant at a 95 per cent confidence level.

[32] There are 59 male buyers compared to 18 females and 68 male vendors compared to 25 females.

although a little more biased towards men when they sell land.[33] Overall, female participation in the land market was more frequent than might be anticipated from the evidence from land registers. Rowlandson noted for Oxyrhynchite nome sales that women are 'actually over-represented in these transactions' compared to the percentage ownership by females in the land registers.[34] Bagnall suggested that there was no more than 25 per cent female ownership of the land area, whilst Tacoma notes that the proportion of female landowners might be 'set in the range of 10 to 20 per cent', although also noting some higher proportions from other isolated documents.[35] The relatively high number of female participants in real estate sales was also noted by Bogaert when he examined transactions involving banks, but neither he nor Rowlandson offered any explanation as to why this difference arose.[36] He also noted that women actually form the majority of buyers of real estate sold by the state.

Based on land registers, Tacoma identified three patterns in female ownership: that female ownership was more frequent in villages than towns, that women had a stronger preference than men for intensively cultivated land such as vineyards and that female land ownership declined over time, although he finds it difficult to find rationales for such patterns.[37] Does the evidence from land sales, as opposed to land registers, support Tacoma's patterns? Dealing first with the number of women landowners in villages and towns, I would agree that it does appear that women were somewhat more active in the land market in villages than cities, but this cannot be stated with 95 per cent confidence. As regards the possible pattern of a preference for women to own intensively cultivated rather than arable land, women bought and sold such land more frequently than men. Some 17 per cent of their land transactions related to intensively cultivated land compared to 13 per cent for men. Once again, the data would appear to suggest a preference for such land types for women, but this cannot be stated with 95 per cent confidence.

33 The male/female proportions are 60:40 (n = 357) for buyers and 64:36 (n = 318) for vendors. Similar proportions apply if the analysis is made on the basis of the total size of land sold. The tendency for men to be vendors more often than buyers is not statistically significant at a 95 per cent confidence level.

34 Rowlandson 1996: 182.

35 Bagnall 1993a: 130; Tacoma 2006: 108. Rathbone 2009b: 224 noted the high variability in the rates of female ownership in different registers. Melaerts 2002: 224 for Tebtunis suggested a somewhat higher level but warned against generalising from local village studies to the general position for Roman Egypt. For the later part of the period considered, Bagnall 1992: 138 computed that female ownership was 14 per cent.

36 Bogaert 2000: 267–8.

37 Tacoma 2006: 110.

When the data are examined on a diachronic basis, another layer of information is revealed. There is a predominance of male participants in first-century transactions that contrasts strongly with the broad equality of participation in the market in the second century. It should be noted that in each of the periods female buyers outnumber vendors.[38] Thus, in theory, although the numbers are small, there may have been a net shift of property from males to females. Such a conclusion would be counter to Tacoma's somewhat reluctant conclusion that female ownership declined over time.[39]

As in the housing markets, there is some evidence for a preference among both genders for transactions with their own gender. There are in total 174 cases where we know the gender of the counterparty of an adult woman who bought or sold a property that she owned solely. Given the overall proportions of activity we would expect therefore that under 70 of the counterparties would be women. However, the actual number of female counterparties is higher at 81. So there is a clear tendency for women to transact with other women. There is also a tendency for men to transact with other men. Some women could conclude contracts directly without other intervention on the basis of the *ius trium liberorum*. However, most women will usually have concluded their transaction through a guardian who was frequently, but not always, their spouse or a male relative.[40] Despite this male interference, there was a higher number of female to female transactions than would be expected if all other things were equal. I believe that the most likely reason for such a tendency is, as Rowlandson noted, that most transactions were concluded by participants within the same social circle and that social circles would have been different for the two genders.[41] To conclude, therefore, this was a gender-differentiated market with an increasingly important female component over time.

Land leases

Turning to the representation of different genders as landlords and tenants, the most striking statistic is the infrequency of women acting as tenants. Of the 1,088 tenants where we know their gender only 3 per cent are women. In the absence of any known legal restrictions on women taking on a lease of land, the low number of females is likely to be due to social restrictions

[38] Younger women are particularly active in the market as buyers of land, with the median age of 23 for female buyers compared to the median age of men of 36, but I cannot suggest a rationale for this difference.

[39] Tacoma 2006: 110–11.

[40] An example of a woman acting without guardian on the basis of *ius trium liberorum* is *P.Oxy.* XLIX 3498, dating from AD 274.

[41] Rowlandson 1996: 183.

on the ability of women to mobilise the necessary resources to farm land directly, much as was also the case for minors of both sexes. Looking in detail at the few female tenants within the leases or sub-leases where we have significant information, there is a surprising frequency of unusual features that stresses the atypical nature of women acting in this role.

In the case of *P.Mich.* II 121r II i, the tenant was a woman, acting with her son as guardian. The fact that the son was the guardian rather than the husband (which was more common) may suggest that she was acting as the matriarchal head of the family as a widow. She made an advance payment in cash for a lease, which was not to commence for two years. Thus, it would seem that from the point of view of the tenant this deferred lease should be regarded as a rational medium-term 'investment' rather than a lease intended to provide subsistence or immediate income for the family unit. It is likely this female entrepreneur secured the lease with a view to sub-leasing or having it farmed by her family at a later date.[42]

In *P. Harr.* II 224, a substantial body of land of more than 30 arouras, or some six times the median size, is leased by one woman of substance to another. A number of other leases were also from women to other women.[43] *P.Cair.Isid* 104 is a complicated division of inherited property which results almost accidentally in women farming land that in part belongs to a family member. *P.Mert.* II 68 is a lease of land where Heras acts jointly with her nephew to continue to lease the land previously farmed by her presumably deceased/divorced/absconded husband Patynis. Even women acting in consort with their husbands, a common feature of land sales and loans, is relatively rare.

The rarity and atypical nature of these leases show that farming was therefore considered externally an almost universally male responsibility, even though women undertook and shared in many of the tasks such as harvesting. Whilst the public perception of farming may have been a male domain, within the family, wives and matriarchs could exercise considerable practical control and take action. Consider the letter of Ptolema to her absent brother (and/or husband) Antas, where she tells him of the condition of the fields, actions she has taken, including selling and buying at prices that were clearly not decided in advance by him but rather seem to have been at her choice and where the comment that 'hay is very cheap' makes it clear that she has a strong understanding of the local commodities market.[44]

[42] See also *P.Kron.* 19 (AD 145) and *P.Kron.* 19a (AD 145–146) for a similar advanced payment by a woman, but for an even greater total period of 17 years.

[43] See, for instance, *P.Sarap.* 33 (AD 121–122) concerning a vineyard or *SB* XXII 15381, a rent receipt from AD 314.

[44] *P. Hamb.* I 86 (second century).

Women do act more often as landlords of agricultural land rather than tenants, and 24 per cent of the 959 landlords where we know the sex were women. This proportion is lower than in land purchases where they constitute around 40 per cent of buyers and sellers, but is, perhaps logically, more in line with the estimated proportion of land under female ownership.

The credit markets

To a much greater extent than in most other areas of financial activity, the credit market was dominated by men. Some 84 per cent of 1,331 lenders and 79 per cent of 1,834 borrowers were male. Overall, women constituted only 19 per cent of all principals within credit transactions. As with real estate transactions, there was a trend for women to transact with women and men with men. Some 87 per cent of male counterparties were male, and 26 per cent of female counterparties were female, compared to an expected 81 per cent and 19 per cent respectively if there were no trend.[45]

Lerouxel has looked in detail within his more restricted dataset at the activity of women and subdivided their activity between women acting on their own behalf and those who acted with their husband or son. He saw increased lending by women acting singly over time and noted that women had to supply specific security more frequently when borrowing than men.[46] My assessment of the general trend of women's participation is shown in Table 12. The main figures include female activity in consort with male relatives, whilst those in brackets only include women borrowing and lending their own capital. Lerouxel identified a trend for women to have greater access to the credit markets as borrowers after the establishment of the *bibliotheke enkteseon* in AD 70 and my more extensive assessment of female activity would support the feature that Lerouxel identified.[47]

[45] Lerouxel found somewhat higher incidences of female to female transactions, which I believe relates to differences in the geographical distribution of the data sample. For instance, for the period AD 70 to 170 he finds that out of 52 female borrowers, 46 per cent borrowed from other women. Lerouxel 2016: 124. With my wider sample of 125 female borrowers for the same period I find that the proportion of women borrowing from women was 31 per cent. Similar levels of female to female lending are seen if my sample is restricted to adult women acting in their own right, not jointly with another person, so as to reduce any bias from women acting in conjunction with their husbands.

[46] Lerouxel 2016: 73, 123. Whilst this could relate to a perceived difference in credit-worthiness between the genders, 'it also points to the extent to which women's economic role is directly linked to their ownership of real-estate'. Hobson 1983: 317.

[47] Lerouxel 2012b: 962. The main reason for the change in the percentage of female participation in the period to AD 1–70 is that the bulk of the abstract records in the Tebtunis *grapheion* register where females are active show husbands and wives acting in consort, although this may hide different types of activity.

Table 12 Percentage of female principals of all principals by date range

Percentage female n = number of females	**AD 1–70 n = 188 (n = 54)**	**AD 71–170 n = 292 (n = 228)**	**AD 171–273 n = 90 (n = 71)**	**AD 274–350 n = 34 (n = 27)**
Borrower	27% (4%)	21% (14%)	17% (13%)	12% (8%)
Lender	9% (8%)	22% (20%)	18% (15%)	11% (10%)

My data additionally show a reduction in the numbers of females active, both as lenders and borrowers, in the period from AD 274.[48] The levels of lending by women may simply reflect their acquired share of the available capital in the economy. However, women were faced with discrimination as borrowers, given their reduced ability to borrow when operating in their own right compared to when acting in consort with male relatives. We can thus think of the credit markets of Roman Egypt as being limited-access institutions, not only as we saw in Chapter 5, because secured lending was only available to some, but also because there was gender bias. I have the impression that men often borrowed in the joint names of themselves and their wives but lent in their sole name. The numbers in Table 12 would support that impression, since women very rarely lent jointly with their husbands.

Women appear to form a higher than expected proportion of people using pawnbrokers as a method for obtaining credit. This was not restricted to women of lower social status. Consider Euonia, who had luxury goods (garments, metal vessels and jewellery) worth more than 200 drachmas, or around two-thirds of a manual labourer's annual income, pledged with two pawnbrokers, presumably in Oxyrhynchus.[49] Euonia was paying 48 per cent interest when she writes to instruct her correspondent to redeem the goods. At first sight, to borrow money at such a high interest rate appears illogical, when to sell the goods, which she foresees as being necessary if she does not have enough cash available to redeem them, might have been the more appropriate action in the first place. But we do not know the full circumstances of why her goods were pawned originally.

48 I lack the data to confirm or deny Hobson's suggestion that women appear more frequently as borrowers in years of economic distress. Hobson 1984b: 389–90. The decline in activity of females in the market in the fourth century is statistically significant at a 95 per cent level.

49 P.Oxy. I 114 (second to third centuries).

Were women always worse off financially than men?

As we have seen, many of the individuals who needed to use pawnbrokers and paid high interest rates were women.[50] They thus suffered financial consequences since they paid much higher interest rates of sometimes more than 50 per cent per annum and were discriminated against by paying higher conveyancing fees. But did this, plus the other discriminatory features, mean that women were always worse off than men? There was one area where women were advantaged compared to men, and that was in their exemption from the poll tax, which was a significant fiscal demand on men. Since this tax was flat rate rather than income- or asset-related, it was a particular burden on low-income men. A matriarchally led family economic unit, with a high female component but with at least one adult male to help represent the unit in external transactions, would actually be advantaged compared to a patriarchally led family unit with a higher male proportion.

Conclusions

Transactions clearly passed through social networks and there is a tendency in all the transaction types for women to prefer transacting with other women, and men with other men. The social networks that helped create markets were thus gendered. The proportions of women acting within the various markets are summarised in Table 13, where the most striking feature is that women were essentially unable to act as tenants of agricultural land.

Table 13 Female participation proportions in the markets

Lenders n = 1,331	Land buyers n = 357	House buyers n = 293	Land landlords n = 959	House landlords n = 183	Vacant lot buyers n = 78
16%	40%	37%	24%	30%	23%
Borrowers n = 1,834	Land vendors n = 318	House vendors n = 338	Land tenants n = 1,088	House tenants n = 172	Vacant lot vendors n = 93
21%	36%	40%	3%	16%	27%

There is no known legal barrier to women acting in this way, so the reason for this feature is thus likely to be that it was socially unacceptable

50 See, for instance, *SB* XVI 12421 (second century) for a pawnbroker's book of loans where all the borrowers are female.

for women either to farm the land solely with their own labour or to be seen to direct men to do so. The relatively low proportion of women acting as landlords or lenders would also seem to indicate that it was socially difficult for a man to be financially subservient to a woman.

These features should logically have had the following impacts. The liquidity within the land leasing market would have decreased by excluding a significant proportion of the population from acting as tenants and (to a lesser extent) landlords, thus reducing the competitive nature of the market. By contrast, the liquidity of the land sales market might have been expected to increase if women sought to sell inherited land they could not farm themselves, or would find difficulty in leasing, but we do not see this in the evidence. Indeed, women form a larger proportion of the buyers of land (40 per cent) than vendors (36 per cent), and their overall participation in the market is greater than is apparent from the land register evidence.[51]

Turning from land to loans, the percentage of women who had access to credit compared to their proportion of the population was low. There is a parallel here with the modern developing world where there has been considerable debate as to the impacts on women of increasing their access to relatively affordable credit. In the modern world, this has been achieved by microfinance lending institutions, rather than lending between individuals, which was the norm in Roman Egypt.[52] Providing women access to affordable credit is currently seen as encouraging 'virtual spirals', which are viewed as positive from a socio-economic perspective by not only reducing poverty and increasing financial stability but also providing women with economic empowerment that can then increase their political power and help address gender inequality.[53] However, some scholars have questioned whether, in today's developing economies, providing proportionally greater access to credit for women, whilst maintaining the same overall level of lending, really is beneficial for society. Studies have shown that when women borrow money it is often their husbands who benefit.[54] This can be referred to as the 'feminisation of debt', since the legal burden falls on the woman, but she gains no tangible advantage. Also, simply changing the gender balance of borrowers may not address wider social inequality issues

[51] See Kelly 2020: subsection 3.1.4 for a description of the relevant evidence, which also does not find statistically significant evidence that, as Tacoma suggested, women preferred vineyards or other intensively cultivated types of land and no evidence that overall female ownership of land decreased over time. Tacoma 2006: 110.

[52] See Kulkarni 2011: 11–22 for a good summary of the issues.

[53] Mayoux & Hartl 2009: 8.

[54] Kulkarni 2011: 20–1. Similar patterns of husbands controlling and benefiting from their wives' loans have been seen in India, Pakistan and Latin America.

since, as Kabeer pointed out, 'many feminists recognize that poor men are almost as powerless as poor women in access to material resources in the public domain, but remain privileged within the patriarchal structure of the family'.[55] The position of the genders within the patriarchal society of Roman Egypt may have been similar, but for women this would have been modified by the Roman dowry and inheritance systems that separated ownership and maintained continued female control over specific assets, even within the marital sphere.

Turning to how the position of women changed over time, the data appear to show a short-lived period at the end of the first century and into the second century AD when women had relatively good access to the credit markets in their own right (although never to the same extent as men) but that this access declines in the third and fourth centuries. But, whatever the period concerned, we can therefore think of both the credit and land tenant markets as being limited-access institutions for women.

Overall, in a historical context, the women of Roman Egypt enjoyed considerable power to act in their own right, which was stronger than in many other periods. In the context of the three dimensions of female financial empowerment defined by Kabeer, I would conclude that women had limited access to necessary resources (and could use these resources to define and achieve a degree of well-being) but lacked the ultimate agency to exploit such resources fully. This lack of female financial agency would have had significant negative implications for the economy by denying a substantial proportion of the population the ability to exploit their own labour and those of their neighbours and making them pay higher transaction costs. It would also have reduced liquidity in some of the financial markets and distorted activity. As we have seen, men will have used coercion to extort assets from their wives and relatives and we also have evidence for fraudulent behaviour in the markets designed to avoid burdensome legal requirements intended to protect women.[56] Thus, the effects on the markets of discrimination against women were to increase inefficiency, increase transaction costs, reduce liquidity and increase fraud and illegality.

Women could resist these discriminatory pressures. Take one Apollonia from Upper Egypt, in the third century, who it appears was perfectly capable of standing up for herself against conventional pricing and social pressures, even if it did annoy an estate manager. He writes to his employer,

55 Kabeer 1999: 13.

56 See, for instance, *P.Oxy.* II 237, page 150, which describes a decree of Mettius Rufus of AD 89 that is designed to avoid men registering their marriage agreements with a different record office from their land holdings to avoid their wives exerting their legal rights to consultation over the hidden assets.

> You wrote to me about Apollonia, that she had first choice(?) in purchasing grain. But when she came before I sold she refused to take it at the universal price in the city, but she said, 'You will sell for 32 drachmas', and I couldn't bring myself to do it. Moreover … I had to go to her [about aracus or fodder] … and she gave me a half-artaba in loan.

So here is a woman having negotiated preferential access to a source of grain, refusing to be pressured into purchasing it at what was presented to her as a 'universal' price, exercising reasoned financial judgement and then finding herself in a position of power over the, presumably male, manager when he is forced to go on bended knee to borrow fodder.

Chapter 7

Warning

'Investments can go down as well as up'

In this chapter, the investment returns available from different types of financial transactions will be compared. First, I need to address the suggestion that investment in land was effectively the only option available, as otherwise any comparisons would be pointless.[1] Kehoe states in the introduction to his study of estates in Roman Egypt: 'land did not represent one possibility within a range of investments, but rather the pre-eminent form of economic security'. But I would rather follow Bagnall's view of Kehoe's position, which is that it is 'certainly not true from an economic point of view; a diversified portfolio of loans, or participation in loans, was certainly possible'.[2] We have seen that loans were frequent and, in city contexts, individual transactions could be of a similar size to a typical transaction in land. In my view, the credit market provided a credible alternative to investment in land.

When the total volume of transactions is examined – market 'turnover' in modern terms – the credit market is five times larger than the land sale market and more than 12 times larger than the housing market.[3] I would suggest that when capital was invested, agricultural land was certainly an important investment option, but investors had alternatives that included loans, speculation in commodities, housing rental, commerce and long-distance trade. This chapter seeks to assess, in a quantitative way, the risks and returns for the options where we have sufficient data to complete this analysis, in the credit and agricultural land markets.

In the previous chapters, I set out the returns and risks of different types of investments and the combined picture is shown in Figure 33. The use

1 Kehoe 1992: 10.

2 Bagnall 1993a: 128n.5.

3 The figures are: credit market 995,000 drachmas, house sales 74,000 drachmas and land sales 204,000 drachmas. The Muziris maritime loan is not included in the above figures since it is of a different order of magnitude and of a different nature to the other transactions. All figures re-calibrated to AD 150 levels of price inflation, covering AD 1–274.

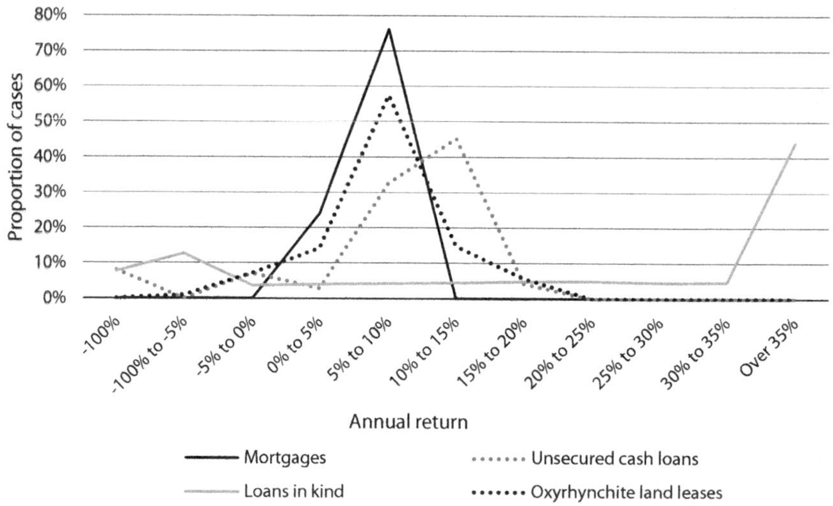

Figure 33 Stochastic return distributions

of the same scale for the horizontal axis for all types of investment clearly shows the wide and unpredictable nature of the returns from loans in kind.[4] The average returns for each investment type are: 24.4 per cent for loans in kind, 7.3 per cent for mortgages, 7.2 per cent for Oxyrhynchite land leases and 0.2 per cent for unsecured cash loans.[5] In comparison, my estimated return on housing, before depreciation and costs, is 6.8 per cent, which does not look particularly attractive compared to land and mortgages.[6]

Modelling different default rates

I was fortunate to have very good solid data as to most of the assumptions that underlie my calculations. However, as noted above, the assumptions as to default for unsecured loans and land leases are perhaps the most debatable and I have run the model on different assumptions. The results for the averages concerned are shown in Table 14. The figures do not

[4] For the mathematically minded reader, the degree of variation can be shown by the standard deviations for each of these return ranges, which are: mortgages 2 per cent, unsecured cash loans 30 per cent, loans in kind 62 per cent and Oxyrhynchite land leases 5 per cent.

[5] The median returns are 28.7 per cent for loans in kind, 9.7 per cent for unsecured cash loans, 8 per cent for mortgages and 7.4 per cent for Oxyrhynchite land leases. The average is much lower than the median for unsecured cash loans given the chance of losing both the capital and the interest if the borrower defaults.

[6] Given the limitations of the data I cannot calculate a distribution of returns for housing in the same way as for other investments.

Table 14 Average yearly returns per investment type

Default rate	0%	2%	4%	8%	12%	16%
Mortgages	7.3%	7.3%	7.3%	7.3%	7.3%	7.3%
Unsecured cash loans	8.8%	6.6%	6.0%	0.2%	−4.3%	−8.5%
Loans in kind	39.2%	35.4%	31.5%	24.4%	17.0%	9.9%
Oxyrhynchite land leases	7.6%	7.4%	7.3%	7.2%	6.8%	6.5%

change for mortgages since the assumption is that if the borrower defaults the lender obtains the mortgaged property, which is equal in value to the capital and interest. In practice, this may underestimate the figures for mortgages since, as we have seen above, the value of the mortgaged security could well be greater than the loan plus outstanding interest.

The comparison between secured mortgages and unsecured loans shows that in order to achieve the same average return on an unsecured loan compared to a mortgage the loan would have to be repaid in more than 98 per cent of the cases, which is equivalent to a default rate of less than 2 per cent. This is because the expected return on mortgages is 7.3 per cent, and even if only 2 per cent of unsecured borrowers default, you expect to earn a lower, 6.6 per cent, return from unsecured lending. To put this another way, lending money without specific security would only make rational financial sense if you were more than 98 per cent sure of getting your money back. This stresses the need for the lender to have good information on the creditworthiness of the borrower, and I believe this would make most unsecured loans between strangers too risky to have been a rational proposition for the lender. Even if the borrower is well known to the lender, this is a highly risky transaction. Loans in kind show good prospective average returns, even if one in six borrowers defaults, but the risk of total loss is substantial.

Reducing risk by diversification

We have seen in the preceding section that whatever reasonable assumption is made as to borrower default, unsecured loans are very risky. There are two ways in which the risk to an investor could have been reduced from these volatile investments. First, the lender may split their investment among a number of transactions of the same type. This tactic will not change the expected average return but will, if it is possible to find and manage a sufficient number of borrowers, possibly reduce the risk of an extreme outcome. For instance, if an investor provides a loan in kind to one individual then the risk of them losing all their money in any particular year is 8 per cent, according to my assumptions, whereas if they split the loan between two independent parties, the risk of losing all their money is reduced to 0.64 per cent, 8 per cent times 8 per cent, in normal circumstances. However, this only applies if the actions of the two borrowers are independent. In my model, and in real life, the likelihood of the default of both parties is dependent on whether that year's harvest has failed, which means that if one defaults the other is likely also to default, meaning that our risk is not substantially reduced by simply splitting a large loan into smaller amounts, although it does reduce the concentration risk related to the assessment of the creditworthiness of a particular borrower.

The other way in which an investor can reduce risk is to diversify among the different investment types, choosing to build a portfolio which balances high risk investments with others that have lower risk characteristics. However, portfolio diversification works best if the values of different investment types move in different, and preferably opposite, ways when there is an outside stimulus such as the general quality of the harvest. Unsecured cash and kind loans and land leasing returns all have a relationship with the quality of the harvest, but one which varies in both the size and nature of the response. Consider, for instance, a Nile flood which is low but not wholly inadequate, so that harvest yields are below average but not disastrous. This is unlikely to impact on the unsecured cash loan, which should still be repaid, and the mortgage holder will similarly receive payment, but there is no upside to the lender. The lender of an unsecured loan in kind should still get paid, but the price of cereals is likely to be higher than normal given the lower harvest yield, and the lender will get a higher than normal return in cash terms. Similarly, the landlord of a leased plot should receive their rent, and when paid in kind it will have a higher than normal cash value. Other harvest results will have different impacts. For instance, a total failure will have disastrous consequences for the return on unsecured loans, but relatively little impact on returns from mortgages. And returns from land leasing will be low, but the value of the land itself is not altered. Therefore, given the fact that different investment types react differently to external events, it makes sense to diversify a portfolio of wealth among these types.

Do we have evidence for investment diversification in Roman Egypt? We can look for evidence in the wills of individuals where one might expect to see a portfolio of different investments that needed to be described and assigned. But although houses and land are frequently described, loans are rarely mentioned as assets in the wills, perhaps because of their typically very short-term nature, which would mean that the information concerned could be out of date by the time of death.[7]

[7] See Nowak 2015 for a comprehensive description of the contents of wills in Roman Egypt and elsewhere in the empire.

Without any other evidence, I do not believe, therefore, that I can make any firm conclusions as to the practice of diversification of assets among investment types by large investors, but families did diversify their economic activity. Evidence from family archives shows that families adopted strategies that would have mitigated the risk of financial ruin, acting at the same time as landlords, tenants, lenders and borrowers.[8] Consider the family of Komon, described by Turner as an 'Oxyrhynchite petit bourgeois family' who both rented and owned land and were involved in the credit market.[9]

It should be stressed that the above discussion of risks and their mitigation is based on the tacit assumption that the risk the individual fears is to lose money in nominal capital terms. This is most likely the key risk in the period under consideration from AD 1 to 274, but there are other potential risks that an individual faced and could have driven behaviour. Although probably of more relevance to the fourth century, an investor may fear the effects of inflation and be satisfied if their assets do not lose real value. An investor may also have specific investment targets that they are aiming to meet – for instance, the accumulation of sufficient wealth to provide a dowry. They may have lost confidence in the value of coinage and would thus favour investments in land and commodities. We can only rarely see what risks investors were willing to take and which they feared, but I believe that capital loss was still probably the main concern of investors in the period to AD 274.

Conclusions

As discussed in the first chapter, I am looking for evidence for drivers of behaviour. Do the risk–return distributions help us to identify these drivers and are they consistent with any of these drivers – in particular the exercise of financial rationality on the basis of exchange value to maximise utility or profit? I can define the exercise of financial rationality as the use of reason to make a comparative decision, seeking to achieve financial goals, having due regard to maximising return and minimising risk. To exercise financial rationality would thus, of necessity, require a comparative assessment of the returns, and risks, expected to be achieved from different investment types. I have modelled what I believe are plausible *actual* returns and risks, but I cannot model those *expected* since this is a function of the mentality of the investors concerned. Unfortunately, it is usually only in the Italian

[8] See, for example, the activities of the family of Sakaon documented within leases and loans in *P.Sakaon*.

[9] Turner 1970: 488.

elite sources that we have direct evidence for the motives of investors in the Roman world.[10]

Despite the shortcomings of examining probable actual risks and returns rather than expected ones, I believe that the risk–return distributions shown above can provide information as to whether the outcomes are consistent with financially rational decisions or reflected other concerns and behaviours. Outcomes that are consistent with financially rational behaviour cannot prove that this behaviour was actually present, but when combined with other evidence, a case can be made, and this will be addressed in the following chapter. If the average outcome is not financially rational, then this proves that the decision was not based on a financially rational judgement, although it cannot prove what alternative considerations drove behaviour. Again this will be considered in the next chapter.

When we look at the outcomes, first we can observe a logical hierarchy of risk and return. Investment in land in the Oxyrhynchite nome in the Nile valley produced a relatively low but stable average return, which I have estimated at 7.2 per cent per annum. The higher returns in the geographically atypical Arsinoite region could reflect possibly a different risk profile, given the reliance on artificial irrigation. Investment in mortgage-backed secured loans, with the associated low risks, provided similar estimated average returns to that of land at 7.3 per cent. Secured lending and investment in land for leasing thus show similar risk characteristics in that their returns have low volatility and similar levels. However, loans in kind provided totally unpredictable returns in cash terms being so dependent on the Nile flood, the resulting harvests and the consequent price levels of cereals. But the average return on these loans in kind was exceptionally high, reflecting the greater risks.

The one type of investment which does not fit comfortably within this hierarchy of risk and return is an unsecured loan. With a typical headline rate of 12 per cent per annum, after allowing for expenses, if even 1 in 50 borrowers defaulted, and I have to believe this is an understatement of default rates given the dependency on the harvest for borrowers to return cash, the average annual return is only 6.6 per cent. The risks are much higher than mortgages, which returned on average 7.3 per cent. It is difficult to make a rational case for a lender to lend to any third party on an unsecured basis at interest rates that were within the legal limit of 12 per cent per annum. It may well be that, in some cases, there was some other side-agreement relating to an obligation, work or benefit accruing to the lender from an unsecured loan which is not visible to us from the documentation. However,

[10] See Kehoe 1997: 71–5 for a summary of the literary evidence for this type of investment, including Columella, Pliny the Elder and Seneca. See Kay 2014: 151–2 for discussion of Cato's views in *De agricultura*.

given the very large number of unsecured loans I do not believe this is a viable explanation for the rationality of the bulk of these loans. Neither do I believe that a rural unsecured loan may be considered financially rational if there is considered to be no other alternative home for the money, given that even with relatively low default rates of 1 borrower in 10 defaulting, the expected return is negative. So we need to look elsewhere than financial rationality to explain the risk–return characteristics of the unsecured loan market. Better bury the money than lend it to an unknown risky borrower if all you are interested in is profit.

In this I am afraid that I disagree with Jesus Christ's view in the parable of the talents, which is in itself a useful indicator of non-Italian contemporary attitudes to investment. For those readers unfamiliar with the parable, a master is going on a journey and entrusts 8 talents to three of his servants to invest. He thus diversifies his risk, and by giving 5 talents to one, 2 to another and only 1 to the third is making rational decisions on investment allocation based on his expectations of risk and return. On his return after a long absence, the first two servants have invested the money and doubled the investment, but the third buried it in the ground for safe-keeping. The master was displeased and punished the third servant, saying 'thou oughtest therefore to have put my money to the exchangers, and then at my coming I should have received mine own with usury'.[11]

I believe that modern institutional investors, who dominate the financial markets, act in a financially rational way, although not always successfully. A comparison of risk–return characteristics of Roman and current US asset classes can help illustrate both the risk–return hierarchy and the irrationality of Roman unsecured lending. Figure 34 shows the average annual return on the x-axis against the risk of volatility of return on the y-axis, which is the standard deviation.[12] It illustrates a number of points. The hierarchy of returns is illustrated by the best-fit line which shows how return by asset class usually increases in line with risk, going from the 'riskless' asset of US cash in government securities in the lower left-hand corner, for which there is no direct Roman comparator, to the high return/high risk of Roman loans in kind in the upper right-hand corner. The extreme volatility of Roman loans in kind is demonstrated by its distance from the other points in the graph, showing more than three times the volatility of investing in today's roller coaster stock market. Nevertheless, an

[11] Matthew 25:14–30.

[12] The US data cover the 15 years from 2004 to 2018, a period of relatively low inflation. The sources of the data are: US cash – US 3-month Treasury Bond rates; US high grade bonds – Barclay's US Aggregate Bond Index; US equities – S&P 500 Index and US high-yield bonds. Bank of America Merrill Lynch US High Yield Master II Index.

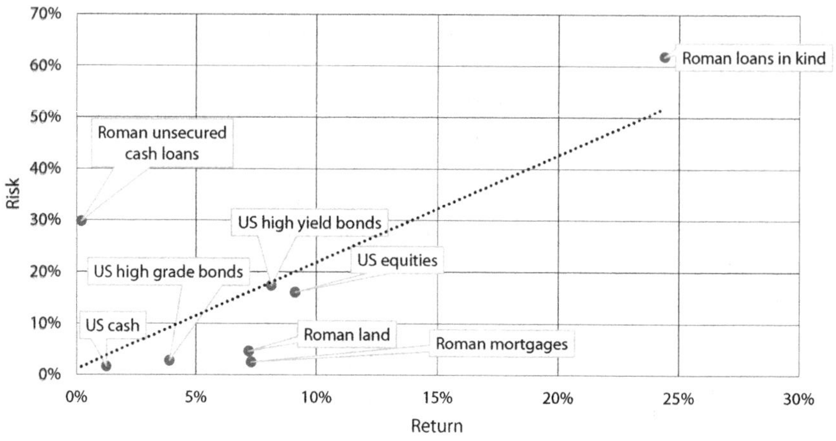

Figure 34 Risk and return characteristics

investor was rewarded appropriately for taking this extreme risk. The clear outlier is the Roman unsecured cash loan (which provides a close to zero return but with a high risk) and cannot, if there were other alternatives, therefore be the result of financial rationality.

It will be noted that if inflation averaged around 1 per cent per annum in the period to AD 274, a secure income of around 7 per cent per annum from mortgages or from leasing land is very attractive, and a 'better' investment than the modern-day equivalent comparator of high yield bonds, which also have some default risk. Investing in land or mortgages in Roman Egypt would, on average, effectively double the real value of an investment over a period of 12 years. There is another consequence of the hierarchy of risk and return that I have outlined above. Foraboschi and Gara noted that if interest rates are higher than the rates of return on productive enterprises then this could lead to economic stagnation.[13] This proposition and my other conclusions from this chapter are addressed further in the final chapter.

13 Foraboschi & Gara 1981: 342.

Chapter 8

Conclusions

The Economy and the Nature of the Markets

I set out in this chapter my main conclusions as to the economy and the markets.

Macroeconomic findings: The Antonine Plague

The growth, decline and general size of the Roman economy has been the subject of a very large body of scholarly endeavour and I hope some of my findings may usefully contribute to the debate.[1] There is no way that the data I have collected can be used to provide direct proxies of the size of the economy and its development over time. However, some clues as to economic activity can be derived from data for financial transactions to provide indicators of economic growth or decline and societal changes. There are three particular periods or events where I have identified diachronic trends: the Antonine Plague, the Third-Century Crisis and the high inflation period from AD 274 to 350.

Dealing first with the Antonine Plague, Duncan-Jones suggested that a reduction in average plot size provides evidence of the immediate economic impact of the Antonine Plague.[2] My own investigation, using bigger data, does not provide any support for this proposition and it is difficult to see any significant impacts in the land markets.[3] We do see a continuation of a decline in the volume of the credit markets (assessed by the proportion of all documents constituted by loans) but this decline starts before the plague hit, with activity in the market peaking at around AD 100. The plague does seem to be responsible for the start of relatively low systemic inflation, but prices do not generally level off once the plague has receded, as Rathbone

1 See, for instance, Bowman & Wilson 2009 or Scheidel & Friesen 2009.

2 Duncan-Jones 1996: 121–2; see also Kelly 2020: subsection 3.2.6.

3 The apparent reduction in real values of land shown in Table 2 (0.3 per cent p.a. compared to 0.8 per cent p.a. for blended inflation for the period AD 160–190) should be viewed with caution since the data are so few.

proposed. Neither is there any strong evidence for wages outstripping inflation, which might be proposed as a neoclassical economic reaction to a reduction in the workforce due to increased mortality.[4] Overall, the impact of the plague on the financial markets is not perhaps as marked as one would expect, which is not to understate its human impact, or to argue against a marked contraction in the overall volume of economic production.

The Third-Century Crisis

During the Third-Century Crisis, the empire was increasingly facing incursions into the border provinces by foreign forces and was beset by civil wars as a succession of short-lived emperors vied for power until a measure of stability and unity was introduced by the accession of Aurelian in AD 270. Add to this the Cyprian plague that struck in the mid-third century and this was certainly a time of crisis. Egypt was not exempt from plagues or unrest and there was a series of revolts and civil wars. There were also incursions from the south by the Blemmyes people. Egypt actually fell to Queen Zenobia of Palmyra in AD 270 but was swiftly reconquered.

Any attempt at economic quantification at a time of crisis requires a thorough understanding of monetary conditions. Thus one of the most important findings within my research is that, in general, prices for most goods, after a period of stability from the middle of the first century to around AD 160, grew during the crisis at an annual average rate of close to 1 per cent. This contradicts the accepted view that a doubling of prices between AD 160 and 190 was the only significant change between AD 45 and 274.[5] Thus, the Third-Century Crisis was a period when inflation continued, but not at a rate that would have hindered growth in the economy or the operation of the financial markets. It is tempting to see a correlation between continued inflation and continued debasement of the coinage in circulation. But correlation does not in itself imply causality and, as I noted in a previous chapter, price inflation is a function of individual and group behaviours that may reflect economic conditions other than the quality of the coinage.

But how is the Third-Century Crisis reflected in the financial markets and can this give us any indication of what the crisis meant for the lives of ordinary people? The most striking feature is the complete collapse in the rural credit markets. I hope I demonstrated in Chapter 5 just how critical the credit markets were to farming families. Without the support of the credit markets, the numbers of families who would have faced ruin increases

[4] See Elliott 2020: 60–1 for a critique of Temin's argumentation on this subject.

[5] Although wheat prices seem to have followed the pattern suggested by Rathbone, with a levelling off of prices in the third century.

to a level where a stable society is unsustainable. More families would have been driven to penury and this would have inevitably increased civil unrest. There would then be a vicious circle where the crisis increased the number of dispossessed people, which in turn magnified the severity of the crisis. My findings do run counter to Rathbone's view of the third-century Appianus estate that 'there are no obvious signs of economic decay. The general picture is of a rural society which was at all levels monetised and economically vigorous'.[6] However, Rathbone was looking at a particular estate and I have taken a wider view.

The collapse of the rural credit market could be taken to reflect the essentially monetary nature of the crisis. However, the city-based credit markets did continue to function, although with fewer transactions than during the preceding years. This may reflect the higher levels of secured rather than unsecured lending in the cities, since the impact of any loss of confidence in the market primarily affects the willingness of the creditor to lend, rather than the debtor to borrow. The lender fears that the coinage he or she receives back will be of less value or that the borrower will default given social instability. A secured loan reduces, but by no means eliminates, these risks and thus the city credit markets may have been more stable.

Apart from monetary debasement, another direct impact of imperial demands in a time of crisis was the introduction of the crown tax. From the landlord's perspective, I have suggested a typical marginal tax take from agricultural activity in the first two centuries AD for landowners of 25 per cent, rising potentially to around 41 per cent if crown tax became annual in the third century.[7] This is much higher than that which has been proposed for the empire as a whole, and is closer perhaps to 'skinning' than 'shearing' the sheep.[8] There would also have been requisition requirements from the military and the wider state.

It is tempting to suggest that the monetary nature of the crisis was caused by a loss in confidence in coinage caused in turn by debasement. However, there are other possible reasons why there would have been a credit squeeze in the rural areas as a result of the crisis. If general economic conditions worsen, particularly when combined with greater redistributive demands from the state, through requisitions and taxation, money will be sucked from the village economy. Less cash will be available for peer to peer lending and the village credit market will collapse. A counter-argument against this would be the evidence for a general increase in money supply

[6] Rathbone 1991: 403.

[7] Kelly 2020: subsection 3.2.19.

[8] See Dio Cassius, *Roman History* 57: 10, 5 describing Tiberius: 'when Aemilius Rectus once sent him from Egypt, which he was governing, more money than was stipulated, he sent back to him the message: "I want my sheep shorn, not shaven"'.

of debased coinage at this time to fund the military, but how much of this cash would have found its way to a village in Egypt? It will also be noted that the relatively low inflation rate experienced is not consistent with a large increase in money supply in the rural economy.[9]

The value traded within the land leasing markets was largely in kind, with rents in the more valuable years in wheat or barley, and cash only being used for rents in the less valuable years when the land was under fodder. The land leasing market was therefore relatively immunised from monetary crises. A number of scholars have suggested that rents for agricultural land declined, with the resultant implications for economic prosperity and activity. However, I would rebut both Muth's and Scheidel's proposals as to declines in land rents and Bagnall's suggested decline in the amount of land leased from the second to the fourth centuries.[10] I would suggest that the apparent decline in attested rents is more likely to be due to regional rather than diachronic differences. The one area where there is strong evidence for greater economic volatility is in the length of leases. Here the data does show a statistically significant reduction in land lease length in the third century continuing into the fourth. I view this, in behavioural finance terms, as reflecting a reduction in an individual's investment horizon in a period of increased volatility, although it does not in itself imply a reduction in overall economic output.

The volume of activity in the land leasing market shows stability from the second century to the third, measured by considering the proportion of land leases as a percentage of all documentary papyri.[11] Similarly, in the other component of the land markets – sales rather than leases – activity in the third century maintains the levels experienced in the second century.[12]

It would be remiss of me not to consider climate as a potential driver or influencer on the experience of ordinary people. Indeed, in a recent

[9] Rathbone argued that the low levels of inflation could be explained by 'a still spreading monetisation of the economy, which … was the sponge which absorbed the cumulatively increasing stock of coinage in circulation without causing price-inflation', but this is not consistent with my new evidence for the collapse of the credit markets. Rathbone 1996: 338.

[10] I disagree with Muth's 'firm' conclusion that the theory that real land rents declined throughout the first three centuries of Roman rule is unfounded. Muth 1994: 220. Muth used data solely from Johnson 1936, did not appear to examine the primary sources and took no account of crop rotation. See also Scheidel 2002: 101 and Bagnall 1985a: 307.

[11] See Kelly 2020: Fig. 5.1.3.

[12] Land sale documents as a proportion of all documentary papyri are: 3.7 per cent in the first century falling to 2 per cent in the second, 1.9 per cent in the third and 0.6 per cent in the first half of the fourth.

publication I argue that climate variability was the key risk that farming families faced.[13] However, there is no strong evidence, from ice cores or elsewhere, of an increase in climate variability in the third century in Egypt. We do see population declines in some of the villages as marginal land in the Arsinoite nome was abandoned, and this could be explainable as reflecting a gradual decline in the irrigation system. It is also a function of the survival bias in the find sites of papyri. Most papyri were found in settlements that were not occupied into modern times. So our papyri are likely to reflect settlements that had been abandoned at some time. Despite this bias, the land markets were remarkably resilient in an undoubted time of crisis but the collapse of the rural credit markets will have fuelled social instability and accentuated the crisis as more families faced ruin and the imperial tax take declined.

High inflation conditions

Turning to the period after AD 274, the wider historical context is dominated by Diocletian's efforts to stabilise both the empire as a whole and the economy in particular, including of course his failed Price Edict of AD 301. I examined the levels of inflation in the period from AD 274 to 350 and confirmed Rathbone's proposal that there was a sharp increase in prices around AD 274.[14] Inflation averaged at around 15 per cent per annum during the first half of the fourth century but we lack sufficient data to conclude whether this average rate hides greater short-term price variations. In the higher inflation conditions from AD 274 to 350, different forms of payment for fodder rents were used as people sought an alternative medium to cash. The duration of leases declined further and share-cropping became more common. These are perfectly rational and sophisticated responses to uncertain conditions.

Other macroeconomic findings

The macroeconomic implications of interest rate structures can be dealt with here. However, a few concepts need to be defined before considering my interpretation of the evidence for Roman Egypt. A key concept in defining any interest rate structure is the 'risk-free' interest rate within the market, where a lender is sure that they will be able to secure both the capital and interest at the end of the loan. In the modern world, this risk-free interest rate is normally determined by the interest applicable to sovereign state borrowing. Higher interest rates are charged by lenders for

13 See Kelly 2021b.

14 Rathbone 1997: 215.

other borrowers who may have a greater chance of default to compensate the lender for the higher risk. The difference, or 'spread', between these higher interest rates and the risk-free interest rate is normally referred to as a 'risk premium'. In Roman Egypt we cannot define the risk-free interest rate by reference to the state's borrowing since we have no evidence that this occurred or that it would have been risk-free. Rather, the proxy for a risk-free rate may be considered to be the average interest rate for secured mortgages, which I have estimated at 7.3 per cent. This 7.3 per cent may be considered therefore as the minimum cost of capital rate for any investor and thus any riskier investment would require a return well in excess of this cost of borrowing if it were to be expected to be profitable, such as investment in a productive concern, like developing land. This borrowing to invest to increase wealth is known as 'gearing'. We have little direct evidence for gearing, despite the very large number of transactions in the databases. This may well reflect the fact that if borrowing rates were around 7.3 per cent and returns on investment in land for leasing were at similar or lower levels, as my analysis suggests, there would not have been any financial incentive to borrow money to invest in land. Finally, neoclassical economic theory states that loans used for productive activity (compared to consumption loans) support economic growth and wealth creation, and thus the relative infrequency of such loans is important.[15]

Turning to the contribution of the financial sectors of the economy, the first point to note is that the credit market was much larger than the real estate markets. For every 1 drachma of turnover in housing, roughly 3 drachmas were invested in land and 13 drachmas were placed in the credit market. This financial activity did not typically involve any development of a secondary service sector related to financial transactions since, when dealing through agents and intermediaries, professional remunerated intermediation was rare. Banks were active in parts of the credit market but their form of remuneration is unclear and I do not believe that income from their activity formed a significant part of the GDP of Roman Egypt. Although banks appear to have taken a position only rarely as a principal in the credit market, their intervention has been taken to imply an increase in the money supply through a 'credit multiplier' or 'money multiplier' effect.[16]

[15] See von Reden 2010: 94–5 for a discussion of the impact of credit on ancient economies and Cumming et al. 2017: 8–9 for consideration of the impacts of microfinance in today's developing countries. Also Bange 2014: 253–7 for the nature of the credit markets in the Roman world.

[16] Harris 2008: 187. As to whether individual lending may be considered to have increased the money supply, Harris took the view that it would not, since one of his preconditions for such a result, the capacity of the lender to recover the debt, is not

This multiplier effect is generally viewed as being positive for the economy in that it increases the liquidity of markets and facilitates productive loans. However, I believe that the potentially positive effects on the economy of the multiplier from banking would have been relatively limited since banks generally only acted as credit transferors rather than lending capital for investment.[17]

Finally, when we consider the macroeconomic features of the Roman economy we must, of course, recognise the influence of the state. It is common for scholars of the ancient Roman economy to emphasise the impact of state institutions, given the NIE framework within which many of them work, but that the Roman state was central to the Roman economy is clear. The state dictated prices for certain goods and influenced markets in more subtle ways. The clearest evidence for state activity is in the wheat market, where the state's actions and pricing structures seem to have dampened price volatility and kept price increases lower than those which applied to other goods. This new evidence of differential pricing argues for a middle ground view of the commodities market, reflecting a 'two-tier' economy with certain sectors of activity where the key actor is the state, and others subject to a greater degree to neoclassical market forces. The state also impacted on the real estate market, through the confiscation of private land in the event of fiscal default or other offence against the state and the sale of the land it owned. These actions had a significant impact on the real estate markets by altering supply and demand.

Another diachronic trend in the credit markets is the increase in transaction size recently identified by Lerouxel as a positive economic impact of the establishment of the *bibliotheke enkteseon*. However, I would suggest that this was largely a phenomenon of the city-based elite and was accompanied by a collapse in the village credit market, and that there is no evidence that an increase in typical loan size would have had any significant macroeconomic benefit. As well as introducing new institutions that facilitated secured lending (in particular the *bibliotheke enkteseon*), the Roman state intervened in the first instance by reducing

met. Harris 2008: 180. He stated that 'the costs of recovering them would have been prohibitive', but I believe he underestimated both the social constraints on debt default, which he mentioned earlier in the article, and the effectiveness of debt recovery as evidenced within the papyri dealing with petitions. Harris 2008: 189, 191. Although it would be impossible to prove, in my view, given that only a relatively small proportion of credit transactions involved banks, the increase in the money supply from person to person lending may well have been of greater significance than that which arose from banking intermediation.

17 In this I would agree with Harris that within the context of the Roman empire the availability of entrepreneurial borrowing is of greater importance than the actual size of the money supply. Harris 2008: 202–3.

the maximum allowable interest rate on cash loans from the 24 per cent allowable in Ptolemaic times to 12 per cent per annum. This action would have been likely to have increased the stability of the economy by reducing the risk of financial ruin for borrowers and in particular for smallholders and tenants.

Another major economic element of the state was the army, for between 11,000 and 16,000 troops were stationed in Egypt throughout the majority of this period.[18] The military must have had a significant influence on the economy, both through their demands for supplies and more subtly through the permeation of ideas and attitudes absorbed by local recruits during their service. In the database of real estate transactions there are few examples of serving soldiers involved as buyers, sellers, landlords or tenants, although veterans are more in evidence. There are a larger number of credit transactions involving serving military personnel. However, the bulk of those involving serving military personnel were internal to the army and did not involve civilians. As Rathbone maintained: 'the sizeable Roman army presence in Egypt introduced to its many local recruits, and the surrounding population ... the Roman economic mentality', but this evidence might indicate that more of this interaction occurred once soldiers had retired as veterans rather than during their active service.[19]

Microeconomic findings

This section deals with conclusions of a microeconomic nature which can be drawn as to the quality of life enjoyed and the challenges faced by the people of Roman Egypt. I have proposed that the normal tax burden on the income of individuals who held land was substantial, with marginal tax rates on rents from leased land estimated at 25 per cent and additional obligations or demands in times of fiscal or social stress. However, for those without substantial land ownership the tax burden would appear to have been relatively low. In a good year, the tenant of a private landlord would be subject to a tax rate which would have been around 5 per cent of their gross income after rent. Typically, rents paid by tenants of state land are considered as taxation, and, if so considered, then the tax rates would have been substantially higher than for private tenants. However, I would question whether the rent paid by a tenant of state land should be classified as a tax. It is certainly part of the state's revenue, but unlike other receipts the payer gains some direct economic advantage from the payment through their exploitation of the land, and thus it is not a tax when viewed from a microeconomic perspective. In summary therefore, contrary to the normal

18 Alston 1995: 31.
19 Rathbone 2007b: 718.

view of Roman taxation, I believe that the tax system in Roman Egypt may be considered as 'progressive' in that lower tax rates applied to lower income groups than to higher ones.

I hope that it is clear that the markets were limited-access institutions, particularly for women, who were driven to rely on the pawnbroker markets for credit, with the higher interest rates this implies, and who were unable to take tenancies on agricultural land. They could also be subject to physical and mental coercion by other family members, particularly in relation to their dowries. However, the women of Roman Egypt were in some respects in a better legal position than historical comparators such as the women of Victorian Britain in that they had the right of independent ownership. They had some tax advantage over men since they were not subject to poll tax and we have many examples of strong successful matriarchally led families and individual women.

If the markets were gendered, they were also influenced by the ages of the participants. The median age of borrowers was higher, at 38, than that of lenders, at 35. Indeed, in their 40s and 50s, people were more likely to be borrowers than lenders. If individuals tended to accumulate capital over their lifetime, we would expect that there would be more lending than borrowing by older people and that borrowers might be more likely to be younger than lenders. This pattern of older lenders, and younger borrowers, is certainly present in most modern developed economies.[20] However, the evidence from Roman Egypt is that older people continued to need to borrow and did not typically have spare capital to lend to younger individuals. This lack of any significant inter-generational lending, with the older generation lending to the younger, can be interpreted as indicating that typically there was no significant accumulation of even moderate savings over a lifetime for ordinary people, with all this implies for social mobility and economic growth.[21]

But the need to borrow was not restricted to older people. Based on the data that Bonneau presented, the chance of the Nile flood failing can be estimated at around 1 year in 12. If a family had not built up sufficient savings to meet subsistence and tax demands then their only recourse would have been to borrow, and this risk of falling into debt is reflected in the fact that borrowing was the most common financial transaction in Roman Egypt. There was also a strong tendency within the credit markets, both those in cash and those in kind, to have a peak in scheduled repayments after the harvest. This demonstrates that many borrowers were dependent on the harvest to be able to make repayment, and if the harvest failed, the

[20] See ONS 2016: 16 for debt by age group in the UK.

[21] This conclusion is confirmed by the modelling of tenant farmer prosperity and financial risk in Kelly 2021b.

borrower would be in a precarious position and the lender might not receive repayment of the loan.

Turning to the place of the credit market, Briggs, in his review of the changing views of credit in the European pre-industrial economy, maintains that

> most current research on European pre-industrial credit adopts an 'optimistic' position and sees lending and borrowing as an important and dynamic element of agrarian societies in the period, frequently used for innovation and investment ... It contrasts with an older 'pessimistic' position which saw little sign of credit structures, and tended to view those that did exist as merely one of several forces leading to poverty cycles and subsistence crises.[22]

I believe that the credit market in Roman Egypt fell between these two extremes. It had the volume of the 'optimistic' view, but credit was rarely used for innovation and investment. However, I also believe that even if our evidence suggests that, for rural markets, credit was largely used for consumption, to tide over family needs in times of shortage, this was an essential feature of agrarian society, increasing social stability. I have demonstrated this by modelling the expected chance of ruin for a tenant farmer in first- or second-century Roman Egypt, over a generation. If access to a relatively cheap credit market is assumed, with an interest rate on cash of 12 per cent, then the model predicts that only 4 per cent of families would face financial ruin. If credit is less easily available (and this is simulated by increasing interest rates to 24 per cent), then the chance of ruin more than doubles. Therefore, the rural credit market, just like efficient granaries, was a key contributor to social stability by acting as a resource, particularly for the poorer classes, which could be accessed when times were hard.

Social inequality and mobility

Turning from those who needed to borrow to those who had capital to spare, I have demonstrated that those investors with larger sums available for investment and who were able to take advantage of the institutions that secured their investment through mortgages or land registers could expect to achieve a very good return net of tax that was well above inflation in the period up to AD 274. However, for those with small sums of money, purchasing land would have been beyond their means. There were also considerable barriers to villagers accessing the mortgage market, including differential literacy rates, scribe fees and geographical access to the mortgage

22 Briggs 2009: 4–5.

registers, which were held in the cities. Thus the credit and land markets can be considered as being limited-access institutions, not just for women, as was proposed above, but also for men of limited means. Villagers with small sums could therefore have been constrained to investing by lending on an unsecured basis, where the likely investment return was close to zero in real terms and where their capital was at considerable risk.

The preceding conclusions lead naturally to the social impacts of attractive, relatively low risk returns in the hands of those who already had capital. This has been addressed by Piketty for more recent historical periods, but his suggestion that if the return on capital, 'r', exceeds gross product growth, 'g', then this would typically lead to a concentration of wealth is equally applicable to ancient economies.[23] My best estimate of the rate of return on capital, 'r', is that available from the leasing of agricultural land, which for the Oxyrhynchite nome for the period prior to AD 274 has a median value of 7.4 per cent. Gross product 'g' is constructed of two elements: general price inflation and real economic growth. I have estimated annual average general price inflation for the period from AD 50 to 270 at 0.6 per cent and I would argue that real economic growth in an essentially agrarian economy would have been relatively low, and certainly below 2 per cent per annum, meaning that 'g' would in all likelihood have been less than 3 per cent per annum. Thus, in Piketty's terms, 'r' was certainly greater than 'g' and, all other things being equal, the rich were getting richer and the poor received a smaller slice of the economic pie. The 'limited access' nature of the financial markets would have further accentuated this impact. It will also be noted that some institutions introduced by the Romans, such as the *bibliotheke enkteseon*, contributed to this trend, but other changes, for instance the reduction in the maximum cash interest rate from 24 per cent to 12 per cent, will have had the opposite effect. As Ogilvie stated, the distributional implications of institutions are just as important as their impact on 'efficiency'.[24]

The question arises whether we have independent evidence for the actual, rather than the predicted, concentration of wealth over the period concerned. Apart from the increase in size of city-based transactions, there is also evidence for the growth of large private estates during the second century.[25] However, we should be aware of a number of counter-factors that would have acted to disperse rather than concentrate wealth in Roman Egypt. First, wealthier families could afford to have more children and therefore inherited wealth would have dispersed. Second, wealthier families would also have been likely to have had better nutrition and lower mortality

23 Piketty 2014: 25–7.
24 Ogilvie 2007: 667–8.
25 Rathbone 1996: 338.

rates, which again would increase the number of survivors from their class into the next generation when compared to poorer families. Finally, war, plagues and rebellions, and Roman Egypt had its share of these events over the period, could act in different ways to redistribute wealth between the state and the people and within the people themselves. Overall, I believe, however, that economic and institutional conditions are more likely to have led to greater social inequality. It is probable that, all other things being equal, despite the progressive tax system, the economic conditions would have concentrated wealth in the existing landed class.

Turning to social mobility of those without capital, my modelling shows that, over a generation, even in benign economic conditions, it was very unlikely that a tenant family could hope to progress socially to own enough land to support their family.

Nature of the markets: frictional costs

The subject of frictional costs in the ancient world has been one of considerable recent scholarly interest.[26] The term 'frictional' is preferred to the more usual 'transactional', given that costs that affect the financial outcome of a transaction can arise beyond the initial transaction date, such as renewal taxes for mortgages or the legal costs of seizing property after a default on a loan. Here, however, I concentrate on frictional costs arising from intermediation since this is the chief area that can be analysed from the data examined. For each of the financial activities discussed in earlier chapters I have determined the percentage of all transactions that definitely involved a third party such as an agent or manager, and these ranged between 4 per cent and 14 per cent.[27] Some transactions may have involved intermediaries, but the evidence for their activity has been lost, or it was not recorded when the document was drawn up. None of the intermediaries concerned appears to have been a professional broker. Overall, I would suggest that these levels are low and that the vast majority of transactions were carried out directly, face to face, between the principals.

The highest levels of intermediation are for land leases and this reflects the geographical dispersion of landlord and tenant and the tendency

[26] See Kehoe et al. 2015 for a recent study on transaction costs and the ancient economy, Lerouxel 2015: 165 for a description of the different categories of transactional costs and Rathbone & Temin 2008 for a consideration of financial intermediation in Rome itself.

[27] The proportions of transactions involving intermediaries are 4 per cent (loans), 4 per cent (house sales), 7 per cent (house leases), 9 per cent (land sales) and 14 per cent (land leases). These percentages are perhaps of more use for comparative rather than absolute analysis purposes, since they must be regarded as minimum levels of intermediation.

for the landlord to delegate leasing to estate managers. It should also be noted that we have no evidence that any of these intermediaries received a remuneration that was directly linked to the transaction. The remuneration of banks within the credit market is also far from clear and we have no evidence for substantial charges. Finally, we have no evidence for the activities of auctioneers in the private real estate markets. This lack of intermediary activity will have kept frictional costs low but will not have helped the second prerequisite for an efficient market, that of good quality information exchange.

Although I have concluded that frictional costs from intermediation were low, if other frictional costs were high, they may have precluded the exercise of financial rationality since they would have impacted on profit to a disproportionate extent. In general, taxes on transactions were sufficiently low to allow for an active market to exist. The relatively high tax on the acquisition of housing, at 10 per cent, could have been amortized over the financial lifetime of the house through personal occupancy or leasing. The 2 per cent tax on mortgages, although high enough to impact significantly the return on a short-term investment, could be considered a rational price to pay for the lender to have greater security. In the commodities market, frictional costs were low enough to allow short-term speculation.[28] However, there are two market sub-sectors where frictional costs may have made it impossible to execute efficient transactions within the formal, recorded, economy. These two sub-sectors are very small loans and housing leases, where the cost of the scribe fees would have been disproportionate, if formal recording was required. I would suggest that, in the main part, activity in these sectors would have been informal and thus largely invisible.

Nature of the markets: information exchange and pricing

Turning to information exchange, the patterns identified within the analysis of the data in the previous chapters can provide insights as to the nature and efficiency of this process. These insights can come from prices, intermediary activity, social networks and the role of state institutions. 'Prices' in this context can also be extended to include rents as the price of occupation and cash interest rates as the price of credit.

Dealing first with price number formats, I would draw a distinction between 'conventional' and 'marginal' pricing. In conventional pricing, prices are rounded, which may reflect institutional constraints or market

[28] When the frictional costs of transactions are high, this tends to discourage short-term speculation, since costs of both buying and selling may impact severely on profit. Frictional costs on long-term investments are less important since they may be amortised over the lifetime of the investment.

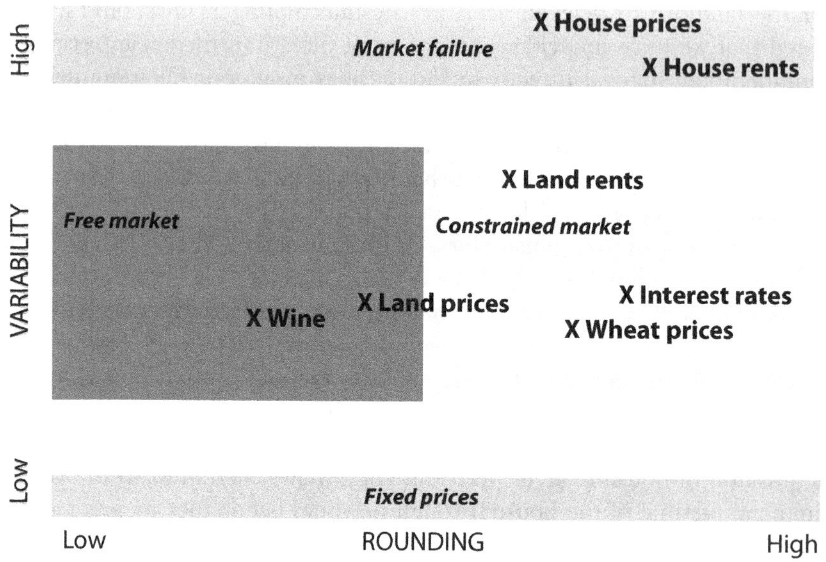

Figure 35 Price rounding and variability for different financial sectors in Roman Egypt

inefficiency. In marginal pricing, the number format is not rounded and this can be considered as evidence for negotiation and competition. Another associated aspect of prices is the degree to which they are variable, since, as Temin noted, 'variable prices then can be used as markers for the presence of market exchange'.[29] Certainly, a relatively small degree of variability in prices would be an indicator of the presence of market forces, but a very high degree of variability may indicate a failure in the pricing mechanism within the market, where participants lack the comparative data to make a rational decision.

The rounding and variability of prices within a low inflation economy are thus indicators of market behaviours. Four different situations can be identified by these indicators: market failure, free market, constrained market and fixed prices. These are displayed in the schematic Figure 35. Along the x-axis, the degree to which rounding is present in the market is shown. Along the y-axis, the variability of prices is shown. Where there is very high variability, this indicates that the market struggled to find a consensus for prices, which in turn implies a failure in the pricing mechanism, most likely due to poor information availability and exchange.

[29] Temin 2013: 8. See also Rathbone 2013: 136–7: 'the more expensive goods and those bought in quantity were subject to fluctuations in price which imply the operation of a free local market'. And for an excellent summary of pricing theory in economics, see Weber 2012.

In short, the market fails to operate efficiently. All markets where exchange value is present, particularly those which are seasonal, or which are examined over a period of time, should show price variability as supply and demand fluctuates. However, exchange value markets will differ in the degree to which prices are rounded. If there is low rounding, then, as noted above, marginal pricing is an indicator of free market exchange. If there is high rounding, exchange value market mechanisms may still operate but they are 'constrained'. There are two reasons why this may occur: the market is constrained either by 'convention' or by market inefficiency. Convention in this context can result from institutional constraints due to state action, coinage unavailability or social factors. Markets may also be constrained by their inefficient nature, particularly with regard to information. If there is insufficient information to enable a debate on price to evolve within the market, participants' opening positions will be far apart and even a negotiated price is likely to be rounded. Finally, where there is no price variability then prices are fixed. This can be as the intended result of state action, such as Diocletian's Price Edict, or in more recent times the attempts of communist regimes to fix uniform prices for goods.

This theoretical framework can be applied to Roman Egypt, but each market needs to be examined separately since the degree to which prices were variable, and/or rounded, differs by market. For instance, in the commodities market, the price of wheat was much more heavily rounded than other similar goods such as barley or wine. I have proposed that the reason for this difference relates to the higher degree to which the state intervened in the strategically important wheat market compared to other sectors of the market. The wheat market is thus an example of a conventionally constrained market. 'Prices' within the credit market, that is interest rates, also showed the features of a constrained market, given that they were heavily rounded to monthly payments defined as a multiple of 1 per 100 of loaned capital, or 12 per cent, but variability is moderate, since when they do differ from 12 per cent there is often a substantial difference. In the land rental market, prices were variable, with rent levels for different plots within the same leases differing according possibly to the level of expected yield. Rounding in this market is more difficult to assess given the rates per aroura are relatively low, but some rounding does occur. By contrast, house rents appear extremely variable and exhibit high rounding, although the diversity of housing stock will have been a factor. Real estate sales were much less frequent than rental agreements and in these sectors of the financial markets, for sales of houses, prices were rounded very frequently, and for land sales, to a lesser extent.

I have placed the market sectors, with wine acting as a proxy for commodities other than wheat, within Figure 35. Along the x-axis, my assessment of the degree to which rounding is present in the market is shown. Along the y-axis the calculated variability of prices is used.[30] In my view, for the housing markets, the presence in the top right quadrant of high, indeed excessive, variability and high levels of rounding indicates that there was insufficient information for individuals to make a reasoned judgement as to prices in these markets. Despite the high rounding, there is no need to assume that this is a result of any specific institutional constraints in the market, and I believe this results from a combination of constraints on competition caused by housing stock fragmentation and associated familial considerations, together with the information deficit. This seems to apply to both the purchase and sale of housing stock and any subsequent lease. Whilst the high variability in prices and rents might be partly explainable by the heterogeneity of the housing stock, I have sought to reduce this impact by the use of 'unit' prices and rents per house and only considering village properties. Heterogeneity in the underlying data cannot, however, explain the high rounding that applies in the housing market, which suggests that prices and rents were set without substantive negotiation given the information deficit. The only datapoint firmly in the 'free market' area, showing moderate volatility and low rounding of prices, which would indicate the operation of an unconstrained market with good exchange of information, is wine. This presumably reflects the relative frequency of these transactions that provided pricing points for reference and the homogeneity of the product. By contrast, the wheat price datapoint shows high rounding but moderate variability, the variability being consistent with the free market in wine, whilst the rounding reflects the intervention of the state as it set conventional prices. In the middle of Figure 35 we find the agricultural land markets, showing some variability that may be attributable to the heterogeneity of the underlying asset as well as the action of the marketplaces.

The above discussion has concerned the period of relatively low annual average inflation to AD 274. However, the final significant point revealed as regards the efficiency of information exchange in the markets concerns the pricing for goods in the high inflationary period of the first half of the fourth century. The market seems to have coped with the pricing of simple, frequently traded goods such as cereals, but the excessively wide variety of pricing of a complex good, donkeys, would indicate that people struggled

[30] The relative standard deviation, which is explained in the glossary, for each of the points is as follows: house prices 132 per cent, house rents 99 per cent, land prices 40 per cent, land rents 65 per cent, wheat prices 38 per cent, wine prices 39 per cent and interest rates 49 per cent. In order to reduce heterogeneity and thus distortion caused by geographical factors, the land rents used are from the Oxyrhynchite nome only, and the house rents are those for village properties only. All prices are re-calibrated to AD 150 general price levels to ensure comparability.

to price these goods at this time, probably due to inefficiencies in the pricing mechanism of the market, which in turn was due to inefficiencies in information exchange. At the risk of being accused of anachronism, buying a donkey in the fourth century would have been like purchasing a second-hand car today without the benefit of price comparison web sites. Not only was the buyer at a disadvantage since he could not know the character of the donkey, but both parties, in a time of high inflation, will have lacked the reference points as to pricing levels that shared experience would have provided in times of more stable prices.

Most transactions occurred within social networks, without intermediaries, and the nature of these networks is key to information exchange. The social networks concerned were gendered and localised. Principals were sometimes linked by family or military ties, or social obligations, which occurred, for instance, when loans were granted from landlord to tenant, but these were relatively rare. The proportions of transactions that we know occurred between family members, military colleagues and landlords/tenants are generally insignificant, at 3 per cent or less, with the exception of land and house sales where 6 per cent and 9 per cent respectively were between family members. Whilst these figures represent the minimum percentage of transactions that can be seen to be between closely connected parties, given that we do not have the full details of the parties for all the transactions, they do look low. The exception is perhaps that of house sales, where the partible inheritance system would have led to fragmentation of house ownership, and with an asset that as we have seen was difficult to price or lease formally, it may have been preferable to sell to a family member rather than a third party. The proportion of intra-family sales for houses is thus much higher than other transaction types. Most transactions must, however, have occurred between people who were not part of the same family. This will have made information exchange more difficult, even if it did mean that transactions were not commonly directly influenced by familial considerations.

Although in some markets asset owners tended to be based in the cities, and tenants or borrowers in the villages, managers employed by the asset owner could bridge this gap and ensure some parity of information. The vast majority of transactions were local, between counterparties from the same village or city, as has been shown by Lerouxel for the credit market for the initial period of Roman rule.[31] I cannot demonstrate the localised nature of the markets with as much conviction as Lerouxel since I have not made the assumption he makes, that when locations are not mentioned then they are the same, but I would agree with his conclusion as to the credit markets and believe that similarly localised

[31] See Lerouxel 2016: 340.

features applied to other markets with the exception of leasing of land.[32] This reflects the concentration of ownership of land, available for leasing, in the city elites.

One other point as regards information exchange is that markets can only work on a large scale if the item being traded is capable of commoditisation, definition and access. This was easy in the land, vacant lot and commodities markets since there were common measures. It was less clear in the donkey or slave markets since the nature and health of the item to be traded may have been clearer to the vendor than the buyer. But there were also issues in the housing market, where it would have been difficult to define exactly what constituted a fraction of a house, either for sale or rent. Which rooms exactly did it mean? What activities/occupations could be performed there? And, probably most importantly, what were the neighbours like?

The final point on information exchange relates to the role of the state in enabling or obstructing the free exchange of information between private parties. I can see no evidence for the state obstructing the exchange of information and I would agree with Lerouxel that the Roman state, by the establishment and maintenance of property registers and the *bibliotheke enkteseon*, would certainly have encouraged the higher value end of the credit and, indeed, the real estate markets through the exchange of information, which confirmed ownership or pledging of assets.[33] The active nature of the state's intervention in the commodities markets, particularly wheat, through requisitions, sales and purchases, will have impacted on the nature of the market and constrained trade.

Overall, I believe that two of the key pre-conditions existed for a relatively efficient credit market and land market – low frictional costs and sufficient information exchange. In the housing markets of rural Roman Egypt, however, the market was far from efficient in both transactional cost and information exchange.

Market drivers and pre-conditions for a neoclassical exchange value market

In this concluding section, I seek to try to determine what behaviours drove the markets. In the preceding discussion we have seen that they were not always driven by a 'rational' profit-making motive. In all the markets we have examples of people's behaviour being driven by gender

32 The proportions of 'closed' to 'open' transactions are 1.8 (loans), 1.3 (land sales), 3.7 (house sales), 0.5 (land leases) and 1.9 (house leases).

33 The state did hinder competition in the real estate markets somewhat by insisting that neighbouring owners be given a preferential ability to make bids.

bias, familial considerations or reciprocity rather than pure rationality. But what conclusions can be reached as to what were the dominant behavioural features in each market drawing on anecdotal, demographic, contractual, pricing and financial outcome evidence? As I set out in the introductory chapter, there are five main types of drivers for behaviours in the markets: pursuit of profit, reciprocity, familial actions, social capital acquisition and redistribution enforced by the state. Whilst people did choose to conduct their business more often with people of their own gender, I would suggest that this was a modifier to their behaviour rather than a driver of the action. An individual first decided that they would loan money, say, to make a profit or gain reciprocity, and only then chose to deal in a gendered segment of the market that suited them and reflected their social network.

Dealing first with profit-driven behaviours, there are certain key pre-conditions to allow for the exercise of financial rationality in a neoclassical market. These are: sufficient information, reasonable frictional costs, mathematical skills and sufficient trade volumes. Although financially rational behaviour can exist in a barter economy, sufficient monetisation to allow cash transactions to crystallise financial return would be a strong enabling factor, if not a strict pre-condition. Finally, the state, and society more broadly, must provide a sufficiently *laissez-faire* institutional structure, without over-riding power imbalances between transactional partners that would force one party to enter into an unfavourable transaction. And societal mores need to allow for the pursuit of financial goals.

The previous discussion has shown that in most financial sectors the necessary 'institutions' existed to ensure that sufficient information exchange could take place. Second, in all sectors, for large transactions, there were relatively low frictional costs. However, when the smaller end of the markets in size terms is examined, I believe that scribe costs would have been disproportionate, which would have increased the tendency to use lower-cost, informal, transaction methods.

Another important pre-condition is the ability to use mathematical skills to allow the use of reason to make a comparative judgement about a transaction. The mathematical skills were certainly in existence as is evidenced by the school exercises that have survived, some of which specifically look at questions related to financial transactions. It should be stressed that the mathematical skills necessary to assess profit are relatively simple: addition, subtraction, division and multiplication. There is no need for any knowledge of double entry book-keeping to satisfy the criterion. Constructing accounts is, as Rathbone showed, an indicator of the exercise of financial rationality but it is not a necessary pre-condition.[34] Assessment of risk may today involve more complicated mathematics, but

[34] Rathbone 1991: 383–6.

in Roman times it could have been on a qualitative basis and it could still be considered as effective. However, the existence within society of these mathematical abilities is no guarantee that they extended across the whole social strata and thus that all market participants had access to these skills.

Markets must also be sufficiently liquid, in the sense that there is sufficient trade volume to support competitive activity to allow comparative judgements to be made. The previous chapters have shown that the volume of transactions varies by market, and credit transactions are particularly frequent. Despite the evidence for the endemic nature of the rural credit market, some scholars have viewed economic life in the Egyptian village as essentially a 'natural, or barter, economy' and that farmers such as 'Kronion and his likes were chronically short of cash and constantly going into short-term debt'.[35] However, this argument fails to distinguish between an economy-wide systemic shortage of cash and a farmer's individual need for cash as the harvest varied according to the quality of the Nile flood and other environmental factors. The evidence from my modelling would suggest that tenant farmers in particular were indeed constantly in need of reciprocal support through the rural credit market. More recently, scholars have viewed rural Roman Egypt as being heavily monetised, and my data from the credit market would support this conclusion, at least for the first and second centuries.[36]

Finally, when we consider the pre-conditions for the existence of a profit-driven market we must recognise the influence of the state and wider society. If the state dictates prices and terms, or influences markets in more subtle ways, then participants, even if they wished to take actions based on financial rationality, may not be able to do so. The clearest evidence for state activity is in the wheat market, where the state's actions and pricing structures seem to have dampened price volatility and kept price increases lower than those that applied to other goods. This new evidence of differential pricing argues for a middle-ground view of the commodities market as reflecting a 'two-tier' economy with certain sectors of activity where the key actor is the state, and others subject to a greater degree to neoclassical market forces. The unpredictability of state actions, notably its demands for additional taxation or requisitioning of goods, will have complicated the assessment of risk. In general, though, there was a sufficiently *laissez-faire* economic institutional framework to allow financial rationality to be exercised in all the related economic sectors, and there were no over-riding societal mores or power imbalances that would have precluded the adoption of this behaviour.

[35] Lewis 1983: 71. See Kelly 2021b for a discussion of the frequency, and reasons, for farmers falling into debt.

[36] Rathbone 1996 and Rathbone 2013.

Anecdotal, demographic and contractual evidence

Anecdotal evidence that would help us understand how people thought about financial decisions is an appropriate area to examine to help answer the question posed. However, as may be expected in any dry collection of financial documents, the insights into how people thought, and possibly rationalised, their views on financial transactions are rare. Perhaps the clearest example, which encompasses both a desire to maximise profit and an understanding of risk, is a letter where the size of the vintage is said to be affecting not just the price of wine but also the price of vineyards as long-term investments.[37] The potential purchaser is seeking to maximise profit by purchasing the land at the most beneficial time, and there is an understanding of the risk of both poor and excessive harvests. Another example of a case where motives are attributed to an investor concerns a lender who has obtained use of a large area of land, seized as a result of failure to repay the loan, and who is receiving rents, and refuses to accept the repayment of the loan, preferring to retain the rents on the land 'having grown covetous of it owing to its great yearly productivity'.[38] This case shows that the decision as to which of two alternative financial transactions was preferable was likely to have been made on the basis of the expected profit, although there is no evidence of consideration of risk. There are other examples where the profit motive is clear. One document provides evidence of speculative activity, where a house is purchased and then immediately sold at a profit, but evidence for risk or for the relative assessment of the level of profit of one investment compared to another is more difficult to identify.[39] As to the actual assessment of the amount of profit for an investment, this is also rare, other than in the school exercises referred to above. But in one case the 'trustees' of a minor's estate calculate not only the gross income from the child's investments but also the net income after costs and taxes.[40] However, despite these partial and rare anecdotal examples of aspects of financial rationality it must be said that there is generally more evidence for behaviours which have no clear relation to profit, although the balance of evidence for motives varies from market to market.[41] Thus, if we are to find substantive evidence for financial rationality it must be derived by indirect means, and possible avenues are examined in the following paragraphs.

[37] *P.Giss.* 79 (*c.*AD 117).

[38] *P.Ryl.* II 119 (AD 62–66).

[39] *P.Lond.* III 1164f (AD 212).

[40] See Kraut 1984: 167–78.

[41] For land sales, investment motives appear to outnumber familial motives, but for house sales and loans respectively, the apparent balance is the opposite.

Table 15 Distribution of financially active population by age

Age Comparison	23–32	33–42	43–52	53–62	63–72	73+
Percentage of adult population[a]	33%	26%	20%	13%	6%	2%
Lenders n = 174	27%	**33%**	**24%**	9%	6%	2%
Borrowers n = 340	31%	26%	**27%**	11%	3%	1%
Land landlords n = 66	30%	21%	**23%**	**23%**	3%	0%
Land tenants n = 129	**36%**	25%	**24%**	10%	5%	1%

[a] Percentage of population over age 22. Activity by people below this age is well below the proportion of the population they represent.

The demographics underlying financial behaviour might provide us with clues as to the motivations of those who participated in the financial markets. In the previous chapters, the demographics of the market participants have been reviewed for different types of financial activity. These can now be brought together and compared with the estimated population structure by age.[42] These are shown in Table 15, for those types of transactions where we have more than 60 cases, with cases in bold indicating where activity was greater than would be expected. It can be seen that relative financial activity peaks in late maturity, from the mid-40s to the early 50s. It is difficult to draw any clear conclusions from this pattern but I suspect it reflects the age when an individual became the head of a wider family unit and had need to access the financial markets, either to support their family or to dispose of excess capital or assets. There is a relative peak in individuals leasing land in their 20s, which may similarly reflect the need to expand farming to meet the requirements of a young family, either within a wider family unit or independently established. There is a corresponding peak in land leasing for older groups in their late 50s and early 60s, which may reflect a declining physical ability in this age group to farm the land themselves, but the total number of available ages is low. This link to life events would tend to suggest that familial considerations were key to a decision, and the profit motive may not have been dominant. For instance, if due to the death of a parent you inherited land which you were unable to farm with your own family's resources you would be forced either to lease or to sell it to avoid it falling into disrepair. In these circumstances, making the deal at the right price may not have been the key factor in your decision-making process. The demographics as to gender may also be examined and the inability of women to act in certain transactions would have distorted the marketplace, with people making sub-optimal decisions

[42] See Kelly 2020: Appendix C for the derivation of the population distribution.

given a preference to contract with members of their own gender and a refusal or avoidance by men of contracting with women in certain roles. This gender bias would have decreased the liquidity and efficiency of the market for everyone.

One final demographic feature needs to be borne in mind when considering what would have been a key driver for behaviour. People would surely have been more willing to help a neighbour than an unconnected third party from another location. But just because someone was your neighbour does not automatically mean that the main driver was reciprocity. Thus localisation can be considered as an admittedly weak, but useful, indicator of reciprocity, and as we saw above, the housing and credit markets are highly localised compared to the agricultural land markets.

Turning to the legal structure of the underlying contracts, this is perhaps the area where we have the most compelling evidence of the rational consideration of the risks that faced each party. The assignment of these risks between the parties and protection against the financial consequences of these risks is often the main object of the clauses of the document. These documents may be considered to be 'relational contracts', with both parties having an interest in a successful conclusion. In the previous chapters, we have seen how complex these contracts were and the similarities with modern terms. Some of the most complex documents tend to relate to the sale of real estate and in many ways they typically resemble modern commercial sale and purchase agreements. As one might imagine, the parties are detailed, the price is provided and the property described. However, there may well be warranties provided by the vendor as to the legal validity of their ownership, the fact that the property is unencumbered by debt and that all taxes have been paid to date. The rights of the buyer and vendor to revenues, in this case usually harvests, are specified from a certain date. The penalties for breach of any warranty are also specified. Finally, the obligations for registering the document and the scope of its validity are laid out. This structure provides some additional security to the buyer, who generally has less information, even after conducting due diligence, than the vendor, and who is exposed to greater risk.

Contracts for leasing real estate are often more complicated than sales documents and tend to be more balanced since both parties are at risk. They impose obligations on the tenant to maintain the property and to return it in a good state at the end of the lease. However, there may also be obligations on the landlord to, for instance, provide oxen for ploughing. Again, this balanced approach to risks is a typical feature of modern leases. The balance between landlords' and tenants' interests is also shown in the rent relief clauses in the case of the Nile not flooding, which are common in Oxyrhynchite leases. These clauses ensured that the lease did not make unreasonable and unenforceable demands on the tenant in times when the

Nile did not flood, and also would have made the lease a more sustainable and stable transaction for the landlord.[43]

In passing, although I would reject any attempt to define any market as 'primitive' or 'modern', there are a striking number of features that are similar to those within historical or modern markets and may indicate similar, 'universal' thought processes and behaviours.[44]

Using outcomes as indicators of rationality

I have spent a great deal of time and ink setting out the outcomes from financial transactions. What was the likely return to an investor and how did those returns relate to the risk that the investor was taking? Did the outcome maximise return for a given risk? It is tempting to link an outcome where return is maximised for a given degree of risk, with the exercise of financial rationality, but this must be considered as circumstantial, rather than definitive, evidence.

A financially rational outcome does not necessarily imply the use of financial rationality in its derivation. A financially rational outcome could arise, not from the exercise of deliberate financial thought and action, but either by chance or from conventional actions which have evolved within society, as we saw above when we considered the 'coincidental' similarities with modern markets. These patterns of actions can arise in an economically evolutionary fashion. Consider a tenant who accepts a financially irrational transaction by leasing land at a high rent. This type of tenant will not survive since they cannot feed their family and prosper financially if they are paying too high a rent. The tenant who rents at a more reasonable rent, providing an equilibrium between landlord and tenant, will survive and prosper, whilst landlords renting at rates below the equilibrium level will tend to disappear and low rents will not be available for tenants. The establishment of this equilibrium level does not necessarily require, at any point, the exercise of any rational assessment on the part of the principals. This proposition is part of the evolutionary efficiency school within economic theory.[45]

[43] For a consideration of the balance of risks between landlords and tenants within the context of wider Roman law, see Kehoe 2015: 239–43, and for a wider consider of the economics behind different forms of land exploitation, see Otsuka et al. 1992.

[44] For instance, state intervention in the wheat markets, the one-third land/two-thirds building cost rule of thumb for the price of a house, the predominance of a 50/50 rent share between landlord and tenant in share-cropping land leases, contractual clauses in the real estate markets which mirror to a large degree those within modern contracts and similar interest rate levels for pawnbroking and mutual support institutions.

[45] See Ogilvie 2007: 656–8 for a discussion of evolutionary efficiency and economic institutions.

Conversely, outcomes which consistently do not meet the requirements of maximising return for a given risk cannot arise from the exercise of pure profit-making. These outcomes, although financially irrational, can still be socially rational. The drivers of behaviour in these cases must have been reciprocity, familial altruism, the acquisition of social capital or the imposed restrictions of the Roman state. Bearing in mind these constraints, the analysis of the different types of financial markets is set out below.

What was the dominant driver in each market?

The first market to examine is the credit market or, rather, the credit markets, since this market had a number of sub-sectors where different rules appear to have applied. The credit market can be split into three sub-sectors: the intra-village cash loan, the generally larger loans involving city-dwellers and loans in kind. Dealing with the intra-village loan, these loans were relatively small in size. They were generally unsecured and presumably in many cases lender and borrower were personally known to each other. Our best evidence as to interest rates suggests that 12 per cent was the typical interest rate, and the analysis of expected returns has shown that a lender would need to be more than 90 per cent confident that a borrower would not default to show even a small return. Also, the timing of the months of repayment show that these loans could typically only be payable after the harvest, and with a chance of the Nile not flooding sufficiently in perhaps 1 year in 12, this implies that many of the borrowers would have defaulted. Thus, an unsecured loan at 12 per cent interest, even to someone known personally by the lender, cannot be considered financially rational if the sole driver was the pursuit of profit. Neither could a deposit, which I have suggested would typically not have attracted any interest. The demographic evidence examined above would also suggest that the localised, gendered village credit market was driven by mutual support/reciprocity. Given the endemic nature of credit within successful agricultural societies it made perfect sense to lend to a neighbour who might then return the favour at some time in the future.

Turning to the second sub-sector of the credit market, cash loans involving city-dwellers were generally of a larger size and were more often secured on specific property than the village transactions. Here we can analyse the outcomes and show that they were indeed financially rational for the lender. There is a clear hierarchy of risk and return that indicates this financially rational nature. Lenders were willing, if the loan were to be secured, to accept a lower return on their investment than on an unsecured loan, at a higher, yet irrational rate. Pawnbrokers operated at interest rates similar to those which apply today, and presumably made a good profit. Larger loans with a single counterparty attracted lower interest rates than the smaller loans. Finally, the economic system was not destabilised by loans at rates of 12 per cent per annum or less. These loans were affordable to the borrower and thus from the lender's perspective this was a sustainable and repeatable investment. All the pre-conditions for the exercise of financial rationality were met in these loans, with the lender able to calculate the profit. And even with a 2 per cent tax on mortgages, large loans had relatively low transaction costs. The detailed clauses within the documentation of secured loans show that the lenders were aware of their risks and took action to mitigate them. And although compound interest was not explicitly provided for, lenders could, and did, effectively obtain the same result by rolling over loans or demanding the payment of interest at year or month end. We have little evidence for gearing, by which is meant borrowing money in order to invest in more productive exercises such as land exploitation, despite the very large number of transactions in the databases. However, this is entirely rational if economic conditions meant that a higher return could not be expected in land investment, and the average returns on land leasing are not sufficiently high to support borrowing costs. Finally, the market reacted rationally to the higher inflationary conditions of the late third or fourth centuries by increasing interest rates accordingly.

However, there was no strong trend to lending in kind, partly reflecting the very unpredictable nature of financial outcomes that I have modelled. The very unpredictable, volatile nature of the returns from lending in kind means that it was like a highly risky bet rather than an investment from the perspective of the lender. I would therefore suggest that this sub-sector of the credit market, along with the small village-based loan market, is unlikely to have been driven by financial rationality, although the very high interest rates do reflect a value framework with a consistent risk–return hierarchy.

Turning to the housing market, I believe that the evidence shows that the pre-conditions for the exercise of financial rationality did not exist. The relatively high frictional costs would have made housing leasing a less attractive investment proposition than leasing land. In addition, the difficulties with regard to information exchange, notably the intangible variability of the experience of sharing living spaces, would have made it problematic to commoditise a portion of a house for sale or rent. Even if the pre-conditions did exist, the evidence for a liquid competitive market is slim. House rents were heavily rounded and look conventional in structure. The liquidity in the market, at least that recorded in the papyri, was low compared to other financial transactions. The average spend per person on housing was also very low as a percentage of total income or expenditure. When we consider the relatively high level of intra-familial transactions and lack of formal leasing documentation, this seems to point to a market that was not primarily driven by the pursuit of profit. Of course, it should be noted that the data come from the rural nomes of Roman Egypt and it may well be that in Alexandria there was scope for commoditisation of the housing market with a larger peripatetic population and larger housing units that could be broken down into standard units and thus commoditised more easily than in the smaller urban sites in the rural nomes.

In contrast to the housing market, the markets for buying and renting land seem to have all the necessary pre-conditions for the exercise of financial rationality to take place, with relatively low frictional costs and sufficient information exchange. There are clear indications of the exercise of financial rationality in the pursuit of profit. Land sale and purchase documents and leases are complex documents. The land sale contracts go some way to protect the buyer against any information deficits they may have as to the nature of the land they are buying, whereas land leases are more balanced between the two parties. These contractual features indicate an understanding of the risks faced by the parties and try to mitigate these risks in a fashion that is entirely consistent with the exercise of financial rationality. This impression of rational behaviour is reinforced by the diversification of crops and plots seen within lease documents. There are no signs of conventional pricing in either land sales or leases, and within both types of documents we can see the exercise of judgement by the fact that in some cases the price of land or the rent applicable may vary for different plots of land within a single lease. Outcomes are financially rational and land ownership is an attractive financial proposition which produces returns that are comparable to those within the only other market available for investment with a similar risk profile, the secured credit market. Land sales show no seasonality of activity, suggesting that buyers and sellers were not driven to transact by poor or good harvests. This would have allowed the exercise of financial rationality after due consideration, rather than the principals being rushed into a decision. However, as may be expected, land leases follow the farming year and leases were generally contracted prior to sowing and rents paid after the harvest. This is also entirely financially rational from the perspective of both the landlord and the tenant. There are relatively few intra-familial transactions that might have been transacted on terms which were financially irrational if family ties and needs played a part. There is also evidence for the symbiotic relationship of landlords and tenants in the frequent instances of landlords dealing sympathetically with rent arrears. Tenants were not strongly tied to private landlords or dependent on them for both housing and land. This was thus not a society where there was typically a large power imbalance between landlord and tenant, which might otherwise have impeded the exercise of financial rationality by both parties. Finally, the land markets reacted to changing conditions in a manner that appears financially rational. In times of instability, such as the later third century, the term of leases decreases as

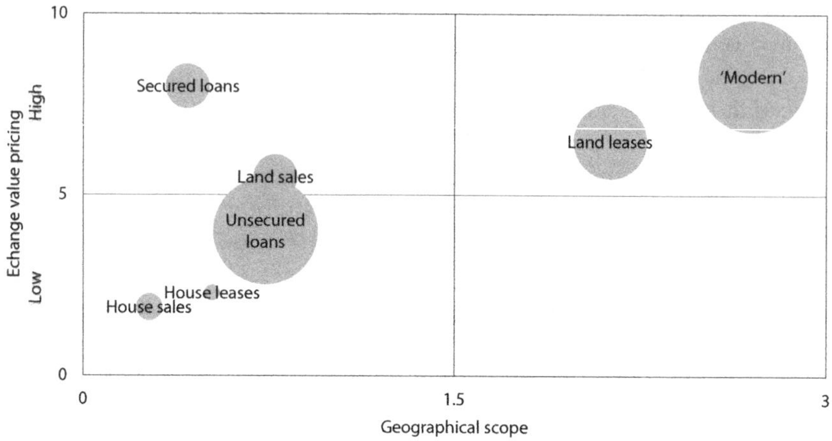

Figure 36 Market schematic

individuals seek to ensure that they have greater flexibility to deal with potentially fast-changing circumstances. In times of high inflation, there is a shift away from payment of rents for fodder land in cash towards other more inflation-proof commodities including cereals.

The nature of the various markets can be presented in the schematic shown in Figure 36, where the size of the circles represents the volume of the market, which is determined by the number of transactions. Along the horizontal axis the geographical scope of the market is plotted, which is based on the localisation ratio I determined above. In turn, the vertical axis is based on my assessment of whether pricing was driven by exchange value – determined by the degree of conventional/fractional and inter-family pricing, as calculated above. The size of the circles reflects the size of the markets concerned, based on the volume of turnover. A plot for a 'modern' geographically dispersed but integrated, competitive, market is provided by way of reference. In general, large circles in the upper right quadrant could be regarded as relatively efficient, geographically integrated, liquid markets. Small circles in the lower left quadrant would suggest inefficient, localised, illiquid markets.

Concluding remarks about the markets

My first conclusion of note is that we must think not of a single market but of a series of sectors and sub-sectors. To talk of 'the' Roman 'market economy' or 'bazaar' is inappropriate. In the commodities markets, we saw that wheat prices exhibited very different formats and developments over time compared to other goods. I have attributed this difference to reflect a two-tier market where the action of the state dampened price movements for the strategically important commodity of wheat whilst leaving other commodities to move more freely.

Turning to the nature of the markets themselves, in general, except for transactions at small amounts, the frictional costs were relatively low and would not have impeded the pursuit of profit by making transactions too costly to undertake. Information exchange would have been influenced and perhaps aided by the fact that most markets were strictly local, gendered and based on social networks. However, in turn, this localised nature and the fact that there is no evidence for professional intermediaries who could have assisted in matching principals and bridging information deficits would have reduced the competitive nature of the markets.

I have little or no direct evidence of the thoughts of market participants, so my assessment of what drove the markets must be derived from other data. My assessment is therefore subjective, and dependent on the emphasis I choose to give on my interpretations of that data. When I started to research the financial markets, reflecting my own life experience, I fully expected to see evidence of the pursuit of profit in all sectors and at all levels of society. However, I have come to the conclusion that the evidence relating to the unsecured loan market, of generally small, village-based, cash loans cannot be considered as a sector driven by financial rationality given the financially sub-optimal outcomes for a lender, but is one where reciprocity dominates. Similarly, lending of commodities has such a wide variability in outcomes that it can only be considered financially rational for a professional gambler. The rural housing market, with its poor liquidity, conventional pricing patterns, relative cheapness and the importance of intra-family transactions, is likely to have been driven by familial concerns.

However, although I cannot prove this indisputably, the secured cash loan and the agricultural land markets show all the features of market sectors driven by financial rationality. In conclusion, I believe that it is highly probable that the agricultural land and the secured credit markets were driven by the pursuit of profit, whilst the housing and unsecured credit markets were driven by familial needs and reciprocity respectively. I hope that these conclusions will assist in answering the central question as to the nature of the markets, which Scheidel described as vital to our understanding of 'the dynamics of Roman economic development and especially its limits and decline', particularly since the conditions and institutions that supported the markets of Roman Egypt also existed in many other provinces.[46]

[46] Scheidel 2012: 9.

Appendix

Assumptions used in modelling of financial outcomes

Details of the reasoning behind most of these assumptions can be found in my contribution to the forthcoming 'The Uncertain Past' volume, but the assumptions underlying the tenant/smallholder/petty landlord model are in the table below.

Number of adults	4
Initial number of children	0
'Farm' size (ha)	4.1
Value of land (dr. per ha)	500
Demography	Mortality and fertility such as to maintain stable population[a]
Wheat yield (multiple per unit seed, net after harvesting losses)	12.8
Wheat price (dr. per kg)	Median 0.265 inversely correlated to that year's wheat yield
Bread price (dr. per kg)	0.232
Year on year wheat yield variability (SD as percentage of mean) due to general conditions	20 per cent (but 8 per cent chance of Nile flood failure)
Yield variability (SD as percentage of mean) due to local factors (farmer skill, experience, soil/seed quality, availability of family labour)	5 per cent
Wheat seed (kg per ha sown)	110
Income from fallow land (dr. per ha)	160
Income from garden produce and hired labour per adult (dr. per year)	15
Income from hired labour per child (dr. per year)	Nil for children under 6, 7.5 for children 6 and over
Rent	50 per cent of total yield from land, rent relief if Nile does not flood

Transport costs to granary (kg wheat per ha)	27.4
Newborn abandonment trigger (normal distribution)	Mean 850 dr., with SD of 38 per cent of mean
Discretionary spend (normal distribution)	Mean 50 per cent of income, with SD of 15 per cent
Spoilage	5 per cent
Proportion fallow	50 per cent
Subsistence adult daily calorie requirement (following 'bare bones' subsistence basket)[b]	1,940
Child costs as percentage of adult	55 per cent
Interest rate on debt (p.a.)	12 per cent on cash, 50 per cent on kind
Return on savings (p.a.)	Average 8 per cent, with SD of 60 per cent of mean
Capitation taxes (adult male)	22.7 dr.
Land tax	1 and 1/7th artabas wheat and 0.5 dr. per aroura

[a] For fertility, the 'Gompertz' curve at Frier 1994: 325 was assumed. For infant mortality and marital data, see Bagnall & Frier 2006: 104, 117.
[b] Allen 2009: Table 16.3.

Assumptions used for returns on investment

The derivation of the principal assumptions for the model which is used to calculate returns on investment can be found in the relevant sections of my PhD thesis[1] and are the following:

- Risk of default (unsecured loans and land leases): 8 per cent
- Most likely cereal prices, where price y (in drachma per artaba) is determined at year x using the following formulae:

  Wheat: $y = -5E - 06x^3 + 0.0024x^2 - 0.2876x + 16.965$
  Barley: $y = 5E - 06x^3 - 0.0017x^2 + 0.173x + 1.818$.

- Wheat price variability: between 50 per cent and 140 per cent of most likely value.
- Barley price variability: between 55 per cent and 150 per cent of most likely value.

[1] Kelly 2020.

- Most likely Oxyrhynchite land prices, where price y (in drachma per aroura) is determined at year x using the following formula:

  Land: $y = 1.5E - 04x^3 - 0.0063x^2 + 10.1x - 56.3$.

- Land price variability: nil.

The size and derivation of frictional costs assumptions for land leasing are as follows.[2] For my purposes, the only relevant costs are those which impacted on the landowner and thus they must be attributed between the principal parties. There are frictional costs payable at the outset of any lease. There would have been fees payable to the scribe to draw up the lease document and there may also have been registration fees and taxes. As regards the scribe fees, or *grammatika*, these one might expect to have been paid for by the party who would have the greatest interest in recording in writing the transaction. Whilst a written lease would establish tenure for the tenant, it was certainly also in the landlord's interest, since having a written document would establish his title to the land, the amount of the rent and his powers over the tenant. However, in *P.Mich.* II 123, the Tebtunis *grapheion* archive, in five out of the six times that the name of the payer is recorded it is the tenant who is responsible for the payment of the *grammatikon*.[3] For the purposes of modelling the return on investment, it is thus assumed that the tenant was responsible for the *grammatikon* or other initial costs or any scribe costs related to rent receipts and no assumption is therefore required as to their size.

Therefore, no frictional costs payable by the landlord have been assumed for the drawing up of the lease. On occasion, however, there are ongoing costs associated with the landlord's obligations under the lease. In *P.Oxy.* LVII 3911 (AD 199), for example, the landlord needs to provide a team of oxen to assist the tenant. These costs are difficult to estimate and are rare so they are ignored. Transportation costs also occurred and would relate to the transport to the threshing floor and onwards to a granary or the taxes associated with such transport. Adams noted that transport costs to the granary were typically paid by the tenant, but there were exceptions such as *P.Tebt.* II 377 (AD 210) or *P.Coll.Youtie* I 27 (AD 165), where the landlord paid the transport costs.[4] When the landlord paid the transport costs, I have assumed that the typical cost was 1 drachma for every 8 artabas of wheat or barley for transport from the field to the threshing

[2] A recent collection of essays has provided some valuable insight into these frictional costs, but it does not provide all the necessary information to construct the assumptions needed for the calculation of returns; see Kehoe et al. 2015.

[3] *P.Mich.* II page 91.

[4] Adams 2007: 168.

floor and on to the granary.[5] This appears feasible when compared with the donkey hire costs and loads quoted by Adams.[6] I have not allowed for any subsequent transportation costs from the granary to any eventual point of sale.[7]

As regards taxation, Rowlandson stated that in almost all cases, taxes on land were met by the landlord and this is indeed the case for the vast majority of the leases I reviewed. A 'monoartaba' or 1 artaba land tax rate applied throughout the province at the start of the Roman period and although the rates of taxation changed under Diocletian, for the period under consideration the 1 artaba land tax is assumed to be applicable.[8] Thus, although there are variations in the taxes payable on private land, unless it is stated otherwise within the lease, it is assumed that the landlord was responsible for a land tax to the value of 1 artaba of wheat for each aroura. A supplement could also be payable and the taxation rate assumed including this supplement is eight-sevenths of an artaba of wheat per aroura.[9] I have assumed that the tax was payable whatever the crop sown or the state of the Nile flood that year given the lack of direct evidence for tax refunds, although if land became habitually dry the land might be re-classified.[10] If the tenant is stated to pay the tax without

[5] I have based my estimated costs on the figures supplied in three documents. The first, *SB* XX 14315 (AD 32–33), where 5 artabas of wheat is stated to be the transportation charges in a lease where the rent is 260 artabas when the land is under wheat. At a typical price of 8 drachmas per artaba, this amounts to 1 drachma for every 6.5 artabas. The second document is *P.Oxy.* LXII 4336 (AD 170), where the rate for transport paid by a tenant is equal to 8 drachmas for just over 73 artabas of wheat and which therefore equates to around 1 drachma for every 9 artabas. The third, *P.Lond.* III 1223 (AD 121), has a charge of one and two-thirds artabas for 100 artabas of barley, which can also be estimated at around 1 drachma for every 9 artabas, assuming a price of barley of 6.5 drachmas per artaba. I have taken an intermediate assumption of 1 drachma for every 8 artabas.

[6] See Adams 2007: 11 for information on the loads and costs of donkey hire. Adams bases his daily cost of half a drachma on Drexhage, but there is evidence for higher rates in, for instance, *P.Mil.Vogl.* VII 302 (AD 151) and *P.Mil.Vogl.* VII 304 (AD 166).

[7] I have also ignored the relatively small taxes related to transportation and the granary such as the *foretron*, *sitologicon* and *sitometricon*. See Johnson 1936: 513 for a description of these taxes.

[8] Wallace 1938: 11–19 details the levels of land taxation by nome and a useful summary of taxation rates for private land is provided in Rowlandson 1987: 292.

[9] See Wallace 1938: 38–41, where he notes that such a surcharge is prescribed in the *gnomon* for taxation of land in the Arsinoite nome, and Rowlandson 1996: 54 for a confirmation of a similar surcharge applying in the Oxyrhynchite. For the equivalent rates in the period after AD 274, see Bagnall 1985a: 300–1.

[10] For the Nile flood question, see Wallace 1938: 19. I am not aware of any document which foresees relief on private land taxation due to the state of the Nile flood. Mountford, whilst arguing that tax relief was granted in cases of insufficient flooding

any reimbursement by the landlord, then the tax is ignored. The tax on land raising grain, the ***dikoinikia***, of 1/20th of wheat per aroura, is also assumed to be payable.[11] Finally, another tax that is normally payable by the landlord is the ***naubion*** tax, which is estimated at half a silver drachma per aroura.[12]

The most difficult tax to estimate is the crown tax. Wallace sees evidence for this tax applying to real estate as being relatively scarce before the late second century when he views it as an annual rather than exceptional extraction and related to land.[13] I have assumed that a crown tax of 8 drachmas per aroura applied on an annual basis from AD 200 onwards. I have not, however, allowed for exceptional demands by the state for requisitions or for any additional costs arising from ***epibole***, an obligation which could apply to ownership of a privately owned piece of land to farm some other, presumably less fertile, plot of public land, on the grounds that the sizes of ***epibole*** land concerned were relatively small and even if a profit was unlikely to be made from this obligation the owner may have been able to cover their costs.[14]

Turning to loans, I made the following assumptions as to frictional costs. Lerouxel separates transaction costs in credit markets into three types: type 1 – initial costs on recording and registering and taxation; type 2 – the cost of intermediation or the 'search costs associated with creditors and debtors finding each other'; and type 3 – the costs associated with a debtor's default.[15] Type 2 search costs are not capable of quantification and may be zero when the parties are known to each other. I would agree with

through *abrochia* declarations of insufficient flooding, admits that 'no declaration, however, makes any express claim for a reduction in tax'. Mountford 2012: 70.

11 Wallace 1938: 12. I have assumed that this is payable only when the land concerned is under wheat and at the same time under the same conditions as the main 1 artaba land tax.

12 *P.Heid.Inv.* G 24 l.10–13 gives 14 drachmas as the cash public charges for two years for 13 arouras – of the same order of magnitude as that within *P.Achm.* 9 (late second century), where the rate is 2.25 obols per aroura.

13 Based on Wallace 1938: 282–4, where he stated that private land in the Oxyrhynchite nome, in the third century, paid at a rate of 8 drachmas per aroura. See also Bowman 1967 for a description of the documents then known to contain references to crown tax, and Johnson 1936: 576 for a general description; for an updated list, see *P.Koeln.* II 91, to which add *BGU* XV 2503–9 and subsequent publications. Note that there is no specific mention of crown tax in any of the 105 leases upon which our estimates of sustainable term return are based, but this is not surprising since when taxes are mentioned generally there is only an overarching reference to public dues.

14 See Rowlandson 1996: 88–90. I have also ignored the *catoecic arithmetikon* on the grounds that it is a form of capitation tax rather than a land tax, following Wallace 1938: 176.

15 Lerouxel 2015: 165.

Lerouxel that it is difficult to know whether intermediation occurred and the costs associated with any intermediation but there is no direct evidence for these costs existing.[16] Type 3 costs are dealt with by modelling the default rate.

Type 1 costs certainly did exist and varied by category of loan. When a mortgage was agreed, there were three costs arising: scribe costs, registration costs and taxes. As regards scribe and registration costs, Lerouxel suggests that since both parties were likely to have 'received a copy of the contract, it is reasonable to assume that the fee … was split and paid jointly'. I follow this assumption and assume that the fee was split 50/50 between lender and borrower.[17] The other type 1 costs associated with a mortgage are taxes and a conveyancing tax amounting to 2 per cent of the value of the loan applied, and I have assumed that this is a cost for the lender.[18] For unsecured cash loans and loans in kind, I have assumed that the scribe costs similarly were split 50/50 but were somewhat less than for mortgages, reflecting the fact that the documentation was simpler.[19] Finally, I have assumed that for loans in kind, any transportation costs were met by the borrower since the loans usually contain provisions for the repayment to be made by the borrower at a specified place.

[16] Lerouxel 2015: 165.

[17] Lerouxel 2015: 166. I have assumed that on average the scribe and registration costs were 12 drachmas, as is the case in *P.Mich.* V 238 l.17–18 (AD 46) but noting that the costs will have depended on how many copies were required and that having the mortgage registered was only an option for the lender, as shown in *P.Oxy.* III 506 (AD 143). Where it is necessary to model the cash value of barley and wheat in loans in kind to compare with type 1 cash costs, the same assumptions as to values per artaba over time as in the previous chapter have been made.

[18] Lerouxel stated that it is certain that the lender alone paid this tax (Lerouxel 2015: 167), and that is the general impression that the papyri present, but there is at least one exception: *P.Oxy.* II 348 (late first century), where the debtor pays the tax. The mortgage conveyancing tax was renewable and paid each year for longer duration loans and I have assumed that the full 2 per cent tax was payable even if the term of the loan was less than one year.

[19] I have assumed 4 drachmas based on the median calculated from the Tebtunis *grapheion* register: Yitfach 2015a: 155n.37. I do not believe that there would have been any obligatory registration fees payable or taxes applicable.

Glossary

Aroura

This is a measure of land area and is assumed to be equivalent to 2,760m^2.

Artaba

This is a measure of dry volume used for produce such as wheat. It is assumed to be equivalent to 38.8 litres. The artaba was divided into choenices, the number varying according to local practice and date. In any calculations I have assumed 40 choenices to the artaba, although there is also evidence for 48 choenices to the artaba being used.

Best-fit regression lines

These are the lines which are the closest fit to the data points on a scatter chart. They reduce the error of the line (the distance from the line to the point) to the minimum by calculating the sum of the squares of the difference between the data points and the line. Regression lines may be either a straight line or curved, as they follow a mathematical function such as a polynomial equation.

Bikos

This is a measure of land area used in urban areas, for instance in defining the size of vacant lots. Its equivalent size in modern terms is unknown.

Correlation coefficients

A correlation coefficient is a numerical measure of the statistical relationship between two variables and in particular it measures how closely they move together. Correlation coefficients vary between −1 and +1, where +1 indicates that the two variables move in tandem and −1 when they move in opposite ways.

Drachma

The principal monetary unit used in Roman Egypt. The silver drachma was normally traded using the Alexandrian silver tetradrachm coin, which had a value of 4 drachmas, and this explains the tendency that we see in the transactions for amounts to be in multiples of four (e.g., 24, 28 drachmas, etc.). For large amounts, these were often expressed in talents, which were each equal to 6,000 silver drachmas.

Certain transactions in the earlier part of the period express prices in bronze drachmas but these prices may be considered as conventional in nature rather than as exchange values. In the latter part of the period, after AD 274, there appears to be a divergence between different forms of money, with units of account differing from coinage in circulation, and this follows on from Aurelian's currency reform. Given the nominal inflation that occurred in silver drachma units, prices and rents tended to be described in myriads of drachma (10,000) or gold solidi.

Keramion monochoron

This is a measure of liquid volume often used for wine. It is assumed to be equivalent to 7.3 litres. The *keramion* is a jar and there are different types, including: the *dichoron*, which is assumed to be twice the volume of the *monochoron*, and the *oxyrhnchition*, which is assumed to be 1.5 times the volume of the *monchoron*. The *kotule* is a smaller measure and 36 are assumed to the *monochoron*. There are a number of other measures of liquid volume or jar descriptions used within the documents analysed. These are the *chous*, *hemikadion*, *knidion*, *sextarius* and *spathion*.

Logarithmic scale

A logarithmic scale is a non-linear scale used when a quantity has a wide range. It is particularly useful when displaying data which may be growing geometrically.

Mann–Whitney U test

A statistical test to determine whether two samples come from populations with the same distribution.

Monte Carlo simulation

This is the repetition of a process a large number of times using a random number generator to produce a series of possible stochastically derived outcomes.

Obol

A fraction of a drachma. I have generally assumed that there were 7 obols to the silver drachma after AD 190 and 6 obols per drachma for the earlier part of the period unless there is evidence to the contrary. The obol could further be divided into chalkoi and 8 chalkoi are assumed per obol.

Polynomial
An equation consisting of more than two algebraic terms which contains different powers of the same variable. A polynomial is given an order according to the highest order in the equation. For instance, $y = x + 1$ is a first-order polynomial, $y = x^2 + 3x + 2$ is a second-order polynomial and $y = x^3 + 2x^2 - x - 2$ is a third-order polynomial.

Portfolio
A combination of investments held by an individual or a family. In Roman Egypt this could contain commodities (such as slaves or wheat), real estate (whether agricultural, commercial or residential), commercial enterprises and loans. In contrast to a modern investment portfolio, there were no quoted bonds or stocks/shares available for investment. The composition of a portfolio impacts both the return achieved and the risk that the investor faced.

R^2 coefficient
R^2 or r^2, and pronounced 'R squared', is the coefficient of determination, and is the proportion of the variance in the dependent variable that is predictable from the independent variable. It is commonly used to determine the degree to which a line fits the data from a scatter diagram. The higher the R^2 coefficient, the better the line fits the data; if all the data points were on the line the fit would be exact and the coefficient would be equal to 1, and if the data were randomly distributed the coefficient would be 0.

Rate of return
The annual financial benefit to an investor from placing the investment expressed as a percentage of the original investment. In the case of a loan it is equivalent to the interest received, when expressed as a percentage of the principal lent. From other investments it may include both income received and capital gain.

Relative standard deviation
This is a measure for comparing the variability of a sample from one type of data to another. It is the standard deviation divided by the mean of the sample.

Secured loan
A loan whereby the lender has the right to seize specific property in the event of a default by the borrower in repaying the loan or the interest attaching to it. A mortgage is a form of secured loan. An unsecured loan is

one where the lender has no right to any specific property of the borrower but will still have the right to seek redress in the courts if the borrower defaults.

Standard deviation

The standard deviation is a measure that is used to quantify the amount of variability of a set of data points. A low standard deviation indicates that the data points tend to be close to the mean of the set, whilst a high standard deviation indicates that the data points are spread out over a wider range. It measures the sum of the square of the difference between the data points and the mean.

Stochastic model

Stochastic models are models whose inputs and outputs are probability distributions rather than discrete values. In this they differ from deterministic models, which produce a single output or answer. In order to define the probability distribution, assumptions need to be made as to the minimum lower bound, most likely value and maximum upper bound of each variable. A further assumption needs to be made as to the likelihood of a variable taking a value within the range set by the minimum and maximum bounds.

Z-test

When the means (or averages) of two samples are compared, a two-sample Z-test can be used to determine the level of statistical significance of any difference between the means. This compares the means of the two samples and determines the probability that they are the same.

Bibliography

Adams, C. (2007) *Land Transport in Roman Egypt: A Study of Economics and Administration in a Roman Province.* Oxford.

Allen, R.C. (2009) 'How Prosperous Were the Romans? Evidence from Diocletian's Price Edict (AD 301)', in A.K. Bowman and A. Wilson (eds), *Quantifying the Roman Economy: Methods and Problems.* Oxford: 327–45.

Alston, R. (1995) *Soldier and Society in Roman Egypt: A Social History.* London.

——. (2002) *The City in Roman and Byzantine Egypt.* London.

Andreau, J. (1999) *Banking and Business in the Roman World.* Cambridge.

——. (2000) 'Les Intérêts des prêts dans les tablettes de Murecine', *Cahiers du Centre Gustave Glotz* 11: 151–9.

——. (2010) *L'Économie du monde romain.* Paris.

——. (2020) 'Capital and Investment in the Campanian Tablets', in P. Erdkamp et al. (eds), *Capital, Investment, and Innovation in the Roman World.* Oxford: 417–33.

Andreau, J. and J. Maucourant (1999) 'À propos de la rationalité économique dans l'antiquité gréco-romaine: Une interprétation des thèses de D. Rathbone', *Topoi* 9: 47–102.

Bagnall, R.S. (1977) 'Price in "Sales on Delivery"', *Greek, Roman and Byzantine Studies* 18: 85–96.

——. (1985a) 'Agricultural Productivity and Taxation in Later Roman Egypt', *Transactions of the American Philological Association* 115: 289–308.

——. (1985b) *Currency and Inflation in Fourth Century Egypt.* Atlanta, GA.

——. (1992) 'Landholding in Late Roman Egypt: The Distribution of Wealth', *Journal of Roman Studies* 82: 128–49.

——. (1993a) 'Managing Estates in Roman Egypt: A Review Article', *Bulletin of the American Society of Papyrologists* 30: 127–35.

——. (1993b) *Egypt in Late Antiquity.* Princeton, NJ.

——. (2002) 'The Effects of Plague: Model and Evidence', *Journal of Roman Archaeology* 15: 114–20.

——. (2011) *Everyday Writing in the Graeco-Roman East.* Berkeley, CA.

Bagnall, R.S. and G. Bransbourg (2020) 'The Constantian Monetary Revolution', in T. Faucher (ed.), *Money Rules! The Monetary Economy of Egypt: From Persians until the Beginning of Islam.* Cairo: 367–92.

Bagnall, R.S and R. Cribiore (2015) *Women's Letters from Ancient Egypt, 300 BC–AD 800.* Ann Arbor, MI.

Bagnall, R.S. and B.W. Frier (2006) *The Demography of Roman Egypt*. Cambridge.

Bandi, L. (1937) 'I conti privati nei papiri dell'Egitto greco-romano', *Aegyptus* 17: 349–451.

Banerjee, A.V. and E. Duflo (2011) *Poor Economics*. New York.

Bang, P.F. (2008) *The Roman Bazaar: A Comparative Study of Trade and Markets in a Tributary Empire*. Cambridge.

Bange, M. (2014) *Kreditgeld in der römischen Antike: Ursprünge, Entstehung, Übertragung und Verbreitung*. Rahden.

Beard, M. (2015) *SPQR: A History of Ancient Rome*. London.

Biggart, N.W. (2001) 'Banking on Each Other: The Situational Logic of Rotating Savings and Credit Associations', *Advances in Qualitative Organization Research* 3: 129–52.

Binswanger, H. and M. Rosenzweig (1993) 'Wealth, Weather Risk and the Composition and Profitability of Agricultural Investments', *Economic Journal* 103.416: 56–78.

Blouin, K. (2010) 'An Arsinoite Loan of Money with Interest in Kind', *Bulletin of the American Society of Papyrologists* 47: 93–110.

——. (2014) *Triangular Landscapes: Environment, Society, and the State in the Nile Delta under Roman Rule*. Oxford.

Boak, A. (1955) 'The Population of Roman and Byzantine Karanis', *Historia: Zeitschrift für Alte Geschichte* 4: 157–62.

Boak, A. and H.C. Youtie (1960) *The Archive of Aurelius Isidorus*. Ann Arbor, MI.

Bogaert, R. (2000) 'Les Opérations des banques de l'Égypte romaine', *Ancient Society* 30: 135–269.

Bonneau, D. (1971) *Le Fisc et le Nil: incidences des irrégularités de la crue du Nil sur la fiscalité foncière dans l'Égypte grecque et romaine*. Paris.

Bourdieu, P. (1986) 'The Forms of Capital', in J.G. Richardson (ed.), *Handbook of Theory and Research for the Sociology of Education*. New York: 142–58.

Bowman, A.K. (1967) 'The Crown Tax in Roman Egypt', *Bulletin of the American Society of Papyrologists* 4: 59–74.

——. (1971) *The Town Councils of Roman Egypt*. Toronto.

——. (1985) 'Landholding in the Hermopolite Nome in the Fourth Century AD', *Journal of Roman Studies* 75: 137–63.

——. (2013) 'Agricultural Production in Egypt', in A.K. Bowman and A. Wilson (eds), *The Roman Agricultural Economy: Organization, Investment and Production*. Oxford: 219–54.

Bowman, A.K. and A. Wilson (eds) (2009) *Quantifying the Roman Economy: Methods and Problems*. Oxford.

Bransbourg, G. (2012) 'Rome and the Economic Integration of Empire', Institute for the Study of the Ancient World Papers 3. http://doi.org/2333.1/280gb73f (accessed 20 December 2018).

——. (2014) 'Les Taux d'intérêt flottants des Sulpicii', in C. Apicela, M.-L. Haack and F. Lerouxel (eds), *Les Affaires du Monsieur Andreau: économie et société du monde romain*. Bordeaux: 123–36.

Briggs, C. (2009) *Credit and Village Society in Fourteenth-Century England.* Oxford.
Browne, G.M. (1968) 'Withdrawal from Lease', *Bulletin of the American Society of Papyrologists* 5: 17–24.
Cagan, P. (1956) 'The Monetary Dynamics of Hyperinflation', in M. Friedman (ed.), *Studies in the Quantity Theory of Money.* Chicago: 25–117.
Caldwell, J.C. (2005) 'On Net Intergenerational Wealth Flows: An Update', *Population and Development Review* 2: 721–40.
Camilli, L. and S. Sorda (eds) (1993) *L'inflazione' nel quarto secolo D.C.* Rome.
Carliner, M. and E. Marya (2016) 'Rental Housing: An International Comparison', Harvard Joint Centre for Housing Studies Working Paper. www.jchs.harvard.edu/sites/default/files/international_rental_housing_carliner_marya.pdf (harvard.edu) (accessed 20 July 2021).
Carrié, J.-M. (1997) 'L'Arithmétique sociale de l'économie agraire: prix de la terre, rente foncière et prix des céréales dans l'Égypte romano-byzantine', in J. Andreau, P. Briant and R. Descat (eds), *Économie antique: prix et formation des prix dans les économies antiques.* Saint-Bertrand-de-Comminges: 121–46.
——. (2003) 'Solidus et credit: qu'est-ce que l'or a pu changer', in E. Lo Cascio (ed.), *Credito e moneta nel mondo romano.* Bari: 265–80.
Christesen, P. (2003) 'Economic Rationalism in Fourth Century BCE Athens', *Greece and Rome* 50: 31–56.
CIL [*Corpus Inscriptionum Latinarum*], ed. Theodor Mommsen et al. 17 vols. (Berlin 1853–).
Claytor, W.G. (2013) 'A Schedule of Contracts and a Private Letter: P. Fay. 344', *Bulletin of the American Society of Papyrologists* 50: 77–121.
——. (2015) 'Donkey Sales from the "grapheion" of Kerkesoucha', *Zeitschrift fur Papyrologie und Epigraphik* 194: 201–8.
Connor, A.J. (2014) 'Temples as Economic Agents in Early Roman Egypt: The Case of Tebtunis and Soknopaiou Nesos', unpublished PhD thesis, University of Cincinnati.
Cuomo, S. (2001) *Ancient Mathematics.* London.
Currie, J.M. (1981) *The Economic Theory of Agricultural Land Tenure.* Cambridge.
Cuvigny, H. and K. Lach-Urgacz (2020) 'Ὀρεινὸν κέρμα. Monetary Circulation in the Praesidia of the Eastern Desert during the Principate', in T. Faucher (ed.), *Money Rules! The Monetary Economy of Egypt: From Persians until the Beginning of Islam.* Cairo: 309–41.
Drexhage, H. (1991) *Priese, Mieten/Pachten, Kosten und Lohne im römischen Ägypten bis zum Regierungsantritt Diokletians.* Sankt Katharinen.
Duncan-Jones, R.P. (1996) 'The Impact of the Antonine Plague', *Journal of Roman Archaeology* 9: 108–36.
Elliott, C.P. (2020) *Economic Theory and the Roman Monetary Economy.* Cambridge.

Erdkamp, P. (2005) *The Grain Market in the Roman Empire: A Social, Political and Economic Study*. Cambridge.

Ermatinger, J.W. (1996) *The Economic Reforms of Diocletian*. Sankt Katharinen.

Finckh, E.F. (1962) *Das Zinsrecht der gräko-ägyptischen Papyri*. Nuremberg.

Finley, M.I. (1999) *The Ancient Economy*. London.

Foraboschi, D. and A. Gara (1981) 'Sulla differenza tra tassi di interesse in natura e in moneta nell'Egitto graeco-romano', in R.S. Bagnall, G.M. Browne, A.E. Hanson and L. Koenen (eds), *Proceedings of the Sixteenth International Congress of Papyrology*. Chicago: 335–43.

Fourcade, M. (2007) 'Theories of Markets and Theories of Society', *American Behavorial Scientist* 50: 1015–34.

Foxhall, L. (1990) 'The Dependent Tenant: Land Leasing and Labour in Italy and Greece', *Journal of Roman Studies* 80: 97–114.

France, J. (1998) 'Three Papyri from Theadelpheia in Gent', *Zeitschrift für Papyrologie und Epigraphik* 123: 135–44.

Frier, B.W. (1994) 'Natural Fertility and Family Limitation in Roman Marriage', *Classical Philology* 89: 318–23.

Frier, B.W. and D. Kehoe (2007) 'Law and Economic Institutions', in W. Scheidel, Ian Morris and Richard P. Saller (eds), *The Cambridge Economic History of the Greco-Roman World*. Cambridge: 113–44.

Gallant, T. (1991) *Risk and Survival in Ancient Greece: Reconstructing the Rural Domestic Economy*. Oxford.

Gondal, S. (2015) 'The Dowry System in India: Problem of Dowry Deaths', *Journal of Indian Studies* 1: 37–41.

Graeber, D. (2014) *Debt: The First 5,000 Years*. New York.

Granovetter, M. (1985) 'Economic Action and Social Structure: The Problem of Embeddedness', *American Journal of Sociology* 91.3: 481–510.

Haklai, M. (2011) 'Aurelian's Monetary Reforms: Between Debasement and Public Trust', *Chiron* 41: 1–39.

——. (2020) 'Credit and Financial Capital in Roman Egypt', in P. Erdkamp, K. Verboven and Arjan Zuiderhoek (eds), *Capital, Investment and Innovation in the Roman World*. Oxford: 437–59.

Harl, K.W. (2012) 'From Aurelian to Diocletian: Financing Imperial Recovery by Coinage Debasements and Fiduciary Currencies', in J.H. Munro (ed.), *Money in the Pre-Industrial World*. London: 33–44.

Harper, K. (2016) 'People, Plagues, and Prices in the Roman World: The Evidence from Egypt', *Journal of Economic History* 76: 803–39.

Harris, W. (1993) 'Between Archaic and Modern: Some Current Problems in the History of the Roman Economy', in W. Harris (ed.), *The Inscribed Economy*. Ann Arbor, MI: 11–29.

——. (1994) 'Child-Exposure in the Roman Empire', *Journal of Roman Studies* 84: 1–22.

——. (2006) 'A Revisionist Review of Roman Money', *Journal of Roman Studies* 96: 1–24.

——. (2008) 'The Nature of Roman Money', in W. Harris (ed.), *The Monetary Systems of the Greeks and Romans*. Oxford: 174–207.
——. (2011) 'Poverty and Destitution in the Roman Empire', in W. Harris, *Rome's Imperial Economy*. Oxford: 27–54.
Hennig, D. (1967) *Untersuchungen zur Bodenpacht im ptolemäisch-römischen Ägypten*. Munich.
——. (1972) 'Die Arbeitsverpflichtungen der Pächter in Landpachtverträgen aus dem Faijum', *Zeitschrift für Papyrologie und Epigraphik* 9: 111–31.
Herrmann, J. (1958) *Studien zur Bodenpacht im Recht der graeco-aegyptischen Papyri*. Munich.
——. (1962) 'Zinssätze und Zinsgeschäfte im Recht der gräko-ägyptischen Papyri', *Journal of Juristic Papyrology* 14: 23–31.
Hin, S. (2013) *The Demography of Roman Italy*. Cambridge.
Hobson, D. (1983) 'Women as Property Owners in Roman Egypt', *Transactions of the American Philological Association* 113: 311–21.
——. (1984a) 'Agricultural Land and Economic Life in Soknopaiou Nesos', *Bulletin of the American Society of Papyrologists* 21: 89–109.
——. (1984b) 'The Role of Women in the Economic Life of Roman Egypt: A Case Study from First Century Tebtunis', *Échos du Monde Classique* 28: 373–90.
——. (1985) 'House and Household in Roman Egypt', *Yale Classical Studies* 28: 211–29.
Hollis, M. and E. Nell (1975) *Rational Economic Man: A Philosophical Critique of Neo-Classical Economics*. Cambridge.
Homer, S. (1977) *A History of Interest Rates*. 2nd ed. New Brunswick, NJ.
Hoogendijk, F. (2006) 'P.Vindob. G 31933: Griechische Übersetzung einer demotisch-griechischen Hauskaufurkunde', *Zeitschrift für Papyrologie und Epigraphik* 156: 199–216.
Hopkins, K. (1995–96) 'Rome, Taxes, Rent and Trade', *Kodai: Journal of Ancient History* 6–7: 41–75.
Hopkins, M.K. (1980) 'Brother–Sister Marriage in Roman Egypt', *Comparative Studies in Society and History* 22: 303–54.
Howgego, C. (1992) 'The Supply and Use of Money in the Roman World 200 B.C. to A.D. 300', *Journal of Roman Studies* 82: 1–31.
Howgego, C., K. Butcher, M. Ponting and V. Heuchert (2010) 'Coinage and the Roman Economy in the Antonine Period: The View from Egypt', Oxford Roman Economy Project Working Paper. Oxford.
Huebner, S.R. (2013) *The Family in Roman Egypt: A Comparative Approach to Intergenerational Solidarity and Conflict*. Cambridge.
Husson, G. (1983) *Οἰκία: Le Vocabulaire de la maison privée en Égypte d'après les papyrus grecs*. Paris.
Johnson, A.C. (1936) *Roman Egypt to the Reign of Diocletian*, vol. 2, *An Economic Survey of Ancient Rome*. Baltimore, MD.
Jones, A.H.M. (1964) *The Later Roman Empire, 284–602: A Social, Economic and Administrative Survey*. 2 vols. Oxford.

Kabeer, N. (1999) *The Conditions and Consequences of Choice: Reflections on the Measurement of Women's Empowerment.* Geneva.

Kahneman, D. and A. Tversky (1979) 'Prospect Theory: An Analysis of Decision under Risk', *Econometrica* 47.2: 263–92.

Kay, P. (2014) *Rome's Economic Revolution.* Oxford.

Kehoe, D. (1992) *Management and Investment on Estates in Roman Egypt during the Early Empire.* Bonn.

——. (1997) *Investment, Profit and Tenancy.* Ann Arbor, MI.

——. (2007) *Law and Rural Economy in the Roman Empire.* Ann Arbor, MI.

——. (2015) 'Contracts, Agency and Transaction Costs in the Roman Economy', in D. Kehoe, D. Ratzan and U. Yiftach (eds), *Law and Transaction Costs in the Ancient Economy.* Ann Arbor, MI: 231–52.

Kehoe, D., D. Ratzan and U. Yiftach (eds) (2015) *Law and Transaction Costs in the Ancient Economy.* Ann Arbor, MI.

Kelly, P.V. (2020) 'Risk and Return in Roman Egypt: Were Markets in Roman Egypt Driven by Financial Rationality?' unpublished PhD thesis, King's College London.

——. (2021a) 'Third-Century Inflation Reassessed', *Theoretical Roman Archaeological Journal* 4(1).5: 1–22.

——. (2021b) 'Risks for Farming Families in the Roman World', in P. Erdkamp, J.G. Manning and K. Verboven (eds), *Climate Change and Ancient Societies in Europe and the Near East: Diversity in Collapse and Resilience.* Cham: 485–503.

——. (2022) 'Was r greater than g? Evidence from Roman Egypt', in M. Koedijk and N. Morley (eds), *Capital in Classical Antiquity.* Cham: 261–86.

——. (forthcoming a) 'Children and their Impact on Family Finances in Roman Egypt', in M. Lavan, D. Jew and B. Danon (eds), *The Uncertain Past: Probability in Ancient History.* Cambridge.

——. (forthcoming b) 'The Real Estate Markets in Roman Egypt', in M. Garcia Morcillo and C. Rosillo-López (eds), *The Real Estate Market in the Roman World.* London.

Kraut, B.H. (1984) 'Seven Heidelberg Papyri concerning the Office of Exegetes', *Zeitschrift für Papyrologie und Epigraphik* 55: 167–90.

Kruse, T. and B.E. Woytek (2020) '"(Old) Ptolemaic" and "New" Coins in 3rd-Century AD Egypt: A Reassessment of the Papyrological and Numismatic Evidence', in T. Faucher (ed.), *Money Rules! The Monetary Economy of Egypt: From Persians until the Beginning of Islam.* Cairo: 341–66.

Kulkarni, V.S. (2011) *Women's Empowerment and Microfinance: An Asian Perspective Study.* Rome.

Lavan, M. (2016) 'The Spread of Roman Citizenship, 14–212 CE: Quantification in the Face of High Uncertainty', *Past & Present* 230.1: 3–46.

Lavan, M., D. Jew and B. Danon (eds) (forthcoming) *The Uncertain Past: Probability in Ancient History.* Cambridge.

Lerouxel, F. (2008) 'La Banque privée romaine et le marché du crédit dans les tablettes de Murecine et les papyrus d'Égypte romaine', in K. Verboven, K. Vandorpe and V. Chankowski (eds), *Pistoi dia tèn technèn: Bankers, Loans and Archives in the Ancient World.* Studies in Honour of Raymond Bogaert. Leuven: 169–97.

——. (2012a) 'Des prêts sans intérêt? Le taux d'intérêt dans le nome Oxyrhynchite avant 79 après J.-C.', *Zeitschrift für Papyrologie und Epigraphik* 181: 161–72.

——. (2012b) 'Le Marché du crédit privé, la bibliothèque des acquêts et les tâches publiques en Égypte romaine', *Annales* 4: 943–76.

——. (2015) 'The βιβλιοθήκη ἐγκτήσεων and Transaction Costs in the Credit Market of Roman Egypt (30 B.C.E.–ca. 170 C.E.)', in D. Kehoe, D. Ratzan and U. Yiftach (eds), *Law and Transaction Costs in the Ancient Economy.* Ann Arbor, MI: 162–84.

——. (2016) *Le Marché du crédit dans le monde romain (Égypte et Campanie).* Rome.

Lewis, D. (2018) 'Behavioural Economics and Economic Behaviour in Classical Athens', in M. Canevaro, A. Erskine, B. Gray and J. Ober (eds), *Ancient Greek History and Contemporary Social Science.* Edinburgh: 15–46.

Lewis, N. (1983) *Life in Egypt under Roman Rule.* Oxford.

Litinas, N. (2019) 'References to Sales of Donkeys'. www.philology.uoc.gr/uploads/nikos_litinas_sales_of_donkeys.pdf (accessed 16 September 2019).

Lo Cascio, E. (2007) 'The Early Roman Empire: The State and the Economy', in W. Scheidel, Ian Morris and Richard P. Saller (eds), *The Cambridge Economic History of the Greco-Roman World.* Cambridge: 619–50.

——. (2008) 'The Function of Gold Coinage in the Monetary Economy of the Roman Empire', in W. Harris (ed.), *The Monetary Systems of the Greeks and Romans.* Oxford: 160–73.

Lozano-Gracia, N. and C. Young (2014) 'Housing Consumption and Urbanization', World Bank Policy Research Working Paper 7112. https://elibrary.worldbank.org/doi/epdf/10.1596/1813-9450-7112 (accessed 11 April 2021).

McCloskey, D. (1990) 'Ancients and Moderns', *Social Science History* 14.3: 289–303.

Macve, R. (2002) 'Insights to Be Gained from the Study of Ancient Accounting History: Some Reflections on the New Edition of Finley's the Ancient Economy', *European Accounting Review* 11.2: 453–72.

Markowitz, H. (1952) 'Portfolio Selection', *Journal of Finance* 7.1: 77–91.

Marshall, A. (1890) *The Principles of Economics.* London.

Maucourant, J. (2004) 'Rationalité économique ou comportements socioéconomiques', in J. Andreau, J. France and S. Pittia (eds), *Mentalités et choix économiques des romains.* Bordeaux: 227–40.

Mayoux, L. and M. Hartl (2009) *Gender and Rural Microfinance: Reaching and Empowering Women. A Guide for Practitioners.* Rome.

Melaerts, H. (2002) 'Aspects du rôle économique des femmes à Tebtynis à l'époque romaine', in H. Melaerts and L. Mooren (eds), *Le Rôle et le statut de la femme en Egypte hellénistique, romaine et byzantine*. Leuven: 209–64.

Mickwitz, G. (1932) *Geld und Wirtschaft im römischen Reich des vierten Jahrhunderts n. Chr.* Leipzig.

Millett, P. (1991) *Lending and Borrowing in Ancient Athens*. Cambridge.

Montevecchi, O. (1941) 'Ricerche di sociologia nei documenti dell'Egitto greco-romano: III. – I contratti di compra-vendita', *Aegyptus* 21: 93–151.

——. (1943) 'Ricerche di sociologia nei documenti dell'Egitto greco-romano: III. – I contratti di compra-vendita', *Aegyptus* 23: 11–89.

——. (1984) *I contratti di baliatico*. Milan.

Morley, N. (1996) *Metropolis and Hinterland: The City of Rome and the Italian Economy 200B.C.–A.D.200*. Cambridge.

——. (2007) 'The Early Roman Empire: Distribution', in W. Scheidel, Ian Morris and Richard P. Saller (eds), *The Cambridge Economic History of the Greco-Roman World*. Cambridge: 570–91.

——. (2013) 'The Market in Classical Antiquity', in M. Frass (ed.), *Kauf, Konsum und Märkte: Wirtschaftswelten im Fokus – Von der römischen Antike bis zur Gegenwart*. Wiesbaden: 103–22.

Morris, R. (1975) 'A Study in the Social and Economic History of Oxyrhynchus for the First Two Centuries of Roman Rule', unpublished PhD thesis, Duke University.

Mountford, M. (2012) 'Documentary Papyri from Roman and Byzantine Oxyrhynchus', unpublished PhD thesis, University College London.

Munro, J.H.A. (2004) 'Before and After the Black Death: Money, Prices, and Wages in Fourteenth-Century England', University of Toronto, Department of Economics Working Paper 24.

——. (ed.) (2012) *Money in the Pre-Industrial World: Bullion, Debasements and Coin Substitutes*. London.

Muth, R.F. (1994) 'Real Land Rentals in Early Roman Egypt', *Explorations in Economic History* 31: 210–24.

Nelson, C.A. (1999) 'Three Loans from the Berlin Collection', *Bulletin of the American Society of Papyrologists* 36: 17–25.

North, D.C. (1990) *Institutions, Institutional Change and Economic Performance*. New York.

Nowak, M. (2015) *Wills in the Roman Empire: A Documentary Approach*. Warsaw.

Ogilvie, S. (2007) '"Whatever Is, Is Right"? Economic Institutions in Pre-Industrial Europe', *Economic History Review* 60.4: 649–84.

ONS [Office for National Statistics] (2016) 'Household Debt Inequalities'. www.ons.gov.uk/peoplepopulationandcommunity/personalandhouseholdfinances/debt/articles/householddebtinequalities/2016-04-04/pdf (accessed 11 July 2019).

Otsuka, K., H. Chuma and Y. Hayami (1992) 'Land and Labor Contracts in Agrarian Economies: Theories and Facts', *Journal of Economic Literature* 30.4: 1965–2018.

Parca, M. (2002) 'Violence by and against Women in Documentary Papyri from Ptolemaic and Roman Egypt', in H. Melaerts and L. Mooren (eds), *Le Rôle et le statut de la femme en Égypte hellénistique, romaine et byzantine.* Leuven: 283–96.

Parsons, P.J. (1969) 'Three Documents from Trinity College', *Chronique d'Égypte* 44: 313–24.

Pestman, P.W. (1971) 'Loans Bearing No Interest?', *Journal of Juristic Papyrology* 16–17: 7–29.

——. (1994) *The New Papyrological Primer.* Leiden.

Piketty, T. (2014) *Capital in the Twenty-First Century.* Cambridge, MA.

Poethke, G. (1969) *Epimerismos: Betrachtungen zur Zwangspacht in Ägypten während der Prinzipatszeit.* Brussels.

Polanyi, K. (1944) *The Great Transformation.* Boston.

——. (1957) 'The Economy as Instituted Process', in K. Polanyi, C.M. Arensberg and H.W. Pearson (eds), *Trade and Market in the Early Empires: Economies in History and Theory.* Glencoe, IL: 243–69.

Polanyi, K., C.M. Arensberg and H.W. Pearson (1957) 'The Place of Economies in Societies', in K. Polanyi, C.M. Arensberg and H.W. Pearson (eds), *Trade and Market in the Early Empires: Economies in History and Theory.* Glencoe, IL: 239–42.

Rathbone, D. (1991) *Economic Rationalism and Rural Society in Third-Century A.D. Egypt: The Heroninos Archive and the Appianus Estate.* Cambridge.

——. (1996) 'Monetisation, not Price-inflation, in Third-Century A.D. Egypt?', in C.E. King and D.G. Wigg (eds), *Coin Finds and Coin Use in the Roman World: The Thirteenth Oxford Symposium on Coinage and Monetary History.* Berlin: 321–40.

——. (1997) 'Prices and Price Formation in Roman Egypt', in J. Andreau, P. Briant and R. Descat (eds), *Économie antique: prix et formation des prix dans les économies antiques.* Saint-Bertrand-de-Comminges: 183–244.

——. (2007a) 'Misthoprasia: The Lease-sale of Ships', in B. Palme (ed.), *Akten des 23. Internationalen Papyrologen-Kongresses.* Vienna: 587–93.

——. (2007b) 'Roman Egypt', in W. Scheidel, Ian Morris and Richard P. Saller (eds), *The Cambridge Economic History of the Greco-Roman World.* Cambridge: 698–719.

——. (2009a) 'Earnings and Costs: Living Standards and the Roman Economy (First to Third Centuries AD)', in A.K. Bowman and A. Wilson (eds), *Quantifying the Roman Economy: Methods and Problems.* Oxford: 299–326.

——. (2009b) 'Review of Fragile Hierarchies: The Urban Elites of Third-Century Roman Egypt by L.E. Tacoma', *Classical Review* 59: 224–5.

——. (2013) 'Village Markets in Roman Egypt: The Case of First-Century AD Tebtunis', in M. Frass (ed.), *Kauf, Konsum und Märkte: Wirtschaftswelten im Fokus – Von der Römischen Antike bis zur Gegenwart.* Wiesbaden: 123–44.

Rathbone, D. and S. von Reden (2014) 'Mediterranean Grain Prices in Classical Antiquity', in R.J. van de Spek, B. van Leeuwen and J. Luiten van Zandend (eds), *A History of Market Performance: From Ancient Babylonia to the Modern World*. Abingdon: 149–235.

Rathbone, D. and P. Temin (2008) 'Financial Intermediation in 1st-Century AD Rome and 18th-Century England', in K. Verboven, K. Vandorpe and V. Chankowski (eds), *Pistoi dia tèn technèn: Bankers, Loans and Archives in the Ancient World*. Studies in Honour of Raymond Bogaert. Leuven: 371–419.

Ratzan, D.M. (2015) 'Transaction Costs and Contract in Roman Egypt: A Case Study in Negotiating the Right of Repossession', in D. Kehoe, D. Ratzan and U. Yiftach (eds), *Law and Transaction Costs in the Ancient Economy*. Ann Arbor, MI: 185–230.

Rémondon, R. (1957) 'À propos du papyrus d'Antinoé n° 38', *Chronique d'Égypte* 32: 130–46.

Richards, A. (1982) *Egypt's Agricultural Development 1800–1980*. Boulder, CO.

Rickman, G. (1980) *The Corn Supply of Ancient Rome*. Oxford.

Ritner, R.K. (1998) 'Egypt under Roman Rule: The Legacy of Ancient Egypt', in C. Petry (ed.), *The Cambridge History of Egypt*, vol. 1, *Islamic Egypt, 640–1517* Cambridge: 1–33.

Rostovtzeff, M. (1957) *The Social and Economic History of the Roman Empire*. Oxford.

Roth, W.-D. (1970) *Untersuchungen zur Kredit-Parathēkē im römischen Ägypten. Ein Beitrag zum Zinsrecht der Papyri und zum nómos tōn parathēkōn*. Marburg.

Rowlandson, J. (1981) 'Sales of Land in their Social Context', in R.S. Bagnall, G.M. Browne, A.E. Hanson and L. Koenen (eds), *Proceedings of the Sixteenth International Congress of Papyrology*. Chicago: 371–8.

——. (1987) 'P. Oxy. XLII 3047, VII 1044, and the Land Tax in Kind', *Zeitschrift für Papyrologie und Epigraphik* 67: 283–92.

——. (1996) *Landowners and Tenants in Roman Egypt: The Social Relations of Agriculture in the Oxyrhynchite Nome*. Oxford.

——. (1998) *Women and Society in Greek and Roman Egypt: A Sourcebook*. Cambridge.

——. (1999) 'Agricultural Tenancy and Village Society in Roman Egypt', in A.K. Bowman and E. Rogan (eds), *Agriculture in Egypt from Pharaonic to Modern Times*. Oxford: 139–56.

Scheidel, W. (2002) 'A Model of Demographic and Economic Change in Egypt after the Antonine Plague', *Journal of Roman Archaeology* 15: 97–114.

——. (2008) 'Real Wages in Roman Egypt: A Contribution to Recent Work on Pre-Modern Living Standards', Princeton/Stanford Working Papers in Classics. Princeton, NJ.

——. (2010) 'Real Wages in Early Economies: Evidence for Living Standards from 1800 BCE to 1300 CE', *Journal of the Economic and Social History of the Orient* 53: 425–62.

——. (2012) 'Approaching the Roman Economy', in W. Scheidel (ed.), *The Cambridge Companion to the Roman Economy*. Cambridge: 1–21.

Scheidel, W. and S. Friesen (2009) 'The Size of the Economy and the Distribution of Income in the Roman Empire', *Journal of Roman Studies* 99: 61–91.

Schmidt, S. (2014) *Stadt und Wirtschaft im Römischen Ägypten. Die Finanzen der Gaumetropolen*. Wiesbaden.

Schnebel, M. (1925) *Die Landwirtschaft im hellenistischen Ägypten*. Munich.

Schubert, P. (2007) *Philadelphie: un village égyptien en mutation entre le IIe et le IIIe siècle ap. J.-C.* Basel.

Schwartz, J. (1961) *Les Archives de Sarapion et de ses fils*. Cairo.

Shaw, B.D. (2013) *Bringing in the Sheaves: Economy and Metaphor in the Roman World*. Toronto.

Shelton, J.-A. (1998). *As the Romans Did: A Sourcebook in Roman Social History*. Oxford.

Simon, H.A. (1947) *Administrative Behavior: A Study of Decision-Making Processes in Administrative Organization*. New York.

Smith, Adam (1976) [1776] *An Inquiry into the Nature and Causes of the Wealth of Nations*. Oxford.

Smith, J.E. and J. Oeppen (1993) 'Estimating Numbers of Kin in Historical England Using Demographic Microsimulation', in D.S. Reher and R.S. Schofield (eds), *Old and New Methods in Historical Demography*. Oxford: 280–317.

Solow, B.L. (1971) *The Land Question and the Irish Economy, 1870–1903*. Cambridge, MA.

Speidel, M.A. (2014) 'Roman Army Pay Scales Revisited: Responses and Answers', in M. Reddé (ed.), *De l'or pour les braves! Soldes, armées et circulation monétaire dans le monde romain*. Bordeaux: 53–62.

Tacoma, L.E. (2006) *Fragile Hierarchies: The Urban Elites of Third Century Roman Egypt*. Leiden.

——. (2008) 'Urbanisation and Access to Land in Roman Egypt', in R. Alston and O.M. van Nijf (eds), *Feeding the Greek City*. Leuven: 85–108.

Taubenschlag, R. (1955) *The Law of Greco Roman Egypt in the Light of the Papyri*. Warsaw.

Temin, P. (2001) 'A Market Economy in the Early Roman Empire', *Journal of Roman Studies* 91: 169–77.

——. (2012) 'The Contribution of Economics', in W. Scheidel (ed.), *The Cambridge Companion to the Roman Economy*. Cambridge: 45–70.

——. (2013) *The Roman Market Economy*. Princeton, NJ.

Tenger, B. (1993) *Die Verschuldung im römischen Ägypten (1.–2. Jahrhundert n. Chr.)*. Sankt Katharinen.

Turner, E.G. (1970) 'Archive of Komon', in D.H. Samuel (ed.), *Proceedings of the Twelfth International Congress of Papyrology*. Toronto: 485–9.

Udry, C. (1994) 'Risk and Insurance in a Rural Credit Market: An Empirical Investigation in Northern Nigeria', *Review of Economic Studies* 61.3: 495–526.

van Minnen, P. (1997) 'Euergetism in Graeco-Roman Egypt', in L. Mooren (ed.), *Politics, Administration and Society in the Hellenistic and Roman World*. Leuven: 437–69.

——. (2000) 'Agriculture and the Taxes and Trade Model in Roman Egypt', *Zeitschrift für Papyrologie und Epigraphik* 133: 205–20.

——. (2008) 'Money and Credit in Roman Egypt', in W. Harris (ed.), *The Monetary Systems of the Greeks and Romans*. Oxford: 226–41.

——. (2009) 'The Future of Papyrology', in R.S. Bagnall (ed.), *The Oxford Handbook of Papyrology*. Oxford: 644–60.

Venit, M.S. (2016) *Visualizing the Afterlife in the Tombs of Graeco-Roman Egypt*. New York.

Verboven, K. (2020) 'Capital Markets and Financial Entrepreneurs', in P. Erdkamp, K. Verboven and Arjan Zuiderhoek (eds), *Capital, Investment and Innovation in the Roman World*. Oxford: 381–416.

von Reden, S. (2010) *Money in Classical Antiquity*. Cambridge.

Wallace, S.L. (1938) *Taxation in Egypt from Augustus to Diocletian*. Princeton, NJ.

Weber, M. (1978) *Economy and Society*. Berkeley, CA.

Weber, T.A. (2012) 'Price Theory in Economics', in Ö. Özer and R. Phillips (eds), *The Oxford Handbook of Pricing Management*. Oxford: 281–339.

West, L.C. and A.C. Johnson (1944) *Currency in Roman and Byzantine Egypt*. Princeton, NJ.

Williamson, O. (2000) 'The New Institutional Economics: Taking Stock, Looking Ahead', *Journal of Economic Literature* 38: 595–613.

Yitfach, U. (2006) 'Spouses in Wills: A Diachronic Survey (III BC–IV AD)', *Journal of Juristic Papyrology* 36: 153–66.

——. (2015a) 'The Grammatikon: Some Considerations on the Feeing Policies of Legal Documents in the Ptolemaic and Roman Periods', in D. Kehoe, D. Ratzan and U. Yiftach (eds), *Law and Transaction Costs in the Ancient Economy*. Ann Arbor, MI: 145–61.

——. (2015b) 'Family Cooperation in Contracts: Pattern and Trends', *Dike* 18: 97–142.

——. (2015c) 'Metepigraphê: Ptolemaic and Roman Policies on the Alienation of Allotment Land', in É. Jakab (ed.), *Sale and Community: Documents from the Ancient World*. Trieste: 133–51.

Youtie, H.C. (1967) 'Papyrus Madrid 11 SB VI 9621', *Chronique d'Égypte* 42: 384–90.

Index

9781802078336